Destinies of the Disadvantaged

Destinies of the Disadvantaged

The Politics of Teenage Childbearing

Frank F. Furstenberg

Russell Sage Foundation • New York

The Russell Sage Foundation

The Russell Sage Foundation, one of the oldest of America's general purpose foundations, was established in 1907 by Mrs. Margaret Olivia Sage for "the improvement of social and living conditions in the United States." The Foundation seeks to fulfill this mandate by fostering the development and dissemination of knowledge about the country's political, social, and economic problems. While the Foundation endeavors to assure the accuracy and objectivity of each book it publishes, the conclusions and interpretations in Russell Sage Foundation publications are those of the authors and not of the Foundation, its Trustees, or its staff. Publication by Russell Sage, therefore, does not imply Foundation endorsement.

Library of Congress Cataloging-in-Publication Data

Furstenberg, Frank F., 1940–
  Destinies of the disadvantaged : the politics of teenage childbearing / Frank F. Furstenberg.
    p. cm.
  Includes bibliographical references and index.
  ISBN 978-0-87154-274-8 (alk. paper)
  1. Teenage pregnancy—United States. 2. Poverty—United States. 3. United States—Social policy. I. Title.
  HQ759.4.F865 2007
  306.874'3—dc22

                                                                    2007014438

RUSSELL SAGE FOUNDATION
112 East 64th Street, New York, New York 10021
10 9 8 7 6 5 4 3 2 1

Contents

—— About the Author ——

FRANK F. FURSTENBERG is the Zellerbach Family Professor of Sociology and a research associate in the Population Studies Center at the University of Pennsylvania, and Chair of the MacArthur Foundation Research Network on Transitions to Adulthood.

—— **Preface** ——

Tᴎɪꜱ ᴠᴏʟᴜᴍᴇ ɪꜱ the final in a trilogy of books on the Baltimore Study, a project launched in the mid-1960s when I began to follow a cohort of teen mothers who were interviewed during pregnancy and six subsequent times over the next thirty years. Over the last four decades, I have seen the issue of teenage childbearing go from near social invisibility to garner greater and greater national concern. This book provides an updated account of the teen mothers in our study and their offspring, but it attempts to do something more than that as well. My principal objective, explored in the second half of the volume, is to examine the wisdom and efficacy of several lines of public policy that have been established to reduce early childbearing and its possible adverse effects on the lives of young mothers, their partners, and their offspring. As will become clear to readers of this volume, I have grave misgivings about whether these policies have been well crafted to address the issues of social disadvantage that give rise to early and unplanned parenthood.

In the more than forty years that I have worked on this project, I have been supported and aided by so many individuals and institutions that it will be impossible to acknowledge them all. But I would be remiss if I did not make some effort to identify some of the sources of this benevolence.

I begin with the nearly four hundred families who have taken time to participate in the study. Since they remain anonymous, I cannot thank them by name; indeed, I have taken some pains to conceal their identities. From time to time, I receive touching reminders of their interest and involvement in the study, as some participants have written me spontaneously to express their thanks when articles or books have appeared in the past. These expressions have been my most satisfying rewards for undertaking this project. One of the great values of social science research is to provide the perspectives of those who do not have a voice in the public sphere. It is useful, even critical, for policymakers to hear and understand responses from those on whose behalf they presumably take action and with whom they often have no direct contact. As I try to show in this book, there can be a wide disparity between the presumptions of policymakers and the reality of the actors who are the object of public policies.

Over the course of four decades, I have drawn so many colleagues and students into this research that I surely shall not be able to list them all. It is always hazardous to list some individuals by name, because I fear that I will neglect others who also deserve my explicit gratitude. Nonetheless, I cannot ignore the help on this volume that I have received from Marianne Bitler, Marcy Carlson, Andy Cherlin, Robin Rogers-Dillon, Kristen Harknett, Roberta Iversen, Dorothy Mann, Amy Schalet, and Kathy Edin, who have read and often made helpful suggestions for improving the manuscript. Among the many students and former students who have assisted me in the analysis I owe special thanks to Kathleen Foley, Monica Grant, Amy Johnson, Kirsten Smith, Kristin Turney, and Chris Weiss.

The funding of this research reaches far back in time, and I will not attempt to thank again the agencies and foundations that have contributed in the past. The data that I collected in the last round of interviewing simply would not exist were it not for the support from the Robert Wood Johnson Foundation and the MacArthur Foundation. The present volume owes much to the Russell Sage Foundation, which provided both financial and intellectual support during the period when much of the book was drafted. I owe a lot to my friend Eric Wanner, who is the president of Russell Sage and has inspired me, among so many others. Thanks also go to Suzanne Nichols and her expert team at the press for the efficient and supportive way in which they do their business.

Patricia Miller, who has been my research administrator, my not-so-secret collaborator, and my good friend, deserves more praise than I can provide.

Finally, my wife, Nina Segre, whom I thanked in each previous volume, provided another healthy dose of love and support during the decade it took to complete this book. She listened to my ramblings with infinite patience, responded with a wonderfully critical mind, and made me feel it was all worthwhile.

—— Chapter 1 ——

The History of Teenage Childbearing as a Social Problem

A CENTURY FROM NOW, social and demographic historians may be pondering the question of why the topic of teenage childbearing suddenly became so prominent in America during the last several decades of the twentieth century. The issue emerged from social invisibility during the 1950s and early 1960s, when rates of childbearing among teens reached historical peaks, and rose to a level of public obsession just as rates of teenage childbearing began to plummet in the late 1960s and early 1970s. In 1995, in his State of the Union address, President Bill Clinton singled out teenage childbearing as "our most serious social problem." When he issued this bit of hyperbole, the overall rate of teenage childbearing was barely more than half of what it had been several decades earlier, and even the rate of *nonmarital* childbearing among teenagers had begun a decline that has continued for more than a decade (U.S. Bureau of the Census 2007; Ventura, Mathews, and Hamilton 2001).

Clinton was not the first president to take note of the costs of early childbearing. Beginning with Jimmy Carter's administration, every president since has put the issue high on his domestic agenda. Americans appear to agree with this emphasis. An advocacy group aimed at preventing teenage pregnancy, reporting on the results of a poll conducted in 1995, concluded that "the number one symptom of erosion in family cohesiveness is the spread of teenage pregnancy" (National Campaign to Prevent Teen Pregnancy 1997, 1). According to the poll, more people were troubled by teenage pregnancy than by the growth of nonmarital childbearing in the

1

population. Most recently, a poll conducted by the Public Policy Institute of California revealed that more than two-fifths of those surveyed in the state regarded teenage pregnancy as a "big problem" in their community, and despite a sharp and steady drop in the rate of pregnancy and childbearing over the past fifteen years, nearly three out of four believed that the problem had been increasing or staying at the same level. Just one in eight Californians knew that early childbearing had been declining.

A veritable industry has grown up over the past several decades producing and disseminating information about teenage pregnancy and childbearing (Alan Guttmacher Institute 2006a; National Campaign to Prevent Teenage Pregnancy 1997). When I began my study on the consequences of early childbearing in 1965 in Baltimore, it was possible to read virtually *every* study that had ever been done on the subject by social scientists and medical researchers. "Teenage parenthood," "adolescent mothers," or similar terms to describe early childbearing were not even mentioned in the *Reader's Guide to Periodical Literature* or in any of the standard medical and social sciences indexes because the issue was simply absent from public discussion.

What an extraordinary contrast to today, when it is virtually impossible to read all the studies produced in a *single year*. Over the years, I have amassed an entire library of professional and popular books and articles on the topic, and no doubt it represents but a small fraction of the studies published on the subject. A recent search on Google of the term "teenage childbearing" yielded more than half a million references and counting.

How did the United States traverse from indifference to public concern to moral crisis in a matter of two or three decades? Was the political, policy, and public concern justified by the evidence? If not, why has the issue loomed so large on the public agenda? Will social historians be intrigued and mystified by our nation's fixation on teenage childbearing, as they are with our other periodic bouts of moral concern, or will they regard the singular attention given to adolescent childbearing as plausible, if not self-evident? This book seeks answers to these questions, building on my own research over the past four decades as well as the considerable contributions of the social scientists and policy analysts who have thought about and studied the causes and consequences of early childbearing.

Of course, the answer I craft must confront a blend of "reality" drawn not only from demographic and social research but also from the popular perception promulgated by the media, political figures, and policy analysts from both the left and the right. Surely, no one could dispute that a dramatic transformation took place in patterns of family formation in the United States and elsewhere beginning in the 1960s. Whether this shift justified the intense focus on the perils of adolescent childbearing is another question altogether. Many of the apprehensions about the powerful and lasting consequences of early parenthood, I will show, have not been substantiated by social science research. But many policymakers and most Americans continue to believe that eliminating early childbearing would produce great dividends for young people, their families, and society at large. More importantly, many of the policies adopted to deter pregnancy and childbearing among young people or to ameliorate its effects may have made matters worse.

Let me be clear about my own position from the start. I do not contend that the issue has been merely contrived by social scientists and advocates, for either worthy or unworthy purposes. As with most other social problems, the public and private costs of early childbearing have a basis in reality; however, our response to the issue has both exaggerated these costs and produced remedies that are either ineffectual or counterproductive, mainly because the problem has come to signify something more than and something different from the reality of young couples having children before they may be fully prepared to enter parenthood. The causes and the consequences of early childbearing, I argue in this book, have been misunderstood, distorted, and exaggerated because they are refracted through a peculiarly American lens strongly tinted by our distinctive political culture.

I am not the only researcher to make this claim. Over the past several decades, a small cadre of feminist scholars, scholars of color, critical theorists, and some social scientists has taken note of how the issue of early childbearing stands for more than the simple proposition that bearing children at a very early age is problematic for young parents and their families (see, for example, the writings of Deborah Rhode, Constance Nathanson, Kristin Luker, and Arline Geronimus, among others who have prominently written about this issue). Our understanding of teenage childbearing was pervaded from the start by a number of preconceptions about the type of women who are willing to bear children in their teens, the families who permit their teenage daughters to become pregnant, and the men who father the children of teenage women. It would not be an exaggeration to describe these beliefs as embodying a series of misunderstandings about the family lives of poor women, of single mothers, of minority males, and even of teenagers more generally. The race or ethnicity, social class, gender, and age of women who have children in their teens all figure into a bundle of American cultural beliefs that have dominated public discourse and social policies surrounding teenage parenthood, such as the assumptions that young women become mothers to receive welfare benefits, that teenage parenthood is the outcome of sexual promiscuity, or that teen mothers are typically irresponsible or indifferent parents (Banfield 1974; Luker 1996; Murray 1984; Nathanson 1991; Wilson 2002).

Any scholar who hopes to comprehend what teenage parenthood is all about must sift through a mountain of evidence on the impact of early childbearing on the lives of young parents and their children as well as take account of how these demographic and social facts have been shaped and interpreted by researchers, the media, politicians, policymakers, advocates, and the public at large. Ultimately, this task is often relegated to intellectual and social historians, but I would like to provide the contemporary perspective of someone who has been a participant-observer of sorts. As a researcher who has been drawn into policy discussions over the past several decades, I have been a player and a witness. Not for a moment would I claim that this double role removes me from my own set of values and preconceptions, which will become evident as I lay out my argument. Yet I do have the advantage (and probably sometimes the disadvantage) that comes with having been steeped in the subject for four decades (Furstenberg 2003).

I report on what the research tells us, though any summary of the literature admittedly involves sorting through studies with differing results. I am convinced that the evidence on the effects of early childbearing on the lives of teen parents and their children does not conform to what most politicians, policymakers, and concerned citizens believe about those effects. If my interpretation of the evidence is correct, it may account for why so many of our policies and prescriptions have been ill crafted, both to prevent early childbearing and to ameliorate its apparent consequences. Indeed, I contend that many of the policies and programs not only miss the mark but have sometimes shot the body politic in the leg, making it harder to address the reasons why young people have children before they want to and often before they are prepared to assume the responsibilities of parenthood.

My conclusions are admittedly controversial, especially when many would argue that our current policies have succeeded in bringing about declining rates of teen childbearing over the past decade—or, depending on how you count it, the last several decades. I show that the drop in teenage childbearing is only loosely connected to many of the public policies that have been instituted in this country. Although we appear to be winning the battle, I argue in later chapters, we are doing so at the cost of losing the war. As happened with other social issues that experienced similar waves of public concern in earlier decades, such as high school dropout rates, gang violence and delinquency, and drug use, most of those concerned about early childbearing have focused myopically on the symptoms of the "disease" rather than on the underlying causes. But to state this thesis is a long way from demonstrating it, so let me turn to the specific contours of the case that I make in this book.

In this chapter and the next, I show why and how teenage childbearing came to stand for something that it is not: a primary explanation for why so many poor people, especially poor minorities, do not succeed in American society. I argue that instead of being a cause of such failure, it primarily represents a marker of marginality and inequality. In later chapters, I examine some of the policies and programs that were devised to curb early childbearing but that have not confronted the underlying problems. We are mainly telling teens to abstain from sex rather than preparing them to make responsible decisions about when, with whom, and why to engage in sex. We have exhorted teens to succeed in school without providing them with the means for doing so. We have changed the welfare system without greatly improving the lives of the families who previously used public assistance. Finally, we are promoting marriage without understanding why a growing share of the population will not or cannot marry. Our collective efforts to address these issues reveal at least as much about how we think about poor minorities and their families as they do about our intentions to address the sources or effects of early childbearing.

THE NATURAL HISTORY
OF A SOCIAL PROBLEM

Long before the issue of teenage childbearing was placed on the hit parade of social problems, there was a subfield of sociology that examined how "deviant" behavior is socially organized, or as Émile Durkheim (1951) contends in his famous book *Suicide,* how it arises from the very nature of social life. Decades before critical theorists began to write about the importance of social and cultural constructions of reality, some social scientists were empirically examining the regularities in how crimes, deviance, and social problems are processed in different societies and cultures. They identified a set of stages in the "natural history" of response to moral concerns (Davis and Blake 1956; Fuller and Myers 1941; Waller 1936).

Simply stated, social problems arise when widespread infractions of social rules (or what used to be called mores) take place. Efforts to deter such behavior follow a course of identifiable phases. Accordingly, researchers must begin their efforts to understand why and how certain actions come to be perceived as deviant or abnormal by exploring the underlying set of standards that they offend. Similarly, social efforts to combat these offenses are themselves rooted in social understandings and arrangements that shape and constrain public response to these problems or efforts to solve them (Becker 1973; Bosk 2005; Gusfield 1963). By failing to take account of the cultural, social, and political values that frame problems and their solutions, we cannot understand why some issues attract attention, especially at particular historical moments, while other equally significant problems are ignored.

The social problems of drugs, alcohol consumption, crime and delinquency, sexual promiscuity, and a litany of other socially disapproved behaviors typically cycle through historical epochs, alternately placed high on the public agenda or relegated to social invisibility. Periods of tolerance or intolerance rise and fall depending on the public agenda. The issues are discovered and rediscovered, or occasionally redefined as normal or, at least, unavoidable. Some problems persist, and others disappear to be replaced by other issues that appear to be more threatening. Habits change, social control diminishes problems, or public initiatives may reduce actions defined as deviant, unnatural, or dangerous.

Several decades ago, the economist Anthony Downs (1972) labeled this process an "issue attention cycle" during which politicians, policymakers and advocates, the media, and service providers and practitioners come to recognize, respond to, and shape policies and assess the effects of those policies. Attention rises from "social invisibility" in the "pre-problem stage" to a period of "alarmed discovery and euphoric excitement" when confidence about illuminating the problem is high. Next, as policymakers and the public come to recognize the costs of making significant progress, public interest wanes, and this gradual decline is a prelude to a twilight period when reformers confront social and political resistance. Finally, Downs identifies a post-problem stage of "lesser attention or spasmodic re-occurrence of interest." Downs's description nicely captures the history of teenage childbearing as a social problem.

TEENAGE CHILDBEARING IN
THE PRE-PROBLEM STAGE

Early childbearing has never been unusual in this country. From the colonial era onward, Americans have always had a distinctly early pattern of family formation, at least compared with Western European nations. There has been great variation over time and place in the age of first marriage and birth, but local birth records, registries, and census data show that a substantial proportion of teenagers became parents before they reached the age of majority (Carter and Glick 1976; Haines and Steckel 2000). Before the twentieth century, early childbearing occurred more frequently in parts of the South, in the border states, and on the western frontier than in the more settled and established sections of New England. Even in the Northeast, however, teen childbearing was not uncommon.

As I discuss in more detail in a later chapter, the timing of family formation is linked to the availability of economic opportunities (Easterlin 1985). When land was cheap and plentiful, Americans began childbearing earlier and had larger families. As resources became scarcer, marriage age rose, and so did the age of first birth. No doubt, the opportunities this nation generally afforded to new settlers and immigrants encouraged the young to establish independence early, especially during earlier times when agriculture was the basis of the family economy.

With the advent of industrialization, the availability of work continued to influence the timing of family formation. Young women worked in the factories, accumulating savings for marriage, while men tried to establish themselves in the new job economy (Hareven 1994). By 1900 the traditionally agricultural economy had been partially transformed, a process that would continue throughout the twentieth century. The timing of marriage and parenthood rose as the country moved from an agrarian to an industrialized nation with a market economy, declining in good times and rising when the economy was bad. Along with older women, teenagers curtailed their fertility during the Great Depression, and rates remained lower during the period leading up to World War II (Haines and Steckel 2000).

This pattern of relatively late family formation abruptly reversed in the postwar period for a complex set of reasons—postponement of family formation in the 1930s and after the outbreak of the war, unbridled optimism with the collapse of Germany and Japan after the Second World War, the hot economy of the 1950s, massive government expenditures on education and housing, and the strong cultural focus on the comforts of hearth and home (Cherlin 1981; Coontz 1992; May 1988). For teenagers, as for older women, this era became a time of domestic mass production. This is shown in figure 1.1, which depicts fertility rates for women of different ages. During the decades between 1955 and 1965, corresponding to the baby boom era, women of all ages began to produce more children. The rise of fertility among teens both led to and resulted from a wave of early marriage that began in the postwar period.

Beginning in the 1960s, American women abruptly shifted course. For women of all ages, childbearing declined significantly. However, young women did not curtail their fertility as quickly as did older women, nor perhaps did they react as swiftly to new economic realities affecting the family (Vinovskis 1988). Whatever signals were leading older women to defer or curb their fertility were not as apparent to teens, particularly teens of color. Demographers now have a pretty good idea of why young women were slower to respond than older women to the social and economic changes

FIGURE 1.1 **Birthrates Among American Women by Age, 1955 to 2004**

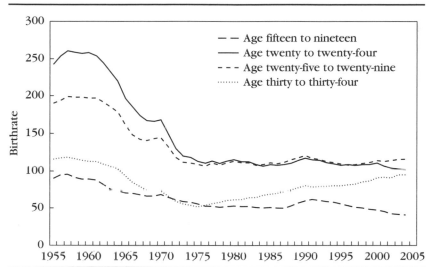

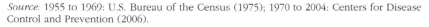

Source: 1955 to 1969: U.S. Bureau of the Census (1975); 1970 to 2004: Centers for Disease Control and Prevention (2006).

that depressed fertility. Teen childbearing was less often planned and hence less regulated by contraception. Moreover, in times past, an ill-timed pregnancy was routinely followed by marriage. However, in the 1960s, early marriage became increasingly difficult, and its swift demise created a painful dilemma for sexually active teenagers who became unintentionally pregnant.

Up until the 1960s, marriage and childbearing had been tightly linked. Researchers have documented relatively high rates of pre-marital pregnancy throughout American history (Bachu 1999; Cutright and Jaffe 1977; Smith and Hindus 1975). In agricultural communities and in the rapidly urbanizing cities, women often became pregnant in the anticipation that their partner would marry them. "Shotgun weddings" were an integral feature of the courtship system in America. Especially in the middle of the past century, pregnancy propelled many couples into marriage earlier than they otherwise might have wed. The fact that nearly half of all teenagers in the 1950s who married were pregnant at the time (O'Connell and Moore 1980) helps to account for both the huge surge in marriage rates and the high rate of teenage parenthood during this era. Black women, as had long been true, were far more likely than whites to have children out-of-wedlock in the 1950s, although most of these women also married either the father or someone else.

Few observers today appreciate how common this pattern was in the past century (and in earlier times as well). As many sociologists in the 1950s and 1960s noted, early marriage was a way of managing the risks associated with premarital sexual activity (Vincent 1961). In many instances, it was women in committed relationships—either formally or informally engaged—who became pregnant. Typically in such cases, a premarital pregnancy merely moved up the timing of a wedding, but sometimes pregnancy led to the collapse of the relationship because one partner pulled out (Green 1941; Whyte 1943). A certain number of forsaken women were left scrambling to find an alternative solution when their partner, in the parlance of the 1950s, refused "to make an honest woman of them" (Vincent 1961).

The alternatives to marriage were not attractive. Illegal abortions were not uncommon, although in the absence of reliable data, we do not know just how prevalent they were. Certainly, among white women, adoption was the most popular remedy for those who were unwilling or unable to obtain abortions. Pregnant black women who did not marry were more likely to foster their children with extended family or friends. Thus, premarital pregnancy during the teenage years was socially managed, albeit imperfectly from a woman's perspective. As the prominent sociologist Clark Vincent (1961, 251) noted in his book *Unmarried Mothers,* the shame inflicted on unwed mothers was designed to support marriage. In a prescient passage that could presage the culture wars, Vincent wrote: "The most vexing complex aspects of trying to decrease the incidence of illegitimacy are results of the contradiction between (a) providing deterrents and punishments that will discourage behavior that undermines legitimate family life, and (b) attempting to facilitate the rehabilitation of the unwed mother, and the development of the illegitimate child, into good and useful citizens."

About the time Vincent completed his study of the veiled practices of unmarried mothers, signs were already evident, especially for teenagers, that these practiced ways of managing unplanned parenthood were becoming less satisfactory. By the mid-1960s, as I have already reported, early marriage was on the wane. This was particularly true for African Americans and other disadvantaged minorities, for whom marriage was becoming a less tenable solution to an unplanned pregnancy. The surge of manufacturing jobs in the postwar era was coming to an end, and the premium on post-secondary education was growing. Minorities were also being affected by the flight of jobs from urban areas to the burgeoning lily-white suburbs as the postwar boom in housing altered the location of jobs (Wilson 1987, 1996).

Sociologists were discovering that early marriages, especially when preceded by a pregnancy, were highly prone to divorce (Weeks 1976). Women were beginning to learn from the experiences of their kin and community that marriage was not a good bet, particularly when their sexual partner was uneducated and under employed, as was often the case among African Americans. As I show in the next chapter, there is little doubt that African American teen mothers were acutely aware of the risks of entering marriage. They were gradually moving toward a view—later adopted by teenage whites and older women in general—that single parenthood was at least as viable a solution to premarital pregnancy as was a hasty marriage or its alternatives (informal adoption or illegal abortion).

In part, their attitudes about nonmarital childbearing reflected a powerful shift of attitudes taking place in the nation as a whole: the stigma associated with premarital sex was on the decline. This change took root in the 1960s, a time when many traditional beliefs were being called into question (Smith 2000). It is difficult to underestimate the powerful role the media played in stimulating a national conversation about premarital sex. Beginning with the release of the first Kinsey report on men in 1948, and especially with the second report on females in 1953, an enormous amount of attention was devoted to the sexual practices of teenagers and young adults. Kinsey and his coauthors reported, whether entirely accurately or not, that premarital sex had long been common in the United States (Kinsey, Pomeroy, and Martin 1948; Kinsey 1953).

As Americans began to perceive that the general standards about sex were more relaxed than they had been led to believe, change in both attitudes and behavior began to snowball. The first nationally representative survey of teenage sexual behavior in the late 1960s and early 1970s, conducted by Melvin Zelnik, John Kantner, and Kathleen Ford (1981), reinforced the findings of the Kinsey reports. Premarital sex was prevalent and rapidly becoming more so. For example, the proportion of teenagers who had ever had sex by age eighteen doubled from about one-fourth of all women born in the 1940s to more than half of women born two decades later (Finer 2007; Laumann et al. 1994).

Premarital sex, it seems, was becoming more common just as early marriage was becoming more problematic—a perfect formula for producing a rapid increase in rates of nonmarital pregnancies and births. From the 1940s onward, nonmarital childbearing climbed steadily for all age groups as nonmarital intercourse increased and contraceptive use lagged far behind. Among older women in their twenties and thirties, a pause in nonmarital childbearing took place in the 1960s and early 1970s, while among teens the pace of nonmarital childbearing picked up, driven by both more sexual risk-taking and fewer marriages (Ventura and Bachrach 2000).

WHY TEENAGE CHILDBEARING
BECAME THE PROBLEM

The demographic disparity created by a rising age of marriage plus the huge number of teens entering the population created by the baby boom first began to be noticed in the 1960s. To most observers, it appeared that teens were suddenly behaving differently from older women. Although unmarried women in their twenties and early thirties actually had a much higher rate of nonmarital births than those age fifteen to nineteen, what initially caught the attention of policymakers and the public was not the changing *rates* of nonmarital childbearing per thousand unmarried women, but the changing *ratio* of nonmarital births—the percentage of all births born to unmarried women. Among teens, this ratio skyrocketed as fewer teenagers married and hence had fewer marital births to offset the growing number of births to single women. Fewer teenagers were actually having children, but more of them who did were electing to have children outside of marriage, creating an increased demand for public assistance and other services for single mothers.

Of course, we know now that older women would follow suit in the last two decades of the century. However, because older women were still marrying in large numbers, it appeared for a time that nonmarital childbearing was reaching epidemic proportions among the young. In fact, the term "epidemic," as some labeled it, was questionable, to say the least. Although a rhetorically effective way of garnering support for young mothers, the word created the impression that a huge wave of early childbearing was sweeping the country (Vinovskis 1988). Teenagers, in effect, were wrongly singled out as demographically deviant from the rest of the population.

African American teens in particular were identified as the main source of the problem because they were the vanguard of change in marriage practices. In fact, the issue of early childbearing was initially identified as a problem that mostly occurred among black teens. The reason why this perception appeared to be plausible is illustrated in figure 1.2, which shows the rate of births to unmarried women by age and race. Young black women were clearly ahead of white teenagers in patterns of family formation in the rise of nonmarital childbearing, but the exclusive focus on out-of-wedlock childbearing among younger teens was hardly warranted. For a time, it might have appeared that blacks generally and black teenagers specifically might be exhibiting a distinctively different set of family practices from the rest of the population. Young black women, in part because so many came from poor, single-parent households, became emblematic of a much more general change in family formation in the United States that was taking place. I concur with previous authors who contend that black teens were singled out and stereotyped unfairly, though clearly it is easier to see that now than it was at the time (Luker 1996; Nathanson 1991).

In 1965 a young assistant secretary of labor in the Johnson administration, Daniel Patrick Moynihan, helped to place the issue of teenage childbearing on the public agenda when he wrote a highly controversial report on the state of the black family in America. Speaking of blacks, Moynihan (1965, 27) stated: "A cycle is at work; too many children too early make it most difficult for parents to finish school. . . . Low education levels in turn produce low income levels, which deprive children of many opportunities, and so the cycle repeats itself."

FIGURE 1.2 **Birthrates Among Unmarried American Women by Race and Age, 1970 to 2004**

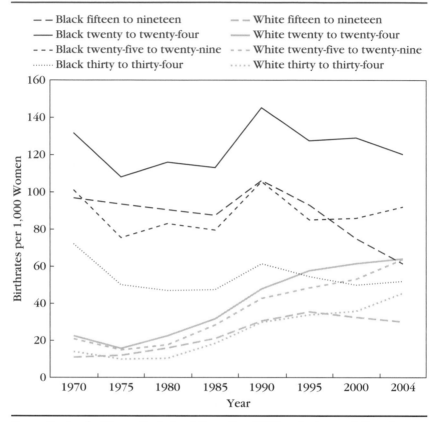

— — Black fifteen to nineteen   — — White fifteen to nineteen
——— Black twenty to twenty-four   ——— White twenty to twenty-four
- - - Black twenty-five to twenty-nine   - - - White twenty-five to twenty-nine
······· Black thirty to thirty-four   ····· White thirty to thirty-four

Source: Centers for Disease Control and Prevention (2000); author's compilation of national vital statistics data from 2000 to 2004.

Moynihan was incorrect in assuming that the growth of non-marital childbearing was confined largely to young black women. By the end of the twentieth century, it was evident that black women were only at the vanguard of a new pattern of family formation that was being rapidly adopted by all teens and eventually by older couples.

Although many left-leaning scholars excoriated Moynihan for singling out the disintegration of the black family, most accepted the proposition that teenage nonmarital childbearing came at a great cost to adolescent parents, their children, and society at large (Rainwater and Yancey 1967). Shortly after the publication of the Moynihan report, interest in the issue grew, even from quarters critical of Moynihan's exclusive focus on the black family (Furstenberg 2007). Several years later, a highly respected demographer, Arthur Campbell (1968, 238), wrote his widely quoted assessment of the consequences of early childbearing for teenage mothers:

> The girl who has an illegitimate child at the age of 16 suddenly has 90 percent of her life's script written for her. She will probably drop out of school; even if someone else in her family helps to take care of the baby, she will probably not be able to find a steady job that pays enough to provide for herself and her child; she may feel impelled to marry someone she might not otherwise have chosen. Her life choices are few, and most of them are bad.

Many advocates for the poor were understandably drawn to the issue, as there appeared to be a rapidly spreading acceptance of single parenthood in urban ghettos. Foremost among them were family planners and sex educators, who believed that the problem resulted from lack of access to contraception and legal restrictions on abortion. They saw the dilemma faced by teenagers as an urgent mission to expand reproductive health services to a population that had little knowledge of or access to reproductive health services. And they were surely right.

The Guttmacher Institute (formerly the Alan Guttmacher Institute, AGI), a research center devoted to reproductive health, led the charge, lobbying for expanded services for unmarried teens, subsidized with federal dollars. Their proposal for serving unmarried teens through the federally funded family planning clinics, considered by many at the time radical and highly controversial, was in fact quickly adopted in the late 1960s and early 1970s, wiping away many of the existing strictures against providing contraception to the young, the unmarried, and the poor.

In a series of reports and publications from the late 1960s and throughout the 1970s, AGI blended alarming demographic data with dire predictions about the adverse consequences of early childbearing, drawing on the relatively primitive research of the time to advocate for funding not only for family planning and service programs to increase contraceptive use among teenagers but also for providing prenatal and postnatal assistance. Indeed, it was AGI that created the impression that the United States faced an "epidemic" of teenage childbearing (Vinovskis 1988).

AGI bolstered its claim that United States policies were failing the teenage population by presenting a remarkable set of statistics highlighting the risks of pregnancy and childbearing. Perhaps the most dramatic were international comparisons showing that the United States, by a wide margin, had higher rates of pregnancy and childbearing than European nations and even other Anglophone nations, including Canada.

These international comparisons dramatically highlighted the problem in the United States, but they failed to take account of the early marriage pattern here, which greatly aggravated the issue. As I noted earlier, the United States had a long history of early family formation, especially compared with many of the nations from which our population emigrated. This pattern of early family formation created a quandary for young women as they began to back away from ill-timed marriages. The impression, however, that teenage childbearing was a growing problem because its incidence was rapidly increasing was misleading. The new problem—to the extent that one existed—stemmed not from more teenagers becoming pregnant, or teenagers having different views about nonmarital childbearing than older women, but from the declining desirability of marriage.

Advocates for reproductive health services rightly pointed to the need for reproductive services for sexually active teens, but they did so by focusing on the rapidly rising nonmarital birth ratio as well as the growing number of births to unmarried teens. By doing so, they created an impression that teenage childbearing was on the rise, obscuring the fact that marriage no longer provided the safety net that it once had when premarital pregnancy occurred. In fact, fewer teenagers were getting pregnant, but so many more remained single that teenage parenthood became synonymous with single parenthood. This helped to fashion a social stereotype of teenage mothers as socially deviant. In retrospect, it is difficult to avoid the conclusion that the issue of teenage childbearing was misunderstood from the start. At the very least, there was very little to distinguish the behavior of teens from that of older women, whose rates of unmarried childbearing had also been climbing and would continue to rise again after 1975. In hindsight, we can now see that there was little reason to single out black women or other minorities, other than to note that they began to retreat from marriage earlier than white women did. Of course, it is easier to grasp these patterns now than it was at the time when they were emerging.

THE SEARCH FOR SOLUTIONS

The creation of teenage childbearing as a public issue had profound political and social consequences, stirring up a hornet's nest of loosely connected discussions about the acceptability of premarital sex, the provision of contraception to the young and unmarried, the ethics of legalizing abortion, the costs of providing public assistance to unmarried mothers, and the reasons for the declining attractiveness of adoption. These debates would continue through the rest of the century and indeed show few signs of disappearing in the immediate future.

The federal government during the Johnson, Nixon, and Carter administrations, with congressional support, funded both Title X, the legislation that funded reproductive health, and a wide array of assistance programs to struggling families and young mothers, including a large expansion of Aid to Families with Dependent Children (AFDC).

In light of the critical response to these legislative initiatives in recent decades, it is difficult to assess their effectiveness in addressing the growing tide of nonmarital childbearing. It was not obvious to social demographers at the time just how massive the retreat was from early marriage. Some critics, none more influential than Charles Murray, subsequently blamed the array of supports put in place to address the problem for actually increasing the problem. Murray (1984) claimed that the growth of public assistance created a disincentive to marry; others argued that service programs that aided teenage parents would enable young mothers to have children; and many critics of family planning services for the unmarried have contended that they promote sexual promiscuity and risk-taking (Sklar and Berkov 1974). I assess the empirical evidence on the validity of these arguments in later chapters. For now, one need only recognize that public policy aimed at preventing teenage childbearing and reducing its adverse consequences has from its very inception been contentious in the American context, especially when compared with the political reaction of most other Western nations.

During the last quarter of the twentieth century, contraception became more widely available to teenagers, although its effect on reducing early childbearing was not immediately apparent. For one reason, sexual activity among teens was growing faster than were family planning services, creating an ever-larger pool of teenagers at risk of becoming pregnant. In addition, the methods first available to teens, such as oral contraceptives, the diaphragm, and intrauterine devices, were not easy to use and were often accompanied by annoying and frightening side effects. Because both sex and contraceptive use among teens remained controversial, many young women were not comfortable with the empowerment or responsibility of managing their sexual life, a topic explored in chapter 4. Moreover, until the advent of HIV/AIDS, responsibility fell primarily to women to enforce contraceptive use, a circumstance that frequently led to miscommunication or no communication at all. Many studies, including my own in Baltimore, indicated that merely making birth control more available without actively promoting its practice was an insufficient strategy to cut deeply into the incidence of early and unplanned pregnancies.

Neither did the change in abortion policies, which began in the late 1960s and culminated in *Roe v. Wade,* the Supreme Court decision legalizing abortion, seem to have much effect on the rate of early childbearing. The use of abortion among teenagers rose rapidly in the decade after legalization. From 1973, the ratio of abortions to live births rose from 280 per 1,000 to 462 in 1985, before descending. There is some evidence that abortion policies may have initially reduced early childbearing in the 1970s. Increases in nonmarital birthrates among teenagers (and even more so among older women) slowed in the mid-1970s (and dropped sharply for women in their twenties and thirties). Among black teens, the unmarried birthrate actually dropped during this decade (Ventura and Bachrach 2000). The decline, however, was offset by a rising rate of unmarried births among white teens. (Separate data for Hispanic youth are unavailable until the 1990s.)

The increase in abortion, however, generated a maelstrom of opposition, creating the pro-life movement and its allies. Abortion's availability, it was also argued, encouraged teens to have sex without worrying about the consequences. In the American context, this argument seemed to resonate with a wary public, even among those who favored abortion rights. No sooner had abortion been made widely available than opponents began to create legal and social barriers to abortions in many parts of the country. These obstacles were especially directed at teenagers, who faced a series of special regulations such as parental consent. As legal barriers and political measures began to shrink access to abortion, nonmarital child-bearing rates would resume their steep rise in the 1980s. Even before these restrictions were imposed, however, substantial numbers of women were reluctant to seek abortion because they held scruples against terminating an ill-timed pregnancy. Clearly, abortion, even if it was tolerated politically, did not have as dramatic or imme-diate an effect as might have been expected by its most optimistic proponents.

The option of adoption also provided no easy solution to man-aging the growing rates of nonmarital childbearing. Among African Americans, a public market for adoption had never existed. In any case, African Americans generally disapproved of adoption unless it was a matter of fostering children temporarily or permanently with kin or close friends. As nonmarital childbearing began to become more prevalent among whites, they too began to back away from adoption. As the century progressed, white teens became almost as reluctant as black teens to elect adoption over its alternative, single parenthood.

SOCIAL SCIENCE RESEARCHERS
ARE MOBILIZED

These policies and the advocacy for special services for teenage women, their partners, and offspring were aided by an army of social scientists who began to study the causes and consequences of early childbearing. This flood of research was initially under-written by government funding agencies and private foundations in the belief that by curbing teenage parenthood, they could make a significant dent in poverty and inequality. In effect, they subscribed to the thesis that Arthur Campbell and many other social scientists first articulated in the 1960s and 1970s—that teenage parenthood has devastating consequences for young mothers and their families.

I take up this thesis in the following chapter when I argue that the early social science evidence greatly exaggerated the impact of early childbearing on mothers, and probably its impact on their offspring as well.

Yet, as I have mentioned, the picture from social science research appears far clearer in hindsight than it did when the trends in fertility first emerged. I am not contending that social scientists or the advocates who relied on their research knowingly misled the public to gain support for their initiatives. To the contrary, the social science evidence initially appeared to be quite compelling, albeit for reasons that now seem suspect.

From the perspective of the 1960s and 1970s, however, when teenage childbearing was first discovered as a social problem, few observers recognized the commonalities in the circumstances of teens and older women (Luker 1996). Indeed, it appeared as though teenagers, especially black teenagers, were adopting a "deviant" lifestyle, owing to unemployment, family instability, and distinctive sexual practices. Programs initiated in the era of the Great Society shaped the early wave of response to the issue, although many of these policies were questioned during the Nixon and Carter presidencies. As it became more apparent that such behaviors were not confined to black teens, commentators expanded their definition of the problem, seeking other justifications for curbing childbearing among teens. As the political climate shifted sharply to the right, teenage childbearing was put to a variety of political uses to justify and advance the conservative agenda.

TEENAGE CHILDBEARING
AND POLITICAL BACKLASH

When teenage childbearing was first identified as a social problem in the era of the Great Society, much of the general public believed that it was possible to eradicate poverty through government action. Responses to the issue focused largely on the need to provide preventive and ameliorative services to young mothers and their children. This sympathetic reaction was all but abandoned in the Reagan years of the 1980s, when criticism of these initiatives became widespread in the body politic.

Conservatives and liberals alike agreed on the demographic dimensions of the problem, but they differed sharply on its etiology and on prescriptions for reducing it. The difference can be summed up easily. What liberals argued were the prescriptions for dealing with the problem, conservatives argued had created the problem in the first place.

The unfavorable international comparisons mentioned earlier began to be used against the advocates as conservative critics countered that American teenagers were behaving less responsibly by having sex before they were ready and then seeking abortions as a remedy or turning to the welfare system for support when they elected to bring their pregnancies to term. Unmarried teenage mothers on public assistance became the poster children for spending reductions. Regardless of whether the conservative claims were valid, these arguments struck a sympathetic nerve among politicians and taxpayers, who felt overburdened by the costs of the Great Society programs that had initially been developed in a period of economic abundance. In the aftermath of the Vietnam War and in the lengthy period of stagflation that began during the oil crisis of the 1970s, the Reagan and Bush administrations in the 1980s and early 1990s believed that they had a political mandate to cut back on social welfare spending. Reducing teen childbearing seemed to be a logical means to cutting back on welfare expenditures.

Paradoxically, the curtailment of government spending for social services occurred at the same time as an uptick in the rate of nonmarital childbearing for black teens, whose rates had been declining in the early 1970s; however, beginning in the early 1980s, nonmarital birthrates reversed course. Among whites, nonmarital childbearing had steadily risen in the 1970s, but its pace accelerated throughout the 1980s (see figure 1.2). The cutbacks in services and the rising rates of nonmarital childbearing among women of all ages might be unrelated, but the withdrawal of preventive and ameliorative services was not warranted by the demographic evidence at the time. As I have already said, the driving force in the changing patterns of early childbearing was the retreat from early marriage. It might be said that poor economic conditions in this country and elsewhere were hastening this trend, as fewer young couples felt able to enter marriage regardless of whether they were facing impending parenthood.

It also seems likely that as restrictions on abortion grew in the 1980s, more pregnant women, and unmarried teens especially, became parents who might have terminated their pregnancies had they been given the opportunity to do so. Clearly too, the declining levels of welfare support and social services did little or nothing to discourage sexual activity among teens, which continued to rise throughout the 1980s as a growing number of white adolescents began to have sex without being well prepared to assume the consequences. Whatever the source of the rise in nonmarital childbearing among teens and older women, the heated political debates of the 1980s did little to curb the trend.

Again, it is important to note that marital fertility was also declining throughout this entire period, albeit at a much slower pace than between 1960 and 1975, when couples first began to postpone marriage. This twin trend of declining marital fertility and rising nonmarital fertility had a dramatic effect on the proportion of women, especially teenagers, who gave birth to a child out of wedlock. For reasons that are still incompletely understood, the steep rise in out-of-wedlock childbearing during the 1980s abruptly reversed course in the 1990s. Among older women, nonmarital childbearing merely settled or slightly declined, but among teens rates fell steeply and steadily throughout the decade, and they continued to fall in the early years of the current century (Ventura and Bachrach 2000; Ventura, Mathews, and Hamilton 2001). During the past decade and a half, sexual activity among teenagers peaked and then declined somewhat, perhaps in response to growing public disapproval and also, no doubt, because of a rising fear of HIV/AIDS.

Condom use rose from the late 1980s onward. Also, during the past two decades new and more effective methods of contraception have been introduced, as well as methods of disrupting conception, obviating the need for later-term abortions. In addition, the booming economy of the 1990s may have contributed to enhanced resolve among teens to complete high school. Finally, many argue that welfare reform in 1996 prompted teens to defer parenthood. In later chapters, I assess these claims and sort out the reasons for the recent decline in early childbearing. Although the phenomenon has not gone away, it may now be entering a twilight period when it is being reconsidered as a major social problem. Eventually, I believe, teenage childbearing will probably recede into the shadows of public attention.

This much is already clear about the so-called epidemic of teenage childbearing. First, the problem was initially misunderstood by social scientists, misused by advocates and social critics, and misunderstood by the body politic. Second, there is no evidence to support the belief that the problem occurred because more teens were "deciding" to have children in the period after 1965. Total birthrates among teenagers fell steadily throughout the time when teenage childbearing was becoming a public issue. Teens, especially black teens, switched from having marital to nonmarital births, a troubling development to be sure, but this pattern quickly was adopted by older women as well. It seems that teenagers were merely at the forefront of a trend away from early marriage and "shotgun weddings"—a term that has become all but obsolete.

Whether teenagers deserved the focus of public attention that they received for contributing to the "breakdown of the family" by having babies before they were ready to marry is addressed in the next two chapters, where I discuss whether and how much early childbearing contributes to adversity for young mothers, the men who father their children, and especially their offspring.

Chapter 2

From Teenage Mother to Midlife Matriarch

WHEN ARTHUR CAMPBELL (1968) wrote his scenario of the life course of teenage mothers in 1968, quoted in the previous chapter, only scant evidence existed on the social and economic consequences of teenage childbearing. Campbell was largely surmising the adverse effects of having a child early in life based on cross-sectional comparisons of women whose first birth occurred in their teens with women who had children later in life. If few studies existed at the time on the short-term effects of early childbearing, even less information was available about the long-term consequences of teenage parenthood for the parents or their offspring. Yet his conclusion that 90 percent of a woman's life script was written when she became a mother at age sixteen or so seemed entirely plausible, if not compelling.

THE BALTIMORE STUDY

When I first read Campbell's statement, I had just completed collecting the first wave of interview data from a sample of nearly four hundred young mothers residing in Baltimore who had participated in a random assignment evaluation of one of the nation's first comprehensive care programs for adolescent mothers (Furstenberg, Masnick, and Ricketts 1972). As I have recounted in greater detail elsewhere (Furstenberg 2002a), the study began almost by accident when I was in the midst of my graduate training at Columbia. My mother, a social worker in an experimental program intended to reduce unplanned births among teenagers, recruited me to help design an evaluation. Though I resisted at first, my mother exercised her parental prerogatives and insisted that I help out. And so I did, of course unaware that I was embarking on a research project that would extend over my entire academic career and not be completed, strictly speaking, until more than forty years later.

The Baltimore sample consisted of just the sort of young women whose lives might unfold as Campbell predicted. All pregnant for the first time before the age of eighteen, the teens who delivered babies at Sinai Hospital of Baltimore in the mid-1960s had grown up in relatively precarious circumstances and appeared to have bleak prospects for their later lives. At the time of conception, half were sixteen or younger, three-quarters had not yet completed the tenth grade, and three-quarters had no immediate plans to wed before their first child was born. As much as I was able to detect from local vital statistics records, the young women in the study were reasonably representative of teenage mothers who gave birth in Baltimore City, and more broadly of young mothers from urban areas who delivered their first child in the mid-1960s. As I note later, the careers of these women and their children appear to be remarkably similar to those of several national samples of teenage parents who have been tracked in larger studies. Thus, the story of the Baltimore mothers closely resembles the findings that would have been obtained had I followed any other urban sample of low-income teen mothers.

I describe the members of this sample as "low-income" because all participants came from poor and working-class families who were eligible for medical assistance in 1965 when the study was launched. Thus, the sample excludes women from more affluent families, many of whom would have married or given up their children for adoption. Four out of five of the women were black; according to vital statistics, their racial composition closely resembled that of women whose first birth occurred before age eighteen in Baltimore City (for a more detailed description of the origins of the study, see Furstenberg 1976).

Some of the women came from desperately poor sections of the city that resembled urban ghettos today, though the conditions faced by these women and their families were probably somewhat less harsh than those that now prevail, if only because neighborhoods were less economically segregated, especially for blacks, than they have become in the intervening decades. One-quarter of the sample came from families on public assistance at the time the pregnancy occurred. Half had grown up in a single-parent family, indicating high levels of disadvantage by standards of the period, but the majority grew up in a family headed by one or two working parents. Nonetheless, the families who participated in the program were burdened by large numbers of children (six on average), and only a small fraction of the parents had completed high school. Accordingly, most parents worked at menial or, at best, semiskilled jobs paying low wages. Many of the families had migrated to Baltimore in the postwar period, when manufacturing jobs were still plentiful, and more than a few were beginning to experience the disorganizing effects of the deindustrialization that was beginning to occur in the late 1950s and early 1960s. But it is also evident that, even in this sample of young mothers that excluded women from more affluent families, considerable variation existed in the social and economic circumstances of the parents.

UNPLANNED PARENTHOOD

As I have already described in greater detail elsewhere, most of the young mothers in my study drifted into parenthood (Furstenberg 1976; Furstenberg, Gordis, and Markowitz 1969). By this I mean that only a tiny fraction, according to their own accounts given shortly after their first pregnancy occurred, had planned to become a mother when they did; three out of four reported at the initial interview that they wished they had not become pregnant when they did, and even most of those who were pleased by the prospect of parenthood indicated that the pregnancy was unplanned.

Although it may seem naive by today's levels of sophistication, the vast majority of the young mothers reported that they believed they could not conceive at such a young age or so soon after beginning to have sex. More than a few never realized that they were pregnant until someone else in the family surmised it. We heard over and over again in the interviews, "I never thought it would happen to me," "I didn't think that I could get pregnant the first time that I had sex," or, sometimes, "I thought my boyfriend was protecting me." Much of the research on the process leading up to pregnancy among teenagers is consistent with these accounts, indicating that few women in their early to mid-teens set out to become pregnant deliberately. Conception may have been only rarely planned or intended, but the question of intentionality remains a thorny one, if only because feelings about parenthood appear to fluctuate or to be revised over time (Alan Guttmacher Institute 1976, 1981, 2001; Edin and Kefalas 2005; Rains 1971; Zelnik, Kantner, and Ford 1981). Thus, the accounts provided after pregnancy and birth must be carefully scrutinized in order to assess feelings about impending parenthood. Few studies, even today, have followed sexually active teens over time to determine how commitments to parenthood might change from pre-conception to conception and then to birth.

In recalling their reactions when they first learned that they were pregnant, the vast majority of the teen mothers said that they were unpleasantly surprised, if not shocked and disappointed. Many of them said that they had let their parents down by becoming pregnant, aware of the fact that their mothers had themselves often struggled after giving birth in the 1950s, when early parenthood was so much more common. "I never anticipated it. I never wanted it, and I knew what my mother had gone through," one respondent told us.

Phoenix Dupree, in her second trimester when she was interviewed, recalled her initial response: "I could have died. I couldn't believe it. I was shocked." Phoenix was not alone in having negative feelings, at least initially. Three out of five of the expectant mothers gave an unqualified negative response to the question of how they had felt when they first discovered they were pregnant; another one-fifth provided a mixed reaction like Angie Brown's: "It is nothing to be ashamed of, but it's nothing to be proud of. [I felt] not too good, not too bad." The remaining one-fifth of the sample who recalled that they were happy about becoming pregnant consisted largely of women who were older, who were about to graduate from high school, and who had firm plans to marry the father of the child.

Parents' reactions to their daughter's pregnancy were, if anything, even more negative, though early childbearing was common, if not normative, when their own first child was born (Armstrong and Furstenberg 1998). Of course, a few reported that they were thrilled about prospective grandparenthood (Stack and Burton 1993), but the vast majority believed that their daughter had let them down and compromised her future by becoming pregnant at such an early age and before completing school. Phoenix's mother sighed when she told the interviewer, "I didn't know whether I could have killed her or just died myself."

These sentiments expressed by both the young mothers and their parents moderated considerably over time. In the initial interview, which generally occurred sometime late in the first trimester or early in the second, the pregnant teens and their parents were asked how they first felt when they discovered that they were pregnant and how they now felt (at the time of the interview). Most parents had come to accept the inevitable, and many of the daughters responded more positively about the prospect of becoming a mother after their parents' initial feelings had turned from anger to anticipation. As one parent explained, "Each and every one of us makes a mistake. She has a chance to rectify it—not to do it again." In part, the shifting responses reflected the reality that either parents would share in the responsibilities of child care or, as often occurred, a marriage was expected to follow—if not immediately, then at least in short order.

THE MARRIAGE DECISION

Like so many of the women of that era, some had deliberately risked becoming a parent with a partner whom they thought they would marry. Bea Mays was just sixteen and in the tenth grade when she became pregnant. Looking back on her situation some years later, Bea recounted:

> So when I was in high school and met my husband, he was my first boyfriend. First time having sex, I get pregnant. Okay. You figured it's gonna work, so you get married.

Unlike Bea, the women who married immediately were mostly older teens, the white women in the sample, or the handful of those who were formally or informally engaged before becoming pregnant. Even many of these women and nearly all of the others reported that they had not wanted or deliberately planned to become a parent. At the same time, it is equally evident that many young women, like Bea Mays, believed that they had a fallback position in the event that pregnancy occurred: they could always marry the father of their child, if not immediately, then as soon as they could manage it.

However, a substantial number of the fathers were deemed to be poor prospects for marriage by the pregnant teens. Even more of their parents expressed skepticism in the initial interviews about the value of a hasty marriage compared to the potential benefits of postponing marriage and completing high school. As I reported in the previous chapter, the inception of the Baltimore Study occurred precisely at the time when a growing number of pregnant teens and women and their families were beginning to realize the hazards of early marriage and the ways it could interfere with school and occupational advancement. Annie Fremont, one of the teens interviewed in 1967, replied to a question about her marriage plans: "I think it would be better [to wait to get married] so you can get some money. So it wouldn't be all on her husband when she do get married. I'd like to have a little change for myself. . . . I'll be about twenty when my boyfriend finishes college and then we will get married." Sadly perhaps, it didn't work out that way for Annie. She and her boyfriend went back and forth about getting married for several years before he became involved with another woman and their relationship dissolved.

Many of the pregnant teens were counseled by their parents, often based on their own experiences, to wait to wed until they graduated from high school and gained greater maturity. A number told us that they were too young to get married. As one young woman explained, "If I waited until I was twenty-four or twenty-five, I'd be able to accept the responsibilities of marriage." The vast majority of their parents, who were also interviewed at the time, concurred. As one prospective grandmother put it:

> No use making it worse than it is now. I don't feel a girl has to get married because she is pregnant. If she marries somebody she loves and cares for . . . she has to be happy.

A shift was occurring in perceptions of the relative merits of immediate marriage compared to the potential benefits of gaining more education and labor force experience. Right up to the beginning of the study, married women had been ineligible to attend high school in many localities, though not in Baltimore. In the 1960s, most teens and their parents believed that marriage would bring about the cessation of schooling and the assumption of a domestic role, even though many of the teens' mothers were employed themselves, albeit at low paying jobs. Judging from what happened to most of the teens who did wed immediately, their beliefs were probably justified. Women who wed before completing high school were far less likely to return to school and graduate during the five-year follow-up period. Most teens in the Baltimore Study, particularly blacks, elected to postpone marriage until sometime after the child was born, although many married in the years between the first interview and the five-year follow-up. As reported in the previous chapter, these women were on the cutting edge of a new demographic trend that was to unfold over the succeeding decades.

THE EARLY YEARS OF PARENTHOOD

More than three decades have passed since I published *Unplanned Parenthood: The Social Consequences of Teenage Childbearing* (1976), an account of the early lives of the young Baltimore mothers and their offspring based on a series of follow-up interviews conducted one, three, and five years after the first child was born. Little described in that book disconfirmed Campbell's dreary prognosis for young parents, though there were certainly glimmerings that the adverse consequences of early childbearing might have been overstated. At least when I contrasted the experiences of the young mothers with those of a sample of their former classmates I used as a comparison group, the teenage parents were not faring well in the aftermath of early parenthood. By all standards of achievement, educational attainment, employment and earnings, and life satisfaction, the young mothers were faring much worse than their classmates from the same homerooms they had been in when they became pregnant.

The vast majority of mothers, despite their resolution to delay further childbearing, had become pregnant again at least once, and many more than once, after the birth of their first child. By the five-year follow-up, three-quarters of the mothers had a second child, and one-quarter had given birth to three or more children. Three out of five of the women had relied partly or wholly on public assistance during the five-year period. Many had married the father of the child, but only two-thirds of the marriages had lasted as long as three years. Bea Mays had a second child even though her marriage was not doing well. She reported, "You have one more child. You realize it then, a couple years, it wasn't going to work," and explained that "we fought a lot, so I probably would have been beaten to a pulp." Bea left her marriage after struggling for nearly five years to make it work.

Those who married men who had not fathered their first child entered even more fragile unions. In all, 60 percent had married during the five-year follow-up, but half of those unions had not lasted, and many more dissolved in time (Furstenberg 1976). A far greater percentage of the young mothers had married and separated by the five-year follow-up than had been the case with their former classmates who were either currently married or still single. Clearly, the pregnancies had moved up the timetable for marriage, and generally speaking, the skepticism voiced by many parents about the wisdom of early marriage had been more than justified.

Considerable variation existed, however, within the sample of young mothers on economic indicators of successful adjustment in early adulthood. Some had returned to high school soon after their child was born or had never dropped out at all; others had entered the labor force; and still others remained married at the time of the five-year follow-up. Although almost none had entered college or appeared to be headed for a middle-class life, relatively few of their classmates had achieved such an exalted status either. On balance, the picture seemed to confirm that early parenthood exacted considerable costs for the women in the Baltimore Study, although experience in the immediate aftermath of early parenthood was not uniformly devastating. In the final chapter of *Unplanned Parenthood* (Furstenberg 1976, 217), I concluded with the following assessment:

> [There was a] sharp and regular pattern of differences in the marital, child-bearing, educational, and occupational careers of the adolescent mothers and their classmates. The young mothers consistently experienced greater difficulty in realizing life plans; a gaping disparity existed between the goals they articulated in the first interview and their experiences following delivery.

But I went on to recognize that a number of the women had managed to return to school, find employment, and stay off public assistance, defying the stereotype of the teenage mother. "A sizable proportion of the young mothers in our study [were] able to cope successfully with the problems of early parenthood" (218).

Even so, if the story of the Baltimore Study had ended there, there would have been little reason for me to question the assumption that early childbearing confers considerable disadvantage over and above the hardships that young mothers might face if they put off childbearing. After all, prior to their first birth, the young mothers and their classmates had been in fairly comparable circumstances, and their experiences had diverged substantially during the five-year follow-up—or at least, so it had seemed at the time.

ADOLESCENT MOTHERS IN LATER LIFE

In the early 1980s, I began to think about reinterviewing the women in the Baltimore Study, in large part because the mounting political discussion about the adverse impact of early childbearing was becoming more heated and partisan. The big question, still unsettled, was whether the lives of the women had continued to follow a negative trajectory or whether they had experienced some recovery in the intervening decade. By the time I procured funding to do the study, a dozen years had passed since the five-year follow-up. The participants in the Baltimore Study were now in their mid-thirties, and their oldest child was approximately the same age as they had been when they first gave birth, providing an interesting vantage point from which to compare the circumstances of the two generations. I was especially interested in the extent to which the pattern of early childbearing was passed on from the mothers to their firstborn daughters (for a detailed account of this phase of the study, see Furstenberg, Brooks-Gunn, and Morgan 1987).

I was fortunate enough to be joined in this phase of the study by Jeanne Brooks-Gunn, a developmental psychologist, and Philip Morgan, a social demographer. Our research team had good success in tracing and reinterviewing the women in the study, even though more than a decade had passed. My collaborators and I managed to reinterview nearly three-quarters of the women who had participated in the original study and remained in it for the year after their first child was born. Virtually all of the parents, now in their thirties, consented to let us talk to their adolescent children. Although funding was not available to reinterview the sample of former classmates, we extracted information from several national surveys to construct a comparable group of mothers and their first-born children and provide a benchmark against which to judge the success of the families in the Baltimore Study.

When I first began presenting findings from the seventeen-year follow-up, I would sometimes ask audiences to project the future life of teenage mothers and their offspring, much as Campbell had done in 1968. Given their disadvantaged circumstances even prior to becoming pregnant and the fact that most had had children before they were prepared to support them, how well would these families do over the longer term? How many women would still be on public assistance or unemployed? How many of the children would be high school dropouts, teenage parents, or incarcerated?

Based on the first phase of the study and the prevailing wisdom about the adverse consequences of teenage motherhood, we did not anticipate the results that emerged from the interviews. In contrast to the highly tenuous living conditions of the mothers in the first five years after they became parents, their circumstances had substantially improved during the following decade. There were dramatic changes in education levels and employment as well as a steep decrease in the proportion receiving welfare as the teen mothers reached full maturity compared to their situation at the five-year follow-up. It turned out that more than half of the women continued in or returned to school after the five-year follow-up, leading to improved labor market opportunities. The majority of women who had *ever* received public assistance during the first five years of the study (60 percent) left the welfare rolls to become economically self-sufficient. These changes, incidentally, happened long before welfare reform was even on the public agenda, a fact to keep in mind later on when I discuss the impact of welfare reform.

Perhaps the most surprising result of all was the curtailment of childbearing between the five- and seventeen-year follow-up interviews. Most women had no additional children after their early twenties. Unexpectedly, more than half of the women in the Baltimore Study had elected to become sterilized. Indeed, a number of women told us that they had problems convincing doctors to permit them to obtain sterilizations because they were still so young at the time. Regina Lee's experience was common among women who sought a tubal ligation when they were still in their early twenties:

> I used to take the pill . . . and when I knew I couldn't take it anymore, I said, "Forget it, do something." I had two kids. I was supposed to get it down at Brady Hospital, but they said, "If both of your kids get killed in a car accident, there is only a one percent chance that we can undo this," and blah, blah, blah. So I went to another hospital.

In other important respects, the lives of the women were more consistent with the findings of earlier follow-ups. Most continued to struggle in their relationships with men. A majority had been in and out of marriage or marriage-like unions during the past dozen years. Only about one-third were currently married, and only about half of these married women had been continuously married to the fathers of their first children, a remarkable level of union instability. Because of these fragile relationships, most households were supported wholly or primarily by a single wage earner with limited earning capacity. Only a small fraction—about one-fourth of the entire sample—had gained a middle-class income through employment. Another one-quarter held stable working-class jobs. The half who had not achieved this level of economic security were evenly split between the working poor, who barely made ends meet by holding poor-paying or unstable jobs, and those who relied on a combination of public assistance, the underground economy, and their families for support. Although faring much better than they had earlier in life, the mothers were not doing as well as their counterparts from national surveys who had delayed childbearing. The differences, however, were not nearly as large as most observers would have predicted based on the findings of the five-year follow-up.

The story of the seventeen-year follow-up was sufficiently intriguing that I was compelled to collect information on the sample again after another lengthy interval. In 1995–96, approximately thirty years after I first interviewed the teenage mothers, my collaborators and I revisited the families in the Baltimore Study. By the standards of most longitudinal studies, we had great success in following the participants: nearly two-thirds of the black mothers who had received prenatal services in the hospital and who participated in the first follow-up were reinterviewed.

By this time, the teenage mothers were now in their mid-forties and their firstborn children were young adults in their late

FIGURE 2.1 **Measures of Well-being of Baltimore Mothers Compared to Mothers in the National Longitudinal Survey of Youth (NLSY), 1995 to 1996**

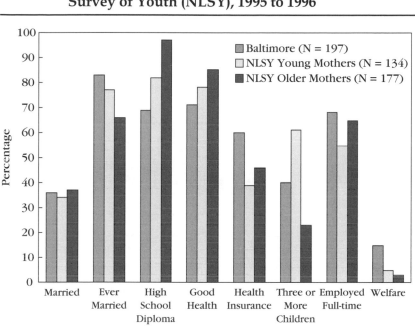

Source: Author's compilation.
Note: Descriptives of the national sample come from the 2004 wave of data collection of the 1979 National Longitudinal Survey of Youth (NLSY79). Sample restricted to black women forty-five years old and older who resided in an urban area. "Young mothers" are those who had their first birth at the age of nineteen or younger; "older mothers" are those who had their first birth when older than nineteen.

twenties. I hoped to get a final reckoning on how the women were doing and at the same time learn the fate of their children as they reached an age when they could be expected to have families or, at least, to be self-supporting. As before, I compared the women with their counterparts in the National Longitudinal Survey of Youth (NLSY), a study that has tracked a nationally representative sample of young adults from the late 1970s to the present. The findings strongly reinforced the lessons learned in the previous waves.

Figure 2.1 shows an array of conventional markers of economic and social success reported by the women in the Baltimore Study and by their counterparts in the National Longitudinal Survey of

Youth (NLSY), and the same set of indicators of success for "comparable" women who postponed parenthood at least until their twenties. Keep in mind that such comparisons actually overstate the differences between teenage mothers and later childbearers because *no* statistical adjustments have been made for the many preexisting differences between these two populations. Thus, although for purposes of this exercise I regard the populations as comparable, in fact they are not strictly so, a problem taken up later in this chapter. Even so, the teen mothers were doing much better by their mid-forties than I—or for that matter most researchers—would have anticipated based on their early adult lives.

TEENAGE MOTHERS IN LATER LIFE

Over time, the differences between the teen mothers and the later childbearers in the national surveys appeared to become less pronounced, though we cannot say for sure, because the numbers in the national surveys dwindle and make comparisons statistically unreliable. The young mothers were not doing as well as those who had delayed motherhood on most of the measures of successful adjustment, but the differences were not nearly as large as had been predicted from the findings reported in the earliest wave of the study, both because the teen mothers did better than might have been anticipated and because the older childbearers, who shared many of the same racial and economic disadvantages, had persistent problems in obtaining good jobs, making stable marriages, and rearing children.

The most unexpected result of the thirty-year follow-up was the unrelenting effort of the Baltimore women to increase their schooling after they had their children (Weiss and Furstenberg 1997). The proportion who failed to complete high school or at least obtain a GED had shrunk to 20 percent, while the number who had completed college rose to one in ten. Over the past dozen years since the seventeen-year follow-up, 43 percent of the women had acquired additional education, mostly in community colleges. On average, these mothers had added more than one year of school between their thirties and forties—an accomplishment that almost no researcher studying the effects of teen childbearing foresaw.

Hillie Andrews, sixteen and a junior in high school at the beginning of the study, was one of the women determined to continue her education. By going to night school, she managed to graduate from high school with her class and began taking college courses when her child entered school. She got an associate's degree in her twenties and went on to college in her thirties, graduating by the time she was forty from a local university. In her forties, Hillie was back in school going for a master's degree. By her mid-forties, Hillie was teaching at a technical college. When asked to explain her success in school, Hillie gave all the credit to her mother, who babysat her child and encouraged her to make something of herself.

> I give it all to her, 100 percent. She backed me up, . . . If I found something in front of me, like a mountain, I'd go to Mom's. . . . She would break it down, show me where to go around it.

Of course, the women's counterparts in the national surveys also gained education, but not as much as did the teenage parents (Jacobs and Stoner-Eby 1998). Accordingly, the differences in economic standing between the early and later childbearers had lessened somewhat, no doubt in part because the teen mothers were at a different stage in their life course. Few had children who were still minors, although many more women had assumed the responsibilities of caring for their grandchildren or other kin.

Jill Roberts's story is not an unfamiliar one. Jill had remained in school, with her mother's help, until she graduated shortly after her child was born. When her mother asked her if she wanted to go to college, Jill remembered replying, " 'Let me go get a job and let me take care of him.' . . . So that's what I did." Jill had been working in a government job for the past thirty years; however, in her forties Jill did finally return to school.

> I have gone back to school and [am] studying law. . . . taking paralegal courses. I mean, even if the grandchild come along, and would have been a welcome pleasure, but it wouldn't have stop me from doing, because I always said, once I got the boys out the way, it was my time to do the things that I want. Didn't do before 'cause [I] make a lot of sacrifices, and I saw my parents make sacrifices for us, so you know, I think that's only nature. It comes natural.

By their mid-forties, only one in six of the women was still receiving public assistance, typically because they were caring for a grandchild. Most held a full-time job, and the majority earned enough to be classified as working- or middle-class, with the rest evenly divided

FIGURE 2.2 **Characteristics of Teenage Mothers, 1972 to 1995 to 1996, Weighted for Attrition (N = 197)**

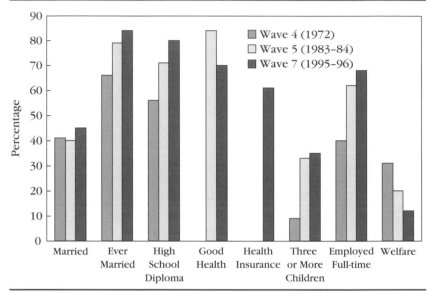

Source: Author's compilation.
Note: Only mothers who participated in all three waves are included on graph.

between the working poor and welfare poor. These figures suggest that they might not have been doing much better economically had they waited to have their first child until they were in their twenties. The minority who had become welfare dependents differed greatly from the rest of the sample: they were considerably less educated, more often suffered from emotional difficulties, and had a particularly difficult time maintaining stable relationships with men.

The thirty-year follow-up produced some other notable results as well, some of which were foreshadowed in earlier waves of the study. For example, all but a few of the young mothers had discontinued childbearing by their late twenties. Their completed family sizes were only modestly larger than the families of women who began childbearing later in life (see figure 2.1). In addition, the differences in the marital distribution between the two populations were not nearly as great as might have been expected, especially in view of the known link between premarital pregnancy and marital dissolution. It appears that the advantage of waiting to have children is not nearly as great as is widely believed, especially considering, as explained before, that the comparisons in figure 2.2 surely overstate the differences between the two groups.

A key to understanding these unexpected trajectories can be found in some of the mental health outcomes that were first measured in 1995–96. We used an identical set of measures that had been included in a national study of the health and well-being of Americans at midlife and developed by a team of researchers funded by the MacArthur Foundation (Brim, Ryff, and Kessler 2004). Among these measures was one that asked the respondents to recall their assessment of well-being in a variety of domains when they were still in their twenties and to compare these evaluations with their current and projected future well-being. Of course, retrospective self-assessments are notoriously unreliable. Nonetheless, the differences between the women in the Baltimore Study and the women in the national survey, who were objectively much better off on average both in the past and at present, are intriguing. They tell us something about how each group thought about the changes in their well-being over the course of their lives.

The patterns depicted in figure 2.3 indicate that the Baltimore mothers perceived their lives to have improved significantly as they moved from early adulthood to middle age. In all respects but their physical health, the women in the Baltimore Study reported that they were better off economically, socially, and in their overall feelings of happiness. By contrast, the women who had better starts in life were not as sanguine about their current circumstances. Although objectively they were doing better than the teen mothers, they felt less well off in many respects than they did before they began to form families. Roberta Rogers, reflecting back on her experiences after the final interview, wistfully remarked:

> I wish I had maybe gone to college or been able to afford to go to college or whatever, which I hadn't been, but it's never too late. Because now, I don't have any children in the home and maybe I can . . . 'cause it's never too late.

In in-depth and open-ended interviews, most women said that their lives had improved as they aged, especially when they looked back to the early years of the study when they first became parents. Although many regretted the timing of their first birth, their reflections

FIGURE 2.3   **Self-Evaluation Over Time: The Well-being of Mothers as They Age from Young Adulthood to Middle Adulthood**

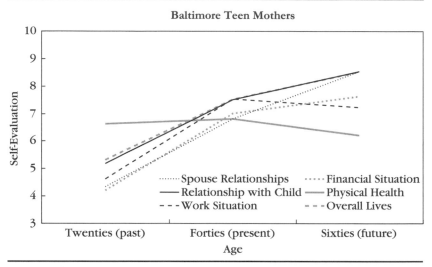

Source: Author's compilation.

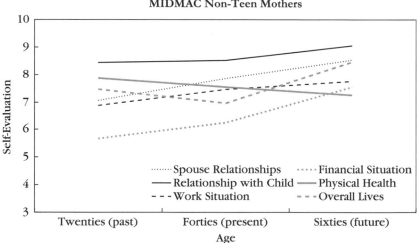

Source: Author's compilation.

on the past indicated two important reasons why they felt much more in control of their circumstances at midlife.

First, they were much better off economically than they had been in the aftermath of their first birth, when most had struggled to stay in school, support themselves, and manage a relationship with the father of their first child. As their economic circumstances improved, so too did their mental health and sense of their own well-being. Many, like Hillie, had been able to return to school and find employment, leaving public assistance and dependency on their parents, though relatively few could match Hillie's educational accomplishments. Still, compared to their modest expectations and their worst fears, a surprising number of the women felt that they had achieved more than they had expected. Dora Pierson, who went back to school and got a job with the Baltimore City school system, remarked:

> I don't know what else I could want out of life. To me, you know, I'm happy. I get up every morning. I go to work. So I don't know what else I could want. Maybe be rich. That's it.

True, their counterparts, who had been better off to begin with, also improved their economic circumstances. Their advancement, however, was more predictable and less dramatic, at least as perceived by the participants in the Baltimore Study. Many of the women in the study believed that they had miraculously escaped a nearly certain destiny, overcoming the odds of being a teen mother. Oddly enough, they were more grateful for their present situations even though they had not accomplished, at least economically, as much as their peers who had waited to have children. As they compared their life circumstances both to where they started and to where they had expected to be at this point, most felt relatively fortunate and even blessed by how far they had managed to journey during the past several decades. Phoenix, when asked how she was doing in life, gave this response: "I could not have prayed for the way my life is. If I had prayed . . . if God had done everything I told him to do, I wouldn't have half the joy I have right now." There were many reasons why so many of the women we talked to were positive about their current circumstances, but almost all referred to how much better things had turned out than they had expected.

Their perspectives, it seems, were shaped in part by the pervasive public stereotypes of teenage parenthood and the negative consequences of early childbearing. Many, wrongly it appears, believed that they were the exceptions to the rule. By dint of family support, help from service providers, and their own considerable efforts to gain education and employment, they thought that they were the lucky ones. Jill reflected back on her experiences and those of some other family members who, like her, got off to a difficult start:

> We've all been pretty much at the same pace. I think each one of us has accomplished almost what [we] thought [could] be done, you know. And people have looked at us. I think we always said we didn't wanna be one of the statistics.

Lest we get completely carried away with these rosy self-assessments, they must be tempered with other more sobering findings that emerged from the thirty-year follow-up. The teenage mothers were not in good physical health. Indeed, nearly 9 percent of the women were no longer alive by their mid-forties, a figure that is 50 percent higher than in the overall population of black women in the United States. No doubt, these cases include a disproportionate share of women who were not faring well on other indicators of well-being, thus inflating our estimates of how well the Baltimore sample was doing.

Some of the information presented in figure 2.4, which reports on stressful events in the lives of the Baltimore mothers, tells a much more problematic story about the frequency of negative and often life-threatening events faced by the families in the study. Crime, illness, homelessness, and substance abuse (undoubtedly underreported) reveal in snapshot fashion a host of ills that the midlife mothers and their family members endured. Add to this list the fact that an alarming number of women reported that they had serious physical or mental health problems. And in separate analyses, we discovered that physical health and depression were directly related to the number of stressful events in their lives. There is little doubt that the women in our study had not attained the relatively untroubled lives of those who grew up in more fortunate circumstances.

Unfortunately, we have no straightforward way of comparing the Baltimore women with their later-childbearing counterparts who grew up in poor or near-poor inner-city neighborhoods, where

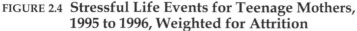

FIGURE 2.4 **Stressful Life Events for Teenage Mothers, 1995 to 1996, Weighted for Attrition**

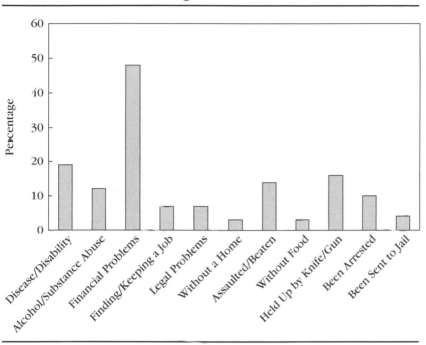

Source: Author's compilation.

stressful events such as the death or incarceration of family members, economic hardship, and substance abuse are all too familiar. Therefore, it is not possible to say for sure from these results whether we would have found any differences in the level of everyday adversities faced by early and later childbearers who came from similar backgrounds. Still, it is important to recognize that however well the teenage mothers did compared with societal or their own expectations, many women in the Baltimore Study were still living close to the margin at midlife, even if they were economically self-sufficient and functioning well socially and psychologically.

Apart from residing in communities that imposed considerable risks on them and their families, the majority of the teen mothers exhibited an extraordinarily high level of life skills, some of which were probably acquired from living a life of adversity. We learned from the qualitative interviews that a high number were working full-time and caring for their own children and those of other kin and friends; active in their local communities, they were also reflective about the journey they had followed since becoming mothers three decades earlier (Armstrong and Furstenberg 1998; McDonald and Armstrong 2001; Rogers-Dillon and Haney 2005). In personal accounts describing the course of their lives, we could observe a huge shift in their self-appraisals. Over the three decades they had been a part of the Baltimore Study, they had moved from being poster children for a negative stereotype to becoming poster women for a more positive image—the family matriarch and protector of the next generation (Furstenberg 2002b).

Missing from these retrospective accounts of the lives of the Baltimore mothers are the impacts experienced by other family members: the children, the fathers and surrogates, and the families who frequently supported and aided the mothers and children in the early decades of the study. Leaving aside the children, whose childhoods and early adult years I recount in the next chapter, I cannot say as much about how other family members were affected by the timing of the first birth from the Baltimore data. Most of the fathers played a major part in the early years, but later on, the great majority of them had effectively disappeared. Relationships between the parents only rarely lasted. As I reported earlier, only one in ten of the couples were continuously married even throughout their children's early lives, and most of the unmarried and previously married fathers drifted out of their children's lives before they reached adolescence.

My collaborators and I took some pains to measure the impact of this loss, comparing fathers who were more or less involved during the children's early years (Furstenberg, Brooks-Gunn, and Morgan 1987; Furstenberg and Harris 1993). It was very difficult to demonstrate much of an impact on the child's development unless the father remained in the home or was highly involved in the child's upbringing, which occurred among only a small minority of the families. From the little that we were able to learn from both prospective and retrospective accounts, relations between the parents were typically acrimonious. The mothers often spoke bitterly about the fathers' failure to support and nurture the children. And the children, too, felt a keen sense of betrayal, perhaps heightened by their mothers' feelings of abandonment.

As for the mothers' kin, who often assumed an active role in providing support and care, the picture is far more positive and reassuring. While conflicts and sometimes permanent resentments did occur as the mothers' kin stepped in to fill the void created by the children's fathers, clearly these were more the exceptions than the general rule. For the most part, the active part played by maternal kin created a lasting sense of obligation to grandmothers and grandfathers, uncles and aunts, and other relatives who shared the burden of child care and support (Furstenberg 1980). As we learned earlier in this chapter, the teen mothers often spoke reverentially about the debt they felt toward their families, who lent support and, in many instances, assumed the major share of parental responsibilities while the mothers gained education and employment experience.

Many, like Hillie Andrews, whom we quoted earlier, gave credit for their success to their mothers. Others cited grandparents, aunts, or neighbors who stepped in to provide guidance, financial support, and child care. It is not easy to reckon the costs and benefits of these family arrangements, whether for the mothers, the children, or the kin who assumed the added kinship responsibilities. There is a tendency in the research on this question of impacts of early childbearing on family members to take one side or the other in assessing the price of helping out (McDonald and Armstrong 2001). After all, it is easy to make a case that already overburdened families are pushed to the brink by assuming the responsibilities of child care for these unplanned children. Alternatively, some observers have claimed that these family arrangements are functional if not optimal in low-income households (Geronimus and Korenman 1992).

In my view, the evidence for one perspective or the other is inconclusive. I am inclined to believe that some families endure a hardship but manage quite well and may even become stronger for the collective involvement, while others cannot handle additional financial and emotional demands. That there is a different set of expectations about helping out in these situations seems undeniable, but I suspect that extended kin are not invariably effective in compensating for the financial and emotional loss of the missing father. At the same time, we must be realistic about how much could or would be provided by the men who faded away; frequently, they did not have much to offer in the way of financial help or emotional support for either the mother or the child. Compared to parenting alone, it is probably safe to assume that most mothers and their children benefited from the help provided, even if it is hard to put a precise figure on the magnitude of that benefit.

One reason why it is so difficult to assess these impacts on the family is that they changed over time. If we had relied on the accounts of the young mothers shortly after they entered parenthood, we would have gotten one picture—not wrong but partial, as it turns out. In interviews conducted at a later age and stage in life, the teen mothers openly and quite explicitly revised their accounts of their own actions and their parents' reactions to the events that transpired at earlier points in their lives. They were generally more reflective and self-critical about their own actions and more sympathetic to their parents as they looked back in time (Armstrong and Furstenberg 1998).

To sum up, based on the Baltimore Study, we have discovered that early parenthood does not necessarily result in a negative trajectory for young mothers. A variety of conditions moderate the impact: the mothers' circumstances at the time of the first birth and, even more important, their psychological ability to respond to the challenges of child rearing. In addition, some were helped or hindered by the men who fathered their children or other males who became surrogate parents. We have also noted the important role played by extended kin in providing assistance and support, as well as the fact that a host of conditions that play out over the life course can strengthen or undermine a woman's ability to manage motherhood. Several factors are critical to her long-term prospects and her ability to manage early motherhood—whether her schooling was interrupted, whether she was able to control additional childbearing, and whether she entered and maintained a stable partnership. It is clear from our data that early parenthood was not the certain path to lifelong disadvantage that many observers believe it to be, but neither could we conclude from the Baltimore Study that it had no adverse effect on teenage parents.

IMPROVING THE RESEARCH, REFINING THE ANSWERS

A body of research has appeared over the past decade or so that generally supports the finding that the long-term effects of teenage childbearing have been overestimated, based on short-term studies of the effects of early childbearing. In 1987, when a panel of the National Research Council (of which I was a member) of the National Academy of Sciences published a broad review of the research on the social and economic consequences of teenage childbearing, most social scientists still believed that the impact was both large and lasting. In summing up the body of research that had been carried out during the 1970s and 1980s, the National Academy's report, entitled *Risking the Future* (Hayes 1987, 132), concluded that, "while the popular image of severe and life-long social and economic disadvantage is exaggerated, women who begin childbearing as teenagers are nevertheless at greater disadvantage than those who delay childbearing." The report also carried this reminder: "It seems important to keep in mind that not all young mothers follow the same recovery route, nor do they achieve educational, financial, and personal success on the same schedule, if at all" (139).

These judicious conclusions were largely ignored in the press coverage of the National Academy report and in the responses of social scientists, politicians, and policymakers that followed its publication. If by the late 1980s we knew that the consequences of early childbearing were neither uniform nor inevitably severe, it has taken a long time for this opinion to be embraced by researchers, not to mention politicians, advocates, and policymakers. During the past two decades, a growing number of studies using more sophisticated techniques have tended to support the opinion that the consequences of early childbearing are far from devastating. Indeed, the causal effect of birth timing appears to be far more modest than we once believed when researchers take fuller account of what is referred to as "selectivity."

The problem that researchers face in assessing the causal effect of early childbearing arises from the fact that teenage childbearing does not occur randomly. Early parenthood happens disproportionately to adolescents (and their partners) who are different in a variety of ways from the teens who typically delay parenthood. Think of it this way: who is more likely to become pregnant and bring the pregnancy to term—a girl who has limited cognitive abilities, has failed a grade or two, and is attending a very poor high school where early parenthood is common, or a girl who is a strong student, gets considerable praise from her teachers, and is in a program for college-bound students? The answer is obvious, but this difference in the proclivity of certain teenagers to have children—to "select themselves" into the role—creates enormous headaches for researchers who want to identify whether and how much teenage childbearing *causes* later outcomes. How much is the effect of early childbearing due to the preexisting differences between early and later childbearers, and how much is due to the timing of the first birth?

Until relatively recently, in attempting to answer this question, most social scientists resorted to using statistical controls in their models that made adjustments for preexisting differences between early and later childbearers. The problem is that researchers have known for a long time that this approach does not adequately deal with the problem of selectivity (Lieberson 1985). Because most surveys contain only a limited number of background controls, a number of unmeasured variables could and no doubt do explain some portion of the differences between the populations being compared. In other words, typically the use of statistical controls results in researchers overestimating the true causal effect of an event like early childbearing.

Statisticians have long wrestled with this problem. Many have concluded that there is no good way of testing for causality except through random assignment experiments, which, if properly performed, can isolate causal influences with some precision. Unfortunately (or probably fortunately for the subjects of social experiments), it is impossible to design random assignment experiments for events such as teenage childbearing—or, for that matter, for many of the other events that interest social scientists and policymakers.

Over the past two decades, researchers have found some very inventive ways of getting around the problem of selectivity, or at least minimizing its impact (Ashcraft and Lang 2006; Geronimus and Korenman 1992; Hoffman, Foster, and Furstenberg 1993; Levine and Painter 2003; Maynard 1997; Wu and Wolfe 2001). For example, some researchers have compared outcomes of siblings, reasoning that such comparisons minimize the environmental differences. Others have capitalized on the fact that some pregnancies end in miscarriage and hence provide a sort of "natural experiment" that allows a comparison between those who involuntarily end a pregnancy and those who are able to bring their children to term. Another researcher compared identical twins, and still another looked at the impact of first and second births in the same family to judge the unique impact of children born in the teen years (for a more detailed review of this literature, see Maynard 1997; Wu and Wolfe 2001).

Generally speaking, these efforts to take account of selectivity (or what economists refer to as endogeneity) reduce the differences between early and later childbearers, who could be presumed to be otherwise identical prior to becoming pregnant. The evidence is still not definitive, but researchers who have employed these different methodological approaches to take better account of selectivity are generally agreed that the impact of early childbearing has been overestimated by the inability to measure accurately the full set of preexisting differences between those who become parents in their teens and those who postpone parenthood until they are older (see, for example, Cherlin 2001).

Arline Geronimus and Sanders Korenman (1992) were among the first researchers to observe the problems of selectivity in the literature on teenage childbearing and to use the technique of comparing sisters in the same family, one of whom had a child in her teens and one of whom did not. By doing so, in effect, they created a better match between early and later childbearers, since presumably the sisters shared genetic and family environments. Initially, I criticized this quasi-experiment, arguing that the sample of sisters used in their analysis was small and that the teen mothers were distinctly unrepresentative of the larger universe of teen mothers (Furstenberg 1991). With Saul Hoffman and Michael Foster, I undertook a replication of the Geronimus and Korenman analysis using a different and larger dataset. Whereas Geronimus and Korenman had found no consistent differences between sister pairs, we found modest to moderate effects in the predicted direction showing that teen mothers had worse outcomes in later life than their sisters who had delayed childbearing. However, even our analysis cut by half the impact of early childbearing that we would have found using the standard regression technique with a generous set of controls for background differences (Hoffman, Foster, and Furstenberg 1993).

For some years thereafter, I continued to believe that early childbearing produces adverse effects on the later lives of teenage mothers. However, as more research has appeared, I am persuaded that the effects of the timing of the first birth would in fact be small to nonexistent were we able to take account of not only individual attributes such as cognitive ability, mental health, and temperament but also family and neighborhood environments. (No study that I know of does *both*.) In fact, whether the impact of early child-bearing is negligible or modest makes only a slight difference for public policy. Admittedly, we still do not know the full answer to that question, and possibly we never will. Part of the reason is that the newer techniques run the danger of "over-controlling" for selection.

Saul Hoffman, an economist, has done a painstaking analysis of different experimental approaches to teasing out the "true" causal significance of early childbearing (Hoffman, Foster, and Furstenberg 1993). His conclusion is that early childbearing has a nontrivial effect on certain outcomes, although the size of the effects on all outcomes is far smaller than is evident in studies that rely on more traditional methods of statistical control (see also Levine and Painter 2003). Although I am inclined to agree with Hoffman that there is likely to be some effect of teenage childbearing, many statisticians might say that any of these methods for detecting selec-tivity are still inadequate. I return to this issue in the next chapter when I address the impact of early childbearing on the next gen-eration. For now, we must consider the distinct possibility that early childbearing has only a modest effect, or conceivably even no effect at all, on the mothers' prospects of having a successful educational, occupational, or marital career. Possibly too, as a few investigators have discovered, early childbearing might even sometimes have a positive effect on the lives of some women who might otherwise have done even worse in later life had they not had a child.

I do not rule out the possibility that early parenthood has a pos-itive effect on some young mothers by galvanizing their motivation to succeed. Numerous women in the Baltimore Study talked in both the ongoing interviews and the retrospective accounts of their lives about how important having a child had been to getting their lives together. Of course, it is entirely possible that many of these women would have gotten their lives together whether or not they had a child. Something else might have made them take more responsibility—finding a job, going to college, or simply getting older. Several of the young mothers, in assessing the impact of early childbearing on their lives, explained that having a child had shifted the focus of their lives. When asked whether she would have done things differently if she had to do it over again, Phoenix first equivocated, but then said, "I think that if I had not had him, I would have been wild with the crowd, you know, that I worked with downtown." She went on to explain that her friends were leading a wild life, whereas "I felt like I had a sense of responsibility."

Whatever the precise effect of early childbearing on women's later lives or its influence on the development and well-being of their children (which I review in the next chapter), we must keep in mind that the effect assessed is an average distributed over a population. On average, we now know that the impact is not large and that it may even be nonexistent for some outcomes. This seemingly improbable result occurs for two separate reasons that have been discussed throughout this chapter. First, most of the women who stumble early on and become pregnant appear to regain their footing over the longer term, as we witnessed with so many of the women in the Baltimore Study. They had a very rough time in the immediate aftermath of becoming a teenage mother, but most eventually found their way back into more conventional roles. The majority returned to school, left welfare, limited their family size, and entered the labor force. Of course, many remained single or went through a series of marriages and partnerships. However, this pattern of family instability was equally characteristic of many of their later-childbearing counterparts, who came from the same sorts of neighborhoods and went to the same sorts of schools.

A second reason why the impact of early childbearing on women's lives has been overestimated is that early research on the topic did not take adequate account of selectivity among those who became teen mothers. While this problem cannot be fully resolved using survey data, newer methods of estimating selection have led to a reappraisal of the magnitude of the effect of birth timing.

Another way of characterizing the findings of the Baltimore Study—as well as the results of the more methodologically sophisticated research—is that teenage childbearing is more a consequence than a cause of economic and social disadvantage (Geronimus and Korenman 1992). To paraphrase Arthur Campbell's (1968) famous prediction: *If you are poor and black and grow up in a disadvantaged community, attend a disadvantaged school, and face an inhospitable labor market, 90 percent of your life's script is written for you.* Teenage childbearing may make matters worse, but waiting three or even five years to have your first child would not greatly improve your chances of doing well in later life, unless your living conditions were to change dramatically.

This conclusion leads us to ask the question: how do we change the living conditions in which most teen mothers grow up? Preventing teenage childbearing has become a mantra for preventing poverty and social disadvantage, but the reverse is rarely given equal consideration: how do we prevent poverty and social disadvantage as a way of reducing early childbearing? It is this question that leads us to examine with a certain degree of skepticism the premises underlying some of the policies that have been devised to prevent teenage childbearing. In chapters four through six of this book, I explore the logic of these policies and ask whether they are appropriate for the intended objective.

Chapter 3

The Next Generation

THE PREVIOUS CHAPTER reviewed the evidence calling into question just how much teenage childbearing compromises the life prospects of young mothers in later life. I concluded that popular accounts in the media, the views often expressed by advocates, and even professional writings overstate the costs to young mothers when taking fuller measure of their circumstances prior to parenthood. Nonetheless, it is possible, even plausible, that early childbearing could still impose significant costs on the offspring of teenage parents. Whether their children fare less well than the children of older childbearers is the topic of this chapter.

There are many reasons to suspect that children of teenage mothers might be disadvantaged. First and foremost, children born to teenage mothers are generally born into poverty, and most grow up enduring spells of poverty throughout their childhood (Ellwood and Bane 1994; Maynard 1997). Related to their precarious economic circumstances is the fact that the fathers of these children typically fade out of their lives (Furstenberg and Harris 1993; King 1994; Mott 1990; Seltzer 1998). All too often, the men who replace them contribute unevenly to their support and development (Garfinkel et al. 1998). The instability of parental figures in the lives of these children creates a level of flux that is often associated with poor outcomes in later life (Cherlin 2006; Wu and Wolfe 2001). Finally, young mothers are frequently forced to juggle school, work, and relationships with the responsibilities of parenting—not an easy task for any parent, but an especially daunting one for mothers in their teens.

The families in the Baltimore Study encountered all of these adversities and more. Many of the children were born into difficult economic circumstances and conflict-ridden families; they typically were reared in impoverished neighborhoods and attended inferior schools; and most endured difficult and dangerous environments throughout much of their childhoods. They attended Baltimore City schools during the 1970s and 1980s, when federal support for urban education was declining. They endured the wave of crime and violence that afflicted their neighborhoods in the 1980s with the spread of crack and other drugs. And they entered adolescence as the risks of HIV/AIDS and incarceration were beginning to take a large toll on the black population. Surely, then, it would seem that this unlucky cohort of young people was destined for disadvantage in later life.

The hard life endured by many of the firstborn children was painfully evident from the earliest interviews that were conducted with them as adolescents in the mid-1980s, when many described the quality of life in their families and communities. Annie Fremont's daughter Sabrina recalled her teenage years:

> The teenage period my mother was my security blanket and the only person I really trusted. . . . And then at sixteen, I felt like she wasn't really there for me. . . . I really had a tough relationship with my stepfather. [Sabrina later moved to her grandmother's house until her mother's marriage broke up and her mother joined Sabrina and her grandmother.] I was the only one in the house working, and I had to help take care of my brother and sister. And I realized . . . that my mother was on drugs. And oh my God, [she] had been all along, and I just didn't know it. I didn't really want to realize it.

The interviews with the children were replete with such stories of hardship, victimization, abandonment, and, not infrequently, abuse. Mixed in—often in the same tale—were accounts of family sacrifice and support. Sabrina described herself as an "outcast" during her adolescent years, commenting: "It was so tough. . . . There's a part of my life I don't remember. I just kinda shut it off, you know. Everybody had tough times as a teenager."

Many, if not most, of the children whose lives we traced for nearly three decades were raised, like Sabrina, under trying circumstances that defy developmental psychology's most elementary principles of what children require to thrive and to succeed. At best, their parents were coping with enormous stresses; at worst, parents were mired in personal problems, as was the case with Annie Fremont, or were absent altogether.

There is ample reason, then, to assume that the offspring of teen mothers, like those we studied in Baltimore, might not fare well during childhood and might face insurmountable obstacles as they enter adulthood. I begin here by reviewing the experience of the children, and then I place the results of the Baltimore Study in the context of the broader research literature on the impact of the timing of first birth on children's development and their success in early adulthood.

THE BALTIMORE CHILDREN COME OF AGE

We began collecting information on the firstborn children of the young mothers in the Baltimore Study in the first-year follow-up, when they were approximately one year old. The focus on the children intensified as the study evolved from a program evaluation to an extended examination of the life course of the teen mothers and their firstborn children. At the five-year follow-up, we administered two tests of cognitive development and attempted (rather unsuccessfully) to interview the children directly using a doll play technique adapted by a developmental psychologist (Furstenberg 1976). At the seventeen-year follow-up, we again interviewed the children, who were by then in their mid-teens. They were interviewed twice again in early adulthood. Finally, in 1995–96, we reinterviewed the sample when the firstborn offspring were in their late twenties (Furstenberg, Hughes, and Brooks-Gunn 1992; Furstenberg, Levine, and Brooks-Gunn 1990; Furstenberg and Weiss 2000).

In the latter stages of the study, the children, by then young adults, were compared to their counterparts drawn from national surveys; we matched them, as best we could, to representative samples of children of teen mothers as well as to children of women who began childbearing later in life. Our aim was similar to the purpose of the procedures we used to follow their mothers. First, we wanted to know whether the children in the Baltimore sample were reasonably similar to their counterparts in nationally representative studies. Second, we wanted to see just how large the differences were between the offspring of early and later childbearers before taking into account differences in their parents' status at the time of their birth. This disparity can be thought of as the maximum possible effect of age at first birth on children's outcomes. Crude as it is, it provides some way of sorting out the effect that is accounted for by differences prior to birth (selection effects), birth timing, or some combination of the two. Finally, we also conducted a series of open-ended interviews with a subsample of the young adults, following them from the end of their teens into their early adult years, with an eye toward understanding the experiences that led to a successful or unsuccessful transition to adulthood. This small-scale qualitative study supplements the analysis of the survey data presented in this chapter.

The earliest assessment of the children, reported in my first book on the study (Furstenberg 1976), found that the preschoolers often faced challenging if not precarious family circumstances. Only one-third were living with both of their biological parents. Of those who were not, nearly one-third of their mothers had been married and separated, either from the child's father or from someone else. Others were living with a stepparent or with their mother and grandparents. About one-fourth were residing in a household headed by their mother with no other adult in the home. About one-tenth of the children had been separated from their mother for some period during their first five years, although most had been reunited by the five-year follow-up.

Caregiving patterns paralleled these living arrangements. Typically, mothers shared responsibility for rearing their child with a partner or a parent. At least by their own accounts, mothers were deeply involved in child rearing. Most spoke proudly of their children's accomplishments, and their houses were decorated with photographs and children's artwork.

Betty Warren had reported that her mother was very upset when she became pregnant, but that her mother had also been "glad in a way." A year after delivery, Betty was caring full-time for the child. "My mom let me be the mother," she explained to the interviewer, "and she was his grandmother." Betty declared that Lawrence, her son, was "a fine little fellow"; though he was doing well at the time of the interview, Lawrence had been hospitalized for tuberculosis. Being a teen mother had been hard, Betty explained years later when she was interviewed. Still, having the help of her mother had provided "a lot of stability and a lot of love."

A significant majority of parents during the early years of the study claimed to take a large share of the responsibility for raising their children. Only a minority reported that they had ceded primary authority to someone else. In a subsequent analysis of the impact of parenting styles, my collaborators and I found no differences when we compared part-time mothers (those who had yielded primary child rearing responsibility to a parent) and full-time mothers (those who had been the exclusive or primary caregiver) in any outcome related to involvement or investment in their children, such as cognitive scores or parent-reported measures of children's adjustment. Apparently, most of the differences in the circumstances of the first-borns resulted from the mothers' degree of involvement in schooling and work outside the home. Of course, we cannot dismiss the possibility that parents were overstating their roles and being overly optimistic about how their children were faring in order to impress the interviewer. But Mrs. Blau, the staff member who conducted most of the interviews in the early years of the study, was genuinely impressed with the intensity of most of the young mothers' emotional involvement with their children and with the level of their development, especially after she had expressed doubts earlier in the study about the mothers' capacity to assume the responsibilities of parenthood.

Reviewing the evidence collected in the first phase of the study is something like sorting through tea leaves for signs of a direction in the lives that were unfolding. Mrs. Blau penciled in marginal notes at the end of the interviews to indicate the baffling shifts in the family circumstances that she followed from year to year. Gladys Beatty, distraught when she was pregnant, according to Mrs. Blau, had recovered a year later. She seemed "sweet, clean, and neat, dressed as if she can't afford to buy her clothes very often." A year later, when Gladys was about to wed her child's father, Mrs. Blau observed, "Gladys looks wonderful. She seems very happy."

Two years later, Gladys was living with her husband and his family and described herself as finally getting her life together. She rated herself as nine out of ten on a happiness scale and, Mrs. Blau commented approvingly, on her skill in raising her two daughters.

Despite the positive reports of most parents and the interviewer, it is evident that ominous events were occurring in many families: a continual stream of household changes, geographical mobility, bouts of extreme poverty, child care problems, illnesses, and problem behaviors among the children. What is less clear is whether or how much the timing of the children's birth contributed to those problems, directly or indirectly. To answer that question, I compared the children of the teen mothers with the children of the mothers' classmates who had given birth by the five-year follow-up. The differences between the two groups were visible, although modest. More of the classmates' children were living in homes with two biological parents and were residing in households living above the poverty line (see Furstenberg 1976, ch. 9).

Test scores on the cognitive measures showed little or no difference between the children of the young mothers and those of their former classmates. On the other hand, there were large differences in the scores of both the offspring of teen mothers and the children of their classmates when compared with children in preschool settings who were given identical tests. Poorer children, especially those not attending preschool, and black children, even holding class constant, performed less well on the cognitive measures. This evidence suggests that the children of both teen mothers and their classmates were not doing well (by national standards) owing more to their class and racial status than to their mother's age at first birth (Furstenberg 1976, ch. 10).

A dozen years elapsed before we gathered any further information on the children.

The next snapshot taken of the offspring when they were in their mid-teens was predictably less flattering than that taken when they were preschoolers. By their mid-teens, just one in ten of the children were living with both of their biological parents, and most of the others had endured a great deal of family flux as fathers, stepfathers, and surrogate fathers moved in and out of the household. A substantial number of children had witnessed violence in the household, and a significant minority had left home on one or more occasions. Many of the families in the study had experienced further spells of unemployment, poverty, and, in a small number of cases, homelessness, victimization, substance abuse problems, and a host of other physical and mental health problems (Furstenberg, Brooks-Gunn, and Morgan 1987).

Just four years after the positive report on Gladys Beatty and her family, Gladys separated from her husband, a policeman, after he suffered a severe psychotic break. Though she received part of his disability payments, Gladys and three of her four children moved in with Gladys's boyfriend. Her oldest, Arlene, moved in with her grandmother because she was having a hard time at home and needed "more freedom." The wear and tear of everyday life, it seemed, was taking its toll on the families in the study, even though many of the parents were living in better conditions than they had been a dozen years earlier.

The vast majority of the children had endured at least one and often many more negative life events—the breakup of parental unions, other parent figures moving in and out, illness, substance abuse and the like—that developmental psychologists and sociologists have linked to poor outcomes for children such as learning difficulties and grade failure, poor adjustment with peers, and physical and mental health problems (Furstenberg 2006). Although we did not examine the children's adjustment in their primary and middle school years, there was certainly cause for concern based on the unsettled and often harsh conditions that they had endured in the interim between the five- and seventeen-year follow-ups.

Not surprisingly, then, as more fully described in *Adolescent Mothers in Later Life,* many of the children were encountering problems during their teen years even though close to a majority, remarkably enough, appeared to be on track for success—or at least for avoiding the obvious pitfalls that might interfere with later life achievement—judging from school performance, lack of involvement with the criminal justice system, avoidance of early motherhood, and other indicators of success. At the same time, this "good enough" standard is not what most affluent parents would hold for their children. By the loftier standards of more privileged American parents, few of the children were on a path for success in the middle class, much less a comfortable life free of economic worries.

It was unclear at the time how many of the youth would outgrow or overcome the problems that they were encountering in their adolescent years, although my coauthors and I wrote at the time:

> The mothers' struggles to avoid poverty may have levied a cost on their children, costs in academic achievement, maladjustment, misbehavior, and possibly early parenthood. (Furstenberg, Brooks-Gunn, and Morgan 1987, 104)

The parents' interviews revealed a sober assessment of the challenges they had faced and were currently encountering in rearing their children. At the same time, most mothers voiced a fervent desire to see their offspring enjoy a better and easier life than they had experienced. As one mother put it, "I hope she does not completely walk in my footsteps because I could have left a few of them out. If she is going to do it, I hope she takes a shortcut to better days."

In 1987, when the children were in their late teens and early twenties, we took another snapshot of their adjustment. The picture of the children's developmental progress was only slightly improved. By the end of their teens, about half had graduated from high school, and nearly one-third were still enrolled in high school or college. Slightly more than half were employed, although most worked low-paying, unskilled jobs. On the negative side, one-third had dropped out of high school, although some of these eventually returned to school. Nearly half reported becoming pregnant or getting someone pregnant, and one-third of the entire sample had had a child by age twenty—almost two-fifths of the females and about one-fourth of the males. Though this figure of second-generation (and sometimes third-generation) teen parents is lower than many observers might have projected, the proportion is nonetheless sizable and troubling. Moreover, one in eight of the offspring, almost all women, were receiving public assistance in their late teens.

Nearly half of the entire sample of youth had been stopped by the police, and one in six, almost all men, had spent time in jail. Perhaps the most damning indicator of their well-being is that only one-third reported that their lives were going well. Consistently, following a pattern established by adolescence, the females in the sample were doing much better than the males on every indicator except early parenthood. In longitudinal analyses aimed at explaining the variation among the youth and using information from earlier interviews, these gender differences overwhelmed all other factors in accounting for the level of overall success in the next generation.

It was at this point that we began to conduct in-depth interviews with some of the firstborn children, contrasting those who were doing well with those who were struggling. Supplementing the interviews with quantitative analysis from the surveys, we were able to identify some of the important precursors of success and failure. Without a doubt, one of the single most powerful predictors of success was whether the mother had succeeded economically during the child's early years. Four out of five children whose mothers had never received public assistance or had received it for a short time were in school, working, or both, compared with only about half of those whose mothers had remained on welfare during most of their childhood. Early childbearing and problems with the law were similarly linked to chronic patterns of public assistance. It was difficult to compare offspring who grew up in stable families with those who did not because so few spent their childhood with both biological parents. Nonetheless, the few who did grow up in intact families did far better on most outcomes.

These findings are in no way surprising: they resemble the results of many other studies that have been carried out on low-income households, whether formed by teen mothers or by older childbearers. Stability in family situations and resources is a potent predictor of success, and these elements were in short supply among the families we studied. Whether and how much the timing of the first birth was implicated in family instability and the absence of material and psychological resources was difficult to ascertain from the Baltimore data, but clearly many, if not most, of the children were struggling to gain a foothold on success as they entered early adulthood.

Let us now fast-forward to the circumstances of the Baltimore youth a decade later, when the firstborn children were young adults in their late twenties. How they were faring in these early adult years gives us a clearer reading of their life chances, though we know some of them will continue to improve their circumstances in their thirties and even forties.

A general picture of how the youth were faring on a number of indicators that are commonly regarded as markers of success for young adults is presented in figure 3.1. Much of the information there is consistent with prior histories, although the pattern of the indicators has become clearer, in large part because more of the firstborn children had either settled into employment and family life by their late twenties or failed to accomplish these transitions. In other words, it is somewhat easier to identify patterns of success than was true a decade earlier.

A striking difference by gender is similar to but far more pronounced than the pattern observed a decade earlier when the firstborn daughters were outperforming the firstborn sons. Whereas 79 percent of the young women were high school graduates by

FIGURE 3.1 **Well-being of the Children of the Baltimore Women, 1995 to 1996**

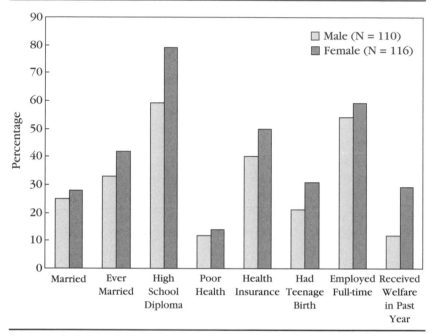

Source: Author's compilation.

their late twenties, only 59 percent of young men had a high school degree. (If anything, these differences are probably understated, because our retention rate for the males is slightly lower than for the females in the study, and the attrition rates for the parents were a bit higher for the mothers who were not faring as well or who were deceased by the later follow-ups.)

A slightly higher proportion of the daughters than the sons had become parents by their late twenties, and sons and daughters had produced roughly the same number of children. A higher proportion of the daughters than the sons, however, were married or living in consensual unions with their child's parent. As I reported earlier, almost two-thirds of the daughters and 80 percent of the sons did *not* become parents while still in their teens. Ten years later, a majority of the males and a substantial minority of the females still had not entered parenthood. Whereas their parents had virtually completed childbearing by their late twenties, close to half of the next generation had not even begun to form families.

Compared with their mothers, a majority of daughters were on a trajectory of economic success that involved postponing parenthood, working, and gaining additional schooling in their twenties. Nearly two-fifths followed in their mother's footsteps by having a birth before age twenty while trying to juggle parenthood, schooling, and work. Most of this minority, like their mothers, cycled on and off of public assistance. (The interviews were conducted the year before passage of the 1996 welfare reform legislation.) Still, the vast majority of the females were self-supporting by their late twenties—a surprising finding in view of the grim prospects their mothers had faced at the time of their birth and the turbulent childhoods that many of them had experienced.

Although we found no differences in the physical health of the younger generation by gender, figure 3.2 shows that men were much more likely than women to run into difficulties with crime and substance abuse. Based on reports by both the young adults and their mothers, we learned that a significant proportion of the males had substance abuse problems, had been incarcerated, or had been victims of violence. Combining youth and parent reports, we found alarmingly high levels of pathology among the males in the study.

The gender differences represent something of a puzzle, given that both males and females profit equally from growing up under conditions of greater stability and more ample resources. From the broader literature in developmental psychology we know that males often are more vulnerable to stressors in the family than females, so part of the difference reflected in the outcomes measured may be a product of that vulnerability (Clarke-Stewart, Dunn, and Rutter 2006; Haggerty et al. 1994; Zaslow and Hayes 1986). The absence of a stable father in the household no doubt could exacerbate these vulnerabilities for males; however, in examinations of the impact of father absence on the children in the Baltimore sample, Kathleen Harris and I found relatively little support for the hypothesis that males suffered more from the absence of the father than did females (Furstenberg and Harris 1993). Still, it is both possible and perhaps even likely that the problems that males encounter when a father is not in the home—such as involvement in the criminal justice system—

FIGURE 3.2 **Negative Outcomes of the Children
of the Baltimore Women, 1995**

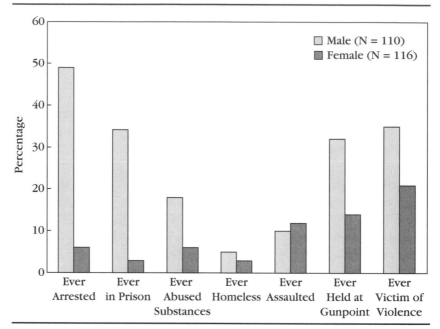

Source: Author's compilation.

produce more lasting consequences, especially in combination with the absence of a committed and protective male figure.

The origin of the gender differences can probably be traced to several related difficulties that combine to limit the progress of low-income minority males in making a successful transition to adult-hood. We know from existing research that low-income males have greater difficulties adjusting to school settings and teachers who may harbor doubts about their abilities and commitment to education. We also know about the influence of neighborhood peer groups—especially in affording opportunities for involvement in crime or with drugs—and the discriminatory treatment of the criminal justice system (Pager and Western 2005a, 2005b). We should probably add to that list of risk factors the difficulty of obtaining gainful employment during adolescence owing to the common fear of employers that minority males may be unreliable or untrustworthy (Holzer and Offner 2001).

Although the sample size in the Baltimore Study is too small to test whether these conditions affected the success of the males more than the females, it appears likely that they did. We compared the youth who had and did not have a stable father figure living in the home until age sixteen; those who were and were not at grade level in school before entering high school; those who did and did not avoid involvement in the criminal justice system during adolescence; those who did and did not participate in pro-social activities in adolescence; and those who did and did not manage to find employment during their mid-teens. Overall, the data suggest that, for males, the pressures to adopt a criminal lifestyle as well as the lack of a stable father figure exert a powerful influence on their later well-being. While living with their biological father was significantly associated with better outcomes in the final interview for both males and females, the presence of a biological father was associated with dramatically lower levels of involvement in the criminal justice system for males. Conversely, avoiding involvement with the criminal justice system was associated with several positive outcomes for men at the final interview, including high school completion, employment and economic well-being, good mental health, and avoidance of drug or substance abuse, homelessness, and physical assault. These findings suggest that, for young urban males, a combination of family, school, and neighborhood effects results in poor outcomes in adolescence that only become stronger in early adulthood. Only a handful of males improved their standing after their teens, whereas females who were doing well during their teens (as well as some who were not) tended to improve their situation after they entered their twenties.

In many respects, the developmental trajectories of the offspring in the Baltimore Study appear to be similar to those traced by many other studies of inner-city, minority populations growing up under circumstances of modest to severe disadvantage (Duncan and Brooks-Gunn 1997; Furstenberg et al. 1999; McLanahan 2004). Considerable variation occurs in outcomes in early adulthood, especially considering the circumstances endured during childhood; nonetheless, the picture emerging is not a very positive one, at least for the males.

The question remains of whether and how much the age of their mothers at the time of their birth contributed to the success in early adulthood of the children in the Baltimore Study. Interestingly, and consistent with the findings of most other studies, the exact age of the mother at the time of first birth (whether she was fifteen or under, sixteen, or seventeen or older), her feelings about the pregnancy when it first occurred (positive or negative), and many other features of the early lives of the children—such as the role of the grandparents, preschool care arrangements, and the involvement of surrogate fathers—were only weakly associated with how well the offspring fared in early adulthood, or not related at all. Indeed, despite the very extensive information that we collected on children's living circumstances, their relations with parents and parental figures, and a host of other factors that might be presumed to account for the variation in how well the children were doing in their late twenties, we were frustrated in our efforts to explain that variation. Despite the abundance of our data on the precursors to problems, our small sample size made it difficult to identify specific sources of success and failure within the Baltimore sample of offspring.

PRIOR STUDIES

There is a large and growing literature in psychology, sociology, and economics on the impact of teen parenthood on children (Geronimus and Korenman 1993; Haveman, Wolfe, and Peterson 1997; Leadbetter and Way 2001; Levine, Emery, and Pollack 2007; Levine, Pollack, and Comfort 2001; Moore, Morrison, and Greene 1997; Whitman et al. 2001). Most studies appear to confirm the seemingly obvious conclusion that teenage childbearing confers considerable hardship on the next generation, though only a small portion of this literature has examined the circumstances of children beyond the childhood years, as we were able to do.

As far back as two decades ago, the National Academy of Sciences panel (Hayes 1987) referred to in the previous chapter summarized the research literature on the children of teen mothers. Sandra Hofferth, a leading authority in the field and the primary author of that review, concluded: "It is clear that being a child of a teenage mother often entails numerous risks." Hofferth went on to enumerate a long list of health problems, cognitive deficits, and developmental problems, including grade failure, socio-emotional difficulties, a higher likelihood of having a fatal accident, early childbearing, and the like. In general, Hofferth concluded, the evidence supported the premise that early childbearing contributes substantially to the cycle of disadvantage by placing children at higher risk of growing up under adverse conditions (Hofferth and Hayes 1987, 174).

Yet, as we learned in examining the consequences of early childbearing on mothers, the research is plagued by the same sorts of methodological problems that call into question the conventional wisdom that teenage parenthood has powerful and deleterious effects on the lives of mothers in later life. Specifically, it is essential not to confound the consequences of early childbearing with its many precursors. Doing so inevitably exaggerates the *causal effects* of early childbearing on the next generation. If we cannot demonstrate that women like Annie Fremont would, herself, have been materially better off by waiting to have Sabrina, can we show that she at least would have been a better and more effective parent for doing so?

Although fewer studies on children of teen mothers exist than on their parents, the history of research on the offspring generally follows the same course that was observed in the previous chapter. The first generation of studies typically revealed large differences between the children of early and later childbearers, in part because they failed to take adequate account of preexisting differences between the two populations. By the time the National Academy issued its report in 1987, the panel conceded that it was difficult to be sure that birth timing was responsible for the poorer development of the children of teen mothers. For example, teenage childbearing conferred health problems on the children not primarily because of the mother's age at the time of birth, but because young mothers were poorer and had less access to health care and prenatal services. Similarly, it was difficult to show that the other developmental risks were directly attributable to the timing of the birth rather than to other circumstances in the mother's life that antedated the birth of her first child. In other words, all we know for sure is that the children did poorly because their parents had numerous problems. Whether they would have done significantly better if their parents had elected to wait until they were older before having their first child (hence avoiding the array of problems facing teen parents) remains an open question (Furstenberg, Levine, and

Brooks-Gunn 1990; Geronimus, Korenman, and Hillemeier 1994; Hofferth and Reid 2002; Moore and Snyder 1991; Nagin, Pogarsky, and Farrington 1997).

A decade after the publication of *Risking the Future,* an important volume of papers, drawing on a fresh set of analyses that showed strong negative impacts of early childbearing on the next generation, was published in the book *Kids Having Kids* (Maynard 1997). Some of the nation's leading researchers presented evidence that children do far less well when their parents are teenagers at the time of their birth on a wide range of outcomes, including physical and emotional health, developmental disadvantage, school achievement, behavioral adjustment and delinquency, and child abuse and foster care placement.

As is so often the case in such studies, the outcomes for children were strongly linked to the mother's socioeconomic status and other social and psychological characteristics prior to the birth of her child, suggesting that the mother's circumstances, not her age, are the source of a sizable portion of the disadvantage incurred by the children. As I noted in the previous chapter, when researchers make statistical adjustments for these disparities, almost invariably the magnitude of the differences shrinks and becomes much more modest. On some outcomes, large and significant differences remain; for others, the differences by age of mother disappear altogether. In most instances, subsequent births to teenage mothers in their twenties fare only slightly better or no better at all than do the children of teen mothers, a finding that might imply either that the disadvantages accrued to the children of teen mothers have ramifications for her other offspring or that the studies are under-controlling for preexisting differences between early and later childbearers.

In the same volume, the economist Jeffrey Grogger reports steep incarceration differences between the sons of early and later childbearers. He acknowledges, however, that

> even though the crime-related costs of early childbearing may be substantial, early childbearing per se explains only a small fraction of the difference in incarceration rates between the children of young teen mothers and the children of older mothers. . . . [W]hat is clear, is that social policy designed to reduce early childbearing will have only relatively small effects on youth crime. (Grogger 1997, 252, 253)

Adolescent parenthood is not, he argues, an important *causal* factor that leads males to commit crimes, but rather a marker for related problems that are implicated in delinquency. Other authors in the volume are more inclined to argue that delaying early child-bearing as such would indeed have sizable impacts on shaping the life course of young adults. However, even proponents of delay acknowledge that they cannot dismiss the alternative possibility that unmeasured differences between early and later childbearers explain the poor outcomes of children of teen mothers (see, for example, Haveman, Wolfe, and Peterson 1997, 277).

A small subset of relatively recent studies have tried to adjust for selectivity beyond using statistical controls. Many of these resemble the efforts discussed in the previous chapter to measure the "true" effect of age of birth on maternal success in later life (Geronimus and Korenman 1993). Several studies have employed clever designs to identify the "age" effect. For example, Arline Geronimus and her collaborators (1994) have compared the children of sisters who gave birth at different ages to take a fuller account of the family and neigh-borhood conditions that might otherwise differ in a random sample. Of course, such comparisons still do not adjust for individual differ-ences between younger and older sisters, such as cognitive levels, mental health, social adjustment, and the like. These differences might account for part of the presumed effect of early childbearing. Even without taking account of the full range of individual differences, the developmental advantage of delaying parenthood, according to the Geronimus analyses, is small or negligible.

Saul Hoffman's (1998) judicious review cautions against reaching definitive conclusions on the magnitude of the effect of teen child-bearing, given that newer studies, taking better account of selec-tivity, have cast considerable doubt on the role that age alone plays in creating negative effects. Nonetheless, Hoffman (1998, 239, 243) argues that compelling evidence has not yet been assembled that would allow policymakers to decide whether "the independent causal effects of teenage parenting are positive, zero, or even just marginally negative." It is hard to disagree with Hoffman's assess-ment. Yet I think it is not rash to conclude that teenage parenting, as such, does not produce the powerful negative effects on children that most commentators predicted years ago and that most of the public still assumes to be almost inevitable.

The question that remains largely unanswered is whether women who live in impoverished circumstances would be better situated to care for, support, and invest in their children if they delayed their first birth. Would they be more likely to form stable and harmonious relationships with the men who father their children, leading to greater involvement of fathers in the home and better material conditions during childhood? Intuitively, it might seem obvious that delaying parenthood by five years on average would yield great dividends for the children. Yet, if the lives of the parents themselves are not significantly improved by the postponement of parenthood, then this seemingly obvious assumption about outcomes for the children does not hold. Judging from the findings in the previous chapter and some of the recent research on the children of teen mothers that takes better account of selectivity, there is some question as to whether the children of poor, minority mothers, especially the males, will experience much better life chances if their mother is twenty-two instead of seventeen when they are born.

CONCLUSION

Although we have identified some of the sources of success (or lack of it) in early adulthood among the firstborn offspring of teen mothers in the Baltimore Study, whether and how much the timing of the mothers' first birth is implicated in the performance of these children remains an open question. Children born to teenage mothers, especially African American males, are likely to experience a host of adverse conditions during childhood that compromise their long-term prospects for a successful transition to adulthood. Being born into and growing up in a poor family, the absence of a stable father in the home, attending low-quality schools, and residing in a disadvantaged neighborhood are factors that place many of the children of teen mothers in jeopardy of acquiring considerable social and educational handicaps.

Whether or how much early parenthood contributes to the circumstances that undermine successful development is still debatable in part because we know that delaying parenthood does not greatly reduce the existing burdens imposed by poverty, race, and low educational attainment. If all women waited until their twenties to begin childbearing, we would not anticipate a sizable dividend for them and their children—even for their sons—*unless* they gained more education, better employment opportunities, and access to marriageable partners in the interim.

Even so, it is difficult to rule out the possibility that delaying childbearing offers children some advantage, if only because mothers are more mature and should be better equipped to assume the parental role. As yet, the evidence on whether maternal skills increase with age (in the absence of additional schooling) is still unsettled. Certainly, a case could be made that young mothers and their children often benefit from living with an older relative who exercises many of the parental prerogatives (see, for example, Geronimus 2003; Smith Battle 1996). Whether the trade-off that comes with greater maturity is offset by losing out on the family support that often accompanies early parenthood is simply unknown. However, the unstable circumstances associated with lone parenthood and with unions that do not survive could make later parenthood no more advantageous for children if mothers are not better off as a result of the delay.

Our finding that the sons of teenage mothers do much worse than the daughters is consistent with a growing literature showing that black males are an endangered demographic group in the United States: they experience higher rates of social pathology than virtually any other population. A cluster of conditions associated with low status helps to explain the precarious situation of young black males, including the absence of male role models, especially fathers, in the family; problems adjusting to school and receiving adequate support and guidance from teachers; the insidious influence of peers in neighborhoods where males are often given free rein; the harsh and sometimes unfair treatment by the juvenile justice system; and the reluctance of employers to give young black males an opportunity to work. These conditions take a huge toll on the prospects of success for young black men. The Baltimore Study did not allow us to determine whether the young men would have done any better if their parents had delayed parenthood; however, there is no compelling reason to believe that they would have done much better unless these crippling conditions were addressed.

In the final chapter of this book, I return to strategies for interrupting the cycle of disadvantage that has become so firmly entrenched in American society for this population. Before doing so, it is necessary to examine more closely the existing policies, which are based on the assumption that delaying parenthood is a promising strategy for reducing poverty. By now, readers should be skeptical that such policies will work, if only because the weight of evidence points to the fact that early parenthood is not an important link in the causal chain connecting one disadvantaged generation to the next. However, for those who still doubt my argument, I try to show that the major policy initiatives have not, in all likelihood, been strongly tied to the decline in teenage childbearing and that the decline in teenage childbearing has not produced the results that policymakers hoped when promoting it as an antipoverty strategy.

Chapter 4

Sexuality and Reproductive Health

IN THE EARLIER chapters of this book, I assembled evidence showing that teenage childbearing has never been quite the problem that most Americans believe it to be. For a host of reasons, the issue has assumed greater political importance and cultural significance than has ever been warranted by either demographic trends or the impact on young mothers and their offspring. Rather than being a primary source of social disadvantage, early childbearing is better understood as a product of disadvantage. As far as researchers have been able to demonstrate, its long-term impact on young mothers and their offspring is modest once we take full account of the selectivity. There are many good reasons for wanting to reduce teen childbearing, but based on existing evidence, its potential as a strategy for decreasing poverty or a means of curtailing the growth of female-headed households has surely been overestimated.

Nonetheless, policymakers, generally believing otherwise, have designed a set of strategies to reduce the incidence of early child-bearing as a means of disrupting the intergenerational cycle of poverty and economic dependency. Thus, teenage parenthood has provided the justification for a series of measures that proponents have claimed will reduce poverty. The logic of the argument goes something like this: (1) early childbearing produces a high rate of single-parent families; (2) children in single-parent families have more academic and social problems and are less likely to succeed in later life; therefore (3) reducing teenage childbearing is a powerful way of reducing poverty because it will both curtail out-of-wedlock unions and save the considerable costs associated with aiding lone-parent households. This argument became more attractive in the wake of the

73

retreat from marriage beginning in the 1960s, especially as out-of-wedlock childbearing replaced divorce as the major source of single parenthood.

The effort to discourage, if not delegitimate, single parenthood, though almost universally endorsed in this country, has considerable appeal to conservatives, for whom the redistributive policies of the New Deal and Great Society were an anathema. Indeed, many critics of proto–welfare state programs and policies have argued with great success that such expenditures on single-parent families are a source of the problem rather than a solution because they ultimately backfire, creating incentives to have children outside of marriage (Blankenhorn 1990; Murray 1984; Wilson 2002). The next several chapters examine a set of diverse policies that emerged in response to rising rates of out-of-wedlock parenthood. Some of these policies, such as those considered in this chapter, are primarily aimed at youth; others are not exclusively so directed, but the population of adolescents and young adults who disproportionately have their first child out-of-wedlock are the major target groups for the marriage and welfare policies discussed in subsequent chapters.

Many of those who believe that single parenthood is the primary culprit in generating high levels of poverty in the United States point to our conspicuously high rate of teenage parenthood as the engine that is driving young people to form families before they are prepared to assume the responsibilities of parenthood (Moynihan, Smeeding, and Rainwater 2004). It seems obvious to most policymakers that a major strategy for curtailing single parenthood involves pregnancy prevention among young adults, especially because so many early births are unplanned and unintended, a conclusion strongly supported by the findings reported in chapter 2. In addition, many scholars have concluded that when parents launch a fertility career disconnected from marriage, ultimately the children's chances of succeeding in later life are damaged (Amato and Booth 1997; McLanahan and Sandefur 1994; Popenoe 1996).

SEXUALITY AND PREGNANCY PREVENTION POLICIES

In explaining the process of "unplanned parenthood," it is necessary to account for a series of discrete events: initiating a sexual relationship, not using contraception effectively, conceiving, and bringing the pregnancy to term (electing not to abort and avoiding a miscarriage). Over the past half-century, social demographers have investigated each of these events in some detail (Bongaarts 1978; Hofferth and Hayes 1987). Beyond academia, advocates and policymakers have used this information to devise various social strategies for reducing teen pregnancy and childbearing. This chapter explores the mismatch between what researchers have discovered and the kinds of public policies that have been crafted to reduce the level of teenage childbearing in the United States. I claim here that a huge gap exists between what young people experience in facing the risk of pregnancy and childbearing and the public policies that have been designed to influence their decisions.

To contend that there is a mismatch between young people's everyday choices about sex and reproduction and the public commitment to pregnancy prevention efforts might at first blush appear to be debatable. After all, during the past half-century we have witnessed a steep decline in birthrates among teenagers, which began in the wake of the baby boom in the late 1950s. A recent government report chronicling the trend in the teenage birthrate concludes: "Teenage childbearing has been on a long-term decline in the United States since the late 1950s, except for a brief, but steep, upward climb in the late 1980s through 1991" (Ventura, Mathews, and Hamilton 2001, 1).

We observed in the first chapter of this book that over the past decade the drop has been especially large, particularly among African American youth. Would it not make sense, then, to celebrate the accomplishments achieved over the past several decades rather than question the impact of public and private efforts to curb teenage childbearing?

This seemingly positive demographic trend has been discounted, or perhaps offset, by the fact that up to the mid-1990s the birthrate for *unmarried* teens had steadily increased as far back as records at the national level exist. The rising birthrates to single young women have overshadowed any satisfaction that might be derived by the overall decline in teenage fertility because of the problems that they seem to pose for lone mothers, their offspring, their families who end up sharing the burden of child care, and taxpayers (Ventura and Bachrach 2000).

The issue of early and out-of-wedlock childbearing in the United States has also commanded public attention because our early birth patterns differ from the patterns of other industrialized nations (Cheeseborough, Ingham, and Massey 1999; Darroch, Singh, and Frost 2001; Jones et al. 1985, 1988; Westoff 1988). Since the 1980s, demographers have noticed that the United States is an extreme outlier in rates of teenage pregnancy and childbearing. We are consistently higher than all other nations (excepting some countries in the former Soviet Union) in rates of teen pregnancies and births. Even more remarkable, we also have higher rates of abortion than nearly all other nations with advanced economies (Darroch, Singh, and Frost 2001; Singh and Darroch 2000).

This dubious distinction occurs not because levels of sexual activity are higher or because teens initiate sexual relations at earlier ages in the United States. Teens in many, if not most, European nations begin to have sex at roughly comparable ages to Americans (Darroch, Singh, and Frost 2001; Smith 1998; Westoff 1988), but they appear to manage the transition more successfully—fewer become pregnant or enter parenthood in their teens or early twenties. Some part of the explanation for these differences can be traced to racial and economic diversity in this country: teenage childbearing tends to be higher in high-income nations with greater levels of poverty and inequality (Furstenberg 1998; Jones et al. 1985; Singh, Darroch, and Frost 2001; Westoff, Calot, and Foster 1983; Westoff 1988). Later in this chapter, I return to the reasons for our relatively poor record of success in controlling early fertility in the United States, at least compared to most other industrialized nations. Since the late 1960s, efforts to provide sex and reproductive health education have been under way here as elsewhere to prevent pregnancies among teenage women and their partners. But in the United States, these reproductive health measures have provoked a fierce debate over the appropriate and most effective strategies for achieving the objective of reducing pregnancy and childbearing among the young.

One party to this debate believes that the best and only way to stop teens from becoming pregnant is to discourage them from initiating sexual relations during their teens, if not until they wed. I refer to this approach—strengthening moral strictures against premarital sex—as an "upstream" strategy. Those who question this approach contend that sexual relationships are inevitable in open societies where teenagers are granted an enormous amount of autonomy. They argue instead for a pragmatic public health approach that includes better access to contraceptive information and services and that, when necessary, offers young people the option of abortion. The second approach espouses "downstream" tactics by encouraging teens to make wiser sexual decisions, promoting contraceptive practice, and permitting abortion when necessary. There is also a third camp of those who believe that both approaches can be more effective in combination rather than either by itself, a balancing act that counsels delay but also, recognizing that not all teens will heed the message, advocates contraceptive education (National Campaign to Prevent Teen Pregnancy 2007).

Obviously, this policy debate rests as much on cultural values as it does on empirical evidence from social science research, although the two elements are often confounded in public discussions. Advocates and policymakers who believe that sexual relationships before marriage are wrong have contended that premarital intercourse among adolescents is inherently risky and can even be deadly because of the threat of HIV/AIDS. This logic has led legislators to fund abstinence-only programs, to encourage parents to speak to their children about the importance of not initiating sex in their teens, and to warn about the potential risks of relying on contraceptives to prevent pregnancy and sexually transmitted diseases.

Many experts, however, believe that it is difficult if not impossible to discourage sexual relationships from occurring during the adolescent years. Since marriage now typically occurs in the twenties or later, proponents of the downstream position believe that teens are better served by being equipped with the information, skills, and resources to manage sexual decisionmaking as they are confronted with the choice of whether and when to initiate sex. Many of the potential risks of having intercourse during the teen years, they argue, can be contained if they are effectively managed by public health policies that promote education, guidance, and supportive health services.

My objective in this chapter is to sort through the available evidence on pregnancy prevention efforts. It would be naïve to believe that my interpretation can be completely severed from this larger discussion of social values. In any case, any discerning reader will quickly recognize that I find myself in the second camp with those who believe that premarital sex in the teen years has been and is likely to remain common. Even if it were not inevitable, I would argue that under the right conditions premarital sex is not harmful and may in fact have positive consequences for the emotional development of young people as they navigate from childhood to adulthood. Indeed, I believe that the American approach to managing sexual relationships is often counterproductive, creates unnecessary risks associated with sexual intercourse, and sometimes ill serves the emotional development of young people (Carpenter 2001). In our highly sexualized society, we provide a baffling array of mixed signals to teenagers, encouraging them to treat sex as an underground, illicit, and uncontrollable urge that is associated with rebellion rather than a part of normal social development. I believe that our inability to resolve the debate over these competing values lies at the heart of the conflicting approaches that have been adopted in this country and undermines the credibility that adults have with adolescents in managing the onset of sexual relationships.

This disagreement over public policy has deep historical roots, but it has taken on a growing intensity during the past several decades. Its history, I believe, is relevant to making an accurate assessment of the effectiveness of the different approaches that have been advocated to manage teen pregnancy and the success of the policies currently in place.

A HISTORICAL PERSPECTIVE

Historians generally agree on two broad observations about premarital sex in America. Going back to the colonial period and continuing throughout the course of our nation's history, Americans have generally disapproved of premarital sex. However, there has never been a time when the norms discouraging sexual relationships were entirely effective. In certain eras and in certain populations, premarital sexual activity was prevalent if not commonplace, judging from the high rates of premarital pregnancy that were recorded in previous centuries (Smith and Hindus 1975).

Recently, historians have discovered that the link between our so-called puritanical roots and present-day policies is far more tenuous than many people believe (D'Emilio and Freedman 1997). First of all, the Puritans were not as sexually chaste prior to marriage as has been widely assumed, though clearly sex outside of marriage was widely condemned in New England. In other parts of the colonies and along the frontier, premarital relationships were more widespread and tolerated. There is even less evidence that Puritan values, such as they were, retained a continuous hold over America's sexual practices after the nation was founded. Over the course of several centuries, sexual permissiveness waxed and waned with the arrival of new immigrant groups and various social movements that promoted or discouraged sexual freedom. In short, many social critics of current behavior have projected backward a highly edited sexual history based more on present-day convictions than realities in the past.

Of course, systematic attitudinal evidence is lacking on how Americans actually felt about premarital sex and on their actual sexual practices, apart from what can be gleaned from birth records and the timing of pregnancies when births and marriages are compared. The historian Carl Degler (1980) uncovered a series of sexual and marital histories of women at the end of the nineteenth century. Degler's findings revealed that our forebears in the late nineteenth and early twentieth centuries were hardly the sexual prudes that we might imagine. A spate of recent historical accounts supports the idea that sexual attitudes and behavior have varied throughout the history of this country, just as we know they did from data collected in the latter part of the last century (Bailey 1988; Coontz 2005; Rothman 1984).

At the middle of the twentieth century, Americans generally held quite conservative views about premarital sex and were shocked to discover that behavior did not conform to the public commitment to virginity before marriage. Premarital sexual behavior was widespread in the United States during this era. This widely heralded discovery was first reported by Alfred Kinsey and his colleagues, who published a volume on the sexual behavior of American males in 1948 and a second volume on females a decade later (Kinsey 1953; Kinsey, Pomeroy, and Martin 1948). Kinsey's studies opened up America's eyes to a reality that shocked the nation and stimulated a public discussion of Americans' sexual behavior that has continued to the present. While their data undoubtedly contain methodological weaknesses, particularly in the sampling method, the Kinsey team demonstrated beyond question that a high rate of premarital (and extramarital) sexual activity prevailed in the United States from the late nineteenth century to the middle of the twentieth. The Kinsey reports also established that levels fluctuated at different times and varied by gender, race, and social class.

When Kinsey collected his data, the double standard was alive and well in the United States (Reiss 1964). Men were far more likely than women to have had sexual experience prior to marriage, and when women had premarital intercourse, they typically engaged in sex with a partner whom they subsequently married (or at least so they reported). The low marriage age in the postwar period reflects the sexual practices of the time; intercourse probably occurred among a majority of males and a substantial minority of females during the teenage years (Finer 2007).

Not until the early 1970s was there a nationally representative study specifically devoted to the teenage population of females age fifteen to nineteen. This pioneering work, conducted by two social demographers, Melvin Zelnik and John Kantner (Zelnik, Kantner, and Ford 1981), had much the same effect as the Kinsey reports: the findings were widely circulated in the press and the revelations startled the country. Sexual activity among teens was far higher than most adults wanted to believe. In 1971, close to half of all females living in metropolitan areas of the United States were nonvirgins by age nineteen. There were significant differences between the levels of sexual experience by race and parental socioeconomic status, but even among white females from well-off families, sex before marriage was common by the end of the teen years.

A second survey conducted by Zelnik and Kantner in 1976 indicated that a significant increase in the level of sexual activity occurred during the first half of the decade. By 1976, rates of sexual activity had trended upward to even higher levels. The overall level of sexual activity for teenagers age fifteen to nineteen had risen from 30.1 percent to 40.9 percent, more than half of teenage women had engaged in sexual intercourse by age eighteen, and more than two out of five had done so by age seventeen.

An important caveat in interpreting these results is that the term "sexual activity" or "sexual experience" implies something more than what is suggested by the data. True, most young people were nonvirgins, but their sexual experience was episodic and typically far less frequent than the media reports of the survey implied. Many teenagers had engaged in intercourse only once or twice, and one-third of the nonvirgins had not been "sexually active" in the past month (which is still the case today). None of the evidence from the period of the late 1960s through the 1970s indicated that teenagers were as promiscuous as was reported in the media accounts of teenage sexual behavior that fed public perceptions that sexual license was growing at an alarming rate. The standard of virginity before marriage was indeed eroding, though not so much as to suggest that most teens were behaving so very differently from their parents or grandparents, many of whom had engaged in sex before marriage. Each generation, it seems, is encouraged to ignore its own sexual history, believing that the next generation should adopt a stricter standard than the one to which it previously adhered.

One large and significant difference in the sexual patterns, however, began to emerge in the 1970s from the preceding periods. Since the marriage age was rising sharply during the same period when the incidence of premarital sex was increasing, and occurring at somewhat earlier ages, sexual initiation, especially for females, was undoubtedly becoming less closely linked to marriage. (It is not clear that it had ever been tightly connected to marriage for males, judging from the Kinsey surveys.) Evidently, many more teens were at risk of becoming pregnant without being able to resort to the time-honored solution of a shotgun wedding.

AN "EPIDEMIC" OF TEENAGE PREGNANCY AND CHILDBEARING?

In the face of this new evidence, a growing alliance among reproductive health professionals, women's groups, and service providers for youth began to advocate more vigorously expanded health services, contraception, and pregnancy prevention programs as well as expanded access to abortion (Levine 2002). The downstreamers contended that more sex education and family planning services were needed in the home, the schools, and the community to serve the growing population "at risk" of pregnancy and sexually transmitted diseases.

Beginning in the late 1960s and throughout most of the next decade, a series of legal challenges had opened up the possibility of extending reproductive health services to the teenage population. Earlier, the Supreme Court in the Griswold case had struck down prohibitions against contraception, establishing a right to privacy that provided the groundwork for a revolutionary change in the government's involvement in population regulation. In 1970 Congress passed the Family Planning Services and Population Research Act (now known as Title X), setting up a nationwide system of family planning clinics that provided health and contraceptive services to poor and single women.

Almost immediately, the advocacy community, led by the Alan Guttmacher Institute (AGI), a newly formed research organization that grew out of Planned Parenthood, issued a series of publications aimed at mobilizing political support for the expansion of reproductive health services for unmarried teenagers, who were initially controversial recipients of Title X services. The Court ultimately supported the right of minors to have access to clinics without requiring parental consent at the very time that demand for pregnancy protection among young, unmarried women was growing.

The Alan Guttmacher Institute published a call to action in a startling 1976 report entitled *Eleven Million Teenagers,* claiming that there was a growing "epidemic" of teenage pregnancy in the United States. In many respects, AGI deserves a large share of the credit—or, I would argue, the responsibility—for putting teenage childbearing on the political map as an urgent social issue. While there is no doubt that the country needed to extend reproductive health services to a growing population who previously had been denied access, the claims in AGI publications sometimes stretched beyond the evidence.

As some critics noted at the time, the term "epidemic" was a rhetorically effective metaphor, but an inaccurate description of what was occurring in the 1970s, even making allowances for its unscientific use (Vinovskis 1988; more recently, see Furstenberg 1998; Levine 2002; Luker 1996). True, rates of sexual intercourse among females (and possibly males as well) were on the rise, but teen pregnancies and births were not. "Eleven million teenagers" referred to the estimated number of teens (female and male) who were "sexually active" (again, bearing in mind that most were not very active). AGI estimated the number of resulting pregnancies to be 1 million per year—by no means an insignificant number. Of those, however, the majority still occurred to married or about-to-be married women who were in their late teens. There were 11 million sexually active teenagers and 1 million pregnancies, but fewer than 200,000 births outside of wedlock. This figure, which is still quite sizable, was prone to some misinterpretation because most of these unmarried mothers were still entering marriage shortly after their child was born, as they had been doing in greater numbers since the 1940s. (Of course, one could claim that most of these marriages contracted by pregnant teens were ill fated, but that had long been true.)

Of the 11 million who were having sex, fewer than 2 percent (including the fathers) ended up producing a single-parent household, at least in the immediate aftermath of birth. Of course, this accounting scheme ignores the more than 300,000 abortions that young women were having annually in the immediate aftermath of *Roe v. Wade*. The rising number of abortions in the 1970s, indeed, created significant apprehension in the upstream camp. They began to express moral outrage at the rapid rise in both the number and ratio of abortions to births among the teenage population.

No doubt, AGI and its allies in the reproductive health rights community could and did make a strong case for the argument that more teens were being seriously underserved by reproductive health services, but the "epidemic" nature of the problem of teenage pregnancy and childbearing was, to say the least, overstated. As observed in the first chapter, the need for contraceptive services among unmarried women was rising for two interconnected reasons: more unmarried teens were having intercourse, and fewer were marrying when pregnancy occurred. Thus, the overall rate of births was declining at the same time that the rate of unmarried fertility was rising for women under twenty (Smith, Morgan, and Koropeckyj-Cox 1996).

Despite these trends that were widely viewed as disturbing evidence that the link between the initiation of sex and marriage was fraying, the *rate of pregnancy* among women in their teens, according to a recently issued report by the Alan Guttmacher Institute (2006b), rose moderately from the early 1970s to 1990, when it hit its recent high, going from 95.1 per 1,000 women in 1972 to 116.9 in 1990. During the following decade, the rate of pregnancy began to drop precipitously, and it has continued its fall to the present. In 2002 it stood at 75.4, well below the rate in 1972 and a drop of more than one-third from its apogee in 1990 (Alan Guttmacher Institute 2006b).

Even in 1990—the most recent high-water mark of teen pregnancy—when over half of all teens had engaged in sexual activity, only slightly more than 6 percent of all women age fifteen to nineteen, both married and unmarried, *had a child* during that year— roughly half of those women who were estimated to have become pregnant in that year. (About one in ten ever had a child before reaching the age of twenty.) Moreover, almost two-thirds of teen pregnancies and births were occurring to eighteen- or nineteenyear-olds (Alan Guttmacher Institute 2006b; Ventura, Mathews, and Hamilton 2001). Nonetheless, the idea that teenage childbearing is at epidemic proportions in the United States continues to be reiterated in the media and is widely believed to this day by the American public. To be sure, the number of pregnancies and births in the United States was troubling because so many conceptions were unintended and preventable, but the public concern was generated at least as much by moral apprehensions about the motivations of young people for having sex, getting pregnant, becoming parents, and not marrying as it was by changing demographic trends.

THE POLITICS OF REPRODUCTIVE HEALTH

The efforts of the reproductive health community to make its case initially produced considerable success. Public opinion began to shift toward favoring a less restrictive approach to managing the sexual transition to young adulthood. Rights to contraceptive and abortion services were granted to minors in the 1970s. During the Carter administration, teenage childbearing became a priority area, and funds were increased to extend remedial and preventive services. In 1978, with the sponsorship of Senate Democrats led by Senator Edward Kennedy, the Carter administration proposed an additional $148 million to increase funding and developed the Adolescent Health, Services, and Pregnancy Prevention Act, which was later passed as part of an omnibus funding bill for health services for pregnant teens and young mothers.

According to Maris Vinovskis (1988, 24), a social historian who as a staff member for the Republicans had an especially good vantage point from which to observe the congressional dealings: "Almost everyone in Washington believed that the problem of adolescent pregnancy constituted a very serious social and health crisis that necessitated an immediate response." A political alliance of sorts was fashioned between the liberals, who favored increased expenditures for publicly funded reproductive health services for pregnant teenagers, and the conservatives, who were troubled by the growth in welfare expenditures and family instability attributed to teenage parenthood as well as by rising levels of abortion.

Undoubtedly, the racial composition of the population of teen mothers played an important part in generating public concern, as some scholars have argued (Luker 1996; Nathanson 1991). Beginning with the Moynihan report issued in 1965, which singled out black family instability as a topic of concern, lawmakers had been looking for ways of intervening to combat the decline in marriage among low-income African Americans. Many believed that young black women were eschewing marriage in favor of welfare support, a theme I return to in the next chapters. Consequently, much of the added funding was directed to remedial programs to serve pregnant teens and young mothers in hopes that early intervention would break the cycle of disadvantage that was presumed to follow adolescent childbearing. A survey of the popular press during this period reflects the view that there was growing sympathy toward helping sexually active teens to avoid becoming pregnant.

In fact, few, if any, existing programs had proven rates of success in primary prevention of pregnancy or childbearing to postpone the first birth or in secondary prevention to curb later births. An important objective of the 1978 Pregnancy Prevention Act was to stimulate research on service interventions that would minimize the costs of nonmarital childbearing in the long run. Liberals could claim that they were helping efforts to prevent pregnancies and the costs of parenthood to young mothers and their families, while conservatives could tell constituents, who were troubled by mounting welfare expenditures, that they were reducing the drain on taxpayers.

In providing an alternative to abortion, considered by many to be morally repugnant, the legislation was attractive to both Democrats and Republicans who were uneasy about the rapidly rising use of abortion services to prevent unwanted pregnancies among women—especially teens, who seemed especially likely to rely on the newly provided abortion services to avoid childbearing. Many experts, policymakers, and advocates, regardless of political persuasion, feared that *Roe v. Wade* was ushering in a wave of recklessness, if not promiscuity, among teenagers. The findings of the Zelnik and Kantner studies, showing a significant rise in the incidence of teenage sexual behavior, seemed to confirm their fears, as did the steady increase in the ratio of abortions to live births in the immediate aftermath of legalization.

No doubt teens were taking advantage of abortion services even as state laws were liberalized leading up to the Supreme Court decision. The abortion rate for teens doubled from 19.1 per 1,000 teenagers in 1972 to 39.7 in 1978 (as it did for older women during the same period), when abortion services became more widely available (Henshaw 1993). Some of the moral alarm felt in the United States probably derived from the appearance of a growing reliance on abortion. However, it is highly likely that women, especially those in their teens and early twenties, were making use of abortion as an alternative to early marriage. In this respect, the rising abortion rates were both a reflection of rising levels of sexual activity in the 1970s, which did boost unintended pregnancies, and declining confidence in marriage as a "solution" to premarital pregnancy.

Again, it is useful to get Vinovskis's insider perspective. He reports that the Carter administration viewed the 1978 act as its alternative to an abortion program (see also Rosoff 1975, 39), commenting that "when many of the 'pro-choice' and 'pro-life' forces united behind the Adolescent Health, Services and Pregnancy Prevention Bill, congressmen found the bill attractive; it permitted them to support positive legislation that seemed to have widespread support and was relatively inexpensive in this highly controversial area."

Without the looming threat of rising abortion rates, the legislation might have failed. In fact, the efforts of the Carter administration to provide a balanced program tailored to satisfy both sides was not the legislative triumph that it appeared to be at the time, nor did it make any mark on the demographic change that was under way. The large increase in proposed funding was never appropriated by Congress, relatively few innovative prevention programs were launched, and abortion and nonmarital childbearing rates continued to rise, albeit at a slower pace.

Opposition to the downstream approach had been visible since the 1960s, when the John Birch Society, an adamantly conservative organization, mounted a campaign against sex education by attacking the policies of the Sexuality Information and Education Council of the United States (SIECUS), an organization formed in 1964 and dedicated to promoting sex education. After *Roe v. Wade,* there was growing opposition to the public health approaches that gave teenagers unrestricted access to family planning services and abortion. During the 1970s, conservatives began to organize at all levels of government to combat what they believed to be a set of counterproductive strategies to curb teenage pregnancy and child-bearing. Many proponents on the right argued that sex education and reproductive health services only encouraged teens to engage in sex, thus increasing rather than decreasing the risk of pregnancy, abortion, and childbearing. This conviction prompted conservatives to claim that the only effective way of curbing teenage pregnancy and childbearing that would not increase abortion was to adopt the upstream approach of deterring premarital sex.

This debate in the United States was hardly a new one, as many social historians have shown. Sex education in the schools, though widely supported by parents in public opinion surveys, was never fully implemented, even in the 1960s and 1970s. Nonetheless, conservative critics of downstream approaches promulgated the impression that liberalized curricula in the schools and family planning services in the community were encouraging teens to engage in sex and to use abortion as a fallback when contraception failed.

In the 1980 presidential election, when Ronald Reagan deposed Jimmy Carter as president, the policy tide began to turn. That same year a freshman senator from Alabama, Jeremiah Denton, proposed the Adolescent Family Life Act, familiarly known at the time as the "chastity law": it provided funding to promote abstinence before marriage. The law restricted access to abortion, promoted adoption as an alternative, and proposed that sex education be required to discourage premarital sex. One critic of this legislative turn of events who chronicles the history of sex education concludes, "Twenty years later, the Right has all but won the sex-education wars" (Levine 2002, 91).

Although the 1980 legislation was widely ridiculed by many on the left, it received a much more sympathetic response from activists and grassroots organizations in many communities throughout the country. Indeed, it is fair to say that the family planning community and its allies from the women's movement were caught flatfooted by the huge wave of opposition to sex education, family planning services, and abortion that was ushered in with the election of Reagan and a majority of Republicans in the Senate in 1980. Conservatives managed to turn the argument that teens needed supportive services on its head, claiming that the message from the public health community favoring sex education and supportive services was not the solution but in fact the source of the problem. The downstreamers have been in retreat ever since, and a huge shift has taken place in the content of sex education, the acceptability of abortion, and, to a lesser extent, the legitimacy of family planning programs for teenagers.

The issue of teenage pregnancy and childbearing was recast by Reagan and the Senate Republicans to advocate a much more restrictive policy for teenagers. Abortion services, which had spread during the 1970s, were rapidly curtailed as legislators began to make it more difficult for teens to terminate their pregnancies without parental notification, a policy that has now been widely adopted by the states (Alan Guttmacher Institute 2007). The curriculum of sex education courses was stripped of explicit discussions about sexual decisionmaking, contraceptive education, and options in the event of pregnancy to focus exclusively on urging teens to postpone sex until marriage. Contraceptive information was withheld in some localities, and many others warned that contraception was ineffective and unreliable (Irvine 2002; Moran 2000). The Republican leadership in the Senate, spearheaded by Orrin Hatch of Utah and Jeremiah Denton, claimed that it was the family planning movement during the previous decade that was responsible for the growing problem of teenage sex, pregnancy, and childbearing, a questionable assertion to say the least. Along with a growing chorus of conservatives, they argued that "the deep pocket of government has funded this intervention between parents and their children in schools and clinics for 10 years. . . . [I]t is little wonder that problems of adolescent sexual activity grow worse" (Levine 2002, 100).

In the early 1980s, it seemed for a time that the restrictive strategies might be paying off. Rates of pregnancy, abortion, and births all leveled off for women under the age of twenty, giving the impression that teens might be either curtailing their sexual behavior or relying more on contraception in response to more restrictive government policies. In fact, what happened is more complicated than the overall figures for *all* teens might initially suggest.

Several simultaneous trends were confounded in most accounts of what actually occurred in the decade of the 1980s. First, early marriage was rapidly declining among younger white women, and the shotgun marriage was going out of favor, just as it had among African Americans two decades earlier. As a result, there were fewer married women in the population. Since married women are far more likely to have births than unmarried women, the teenage birthrate was declining merely because of the postponement of marriage. The nonmarital birthrate continued to climb unabated, if not at an accelerated pace.

This is not the same as saying that the restrictive policies caused the increase in the rate of nonmarital births among teens. In fact, the nonmarital birthrate for all age groups was shooting up during this period, owing in large part to the declining appeal of shotgun weddings and the reduced stigma of bearing a child out-of-wedlock. Still, we can say for certain that no significant decline in sexual behavior, pregnancies, or childbearing among teens took place in the face of mounting disapproval of teenage childbearing at the federal, state, and local levels. The incidence of premarital intercourse among women continued to rise during the decade of the 1980s (Singh and Darroch 1999). The proportion of unmarried teens who ever had premarital intercourse rose from 44 percent in 1982 to 52 percent in 1988, building on the trend that had been observed in the previous decade. This trend drove the rate of births among *unmarried* teens upward from 27.6 per thousand in 1980 to 40.1 in 1989. During this period, the rate of births for married teens remained relatively stable (increasing less than 15 percent during the decade of the 1980s). In other words, the experiment that began during the late 1970s to discourage teenage childbearing by imposing more restrictive policies on contraception and abortion appeared to be a failure, at least in its stated goal of discouraging sexual intercourse and reducing pregnancy and childbearing among teenagers. Rates of sexual intercourse continued to go up, as did rates of nonmarital childbearing among teenagers. Abortion did decrease, shutting off an option for curtailing unintended births that had become more popular in the 1970s with the liberalization of state and federal laws. More restrictive abortion policies may have accounted for the slight uptick in the rate of marital births and the overall birth-rates experienced by teenagers during the late 1980s (for further discussion and explanation of these trends, see Smith, Morgan, and Koropeckyj-Cox 1996).

It appears that teens were using a variety of different strategies during the 1980s to manage their sexual behavior, but it is difficult to conclude that a greater number were heeding the moral messages emanating out of Washington and being championed by conservatives at local levels of government. Abortion, however, was becoming a less popular and less accessible option. At the same time, unmarried teens were gradually becoming more adept at using contraception as the alternatives of abortion or early marriage became less available or attractive.

There is strong evidence that the growing efforts in schools, churches, and communities during the 1980s to promote chastity among teens were largely ineffectual, but that teens were using contraception more often to protect themselves against the risk of pregnancy. During the 1980s, teens gradually began to rely more on the condom, particularly when they first initiated sex and in casual liaisons (Luker 1999; Mauldin 1998; Piccinino and Mosher 1998; see also, for the late 1980s and 1990s, Bankole, Darroch, and Singh 1999; Darroch and Singh 1999). This shift in behavior no doubt occurred because of the perceived threat of HIV/AIDS, not merely as a means of preventing pregnancy (though it is possible that males were also attentive to the efforts of the government in the 1980s to enforce child support payments to unmarried mothers, as discussed in the next chapter). Males in particular began to have more of a stake in the outcome of risky sex during the 1980s as young people became more aware of the risk of HIV/AIDS. As HIV/AIDS began to spread to the heterosexual population, the politics of sex education reached a new level of polarization as the stakes involved in sexual education and access to reproductive health services became even more critical than in the past.

Not surprisingly given the growing concern about the health risks associated with unprotected sexual intercourse, the debate between upstreamers and downstreamers became uglier in the 1980s as a growing coalition on the right argued vociferously that sex education that condoned premarital sex and taught about contraceptive methods was more than immoral and counterproductive. Some of those who adopted these arguments even contended that it was downright dangerous to encourage young people to use condoms, an argument that continues to this very day. In 1986, however, the outspoken, controversial, but highly regarded conservative surgeon general C. Everett Koop broke rank with his allies when he issued a report on the HIV/AIDS threat. Koop argued that sex education had to become more realistic and less monotonic than most conservatives believed it should be. He recommended that sex education begin earlier and be more explicit in covering a range of topics, including homosexuality, premarital sexual behavior, and contraception. The *Surgeon General's Report on Acquired Immune Deficiency Syndrome* (U.S. Public Health Service 1986) provided a shield against the widespread onslaught against contraceptive services that had put family planners and sex educators on the defensive in the late 1970s and early 1980s. Koop helped to maintain the precarious détente between the upstreamers, who advocated teaching chastity, and the downstreamers, who wanted to preserve funding for contraceptive services.

During the first part of the decade, sex education in the schools had been in steady retreat as the federal government tried to promote parental control and restrict school-based efforts unless they were aimed at discouraging teenage sex. A range of religious education initiatives under the guise of community-based grants by the Office of Adolescent Pregnancy Prevention (OAPP) promulgated school curricula that explicitly referred to religious teachings. Litigation efforts beginning in the middle of the decade eventually led to some concessions and forced conservatives to reword religious language in curriculum supported through federal funding. The premarital chastity approach eventually morphed into a curriculum that stressed abstinence only and typically omitted any explicit discussion of topics such as masturbation, homosexuality, abortion, and contraception, but that also removed references to biblical scriptures.

Several historians of this period conclude that the legislation created by the government in the early 1980s laid the foundation for a governmental intervention approach to controlling sexual behavior that survives to the present day (Levine 2002; Luker 1996, 1999). Certainly, the Clinton administration in the 1990s did relatively little to divert public policy from this ideological direction. Whatever Clinton's convictions about the wisest policies for preventing teenage pregnancy—an issue that he described as the nation's greatest problem—he took only cautious steps to alter the conservative agenda to focus the content of sex education in the schools toward a more upstream approach promoting abstinence as the first line of sex education. During his presidency, Clinton softened the hard-line approach followed during the Reagan and George H. W. Bush years, but the public conversation about sexuality was largely one-sided: teenagers were encouraged to "just say no."

Perhaps the lowest point of the Clinton years was his refusal to back Jocelyn Elders, his surgeon general, when she got into hot water with conservatives for proposing that sex education programs mention masturbation as an alternative to intercourse for teens. Elders's explicit mention of masturbation was enough to get her fired from her post, with the president declaring that "that's not what schools are for" (Levine 2002).

Clinton did strongly endorse the formation of a National Campaign to Prevent Teen Pregnancy, a prestigious panel of political figures, advocates from all sides of the political spectrum, and representatives of the media. Over the decade of the 1990s, the campaign mounted a vigorous public conversation through its publications, research initiatives, evaluations, and public events. The idea was to strike a balance by advocating a two-pronged approach that attempted to integrate upstream and downstream messages: a push for postponement of sexual activity (abstinence only during the teenage years) and the recognition that some teens would not heed the message and would require contraceptive services.

Whether this blended approach has built a national consensus on the need for twin tracks or whether it is merely a way of muddling the message can be debated by experts in communication and public policy. In many respects, the message is not unlike what the parents of the teen mothers I studied back in the 1960s told their daughters: "I don't want you to be messing around. But if you do, be sure to protect yourself." This contradictory message—the hallmark of the Clinton policy—did not appear to have a large effect on the sexual behavior of America's teens, at least not initially. The prevalence of sexual intercourse

FIGURE 4.1 **Sexual Activity of High School Students, 1991 to 2005**

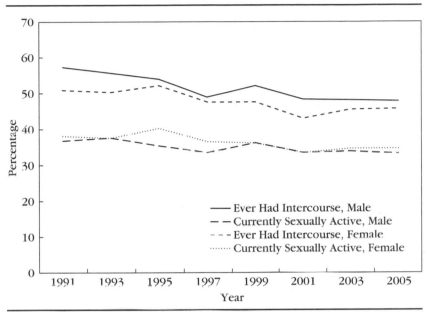

Source: Centers for Disease Control and Prevention (2006).

remained relatively stable, judging from a number of national surveys. Surveys differed somewhat in the samples, the wording of questions, and the method of data collection, but an examination of a number of surveys generally points to a slight rise until the early 1990s in the proportion of women who were nonvirgins, albeit at a much slower pace than the increase in the 1970s and 1980s. Beginning in 1993, there was a more noticeable decline, especially as reported in the school-based survey called the national Youth Risk Behavior Survey (YRBS) funded by the Centers for Disease Control (CDC). A closer inspection of the data suggests that the rates did not decline for white and Hispanic females, though they did appear to drop off significantly for black women. Interestingly, the pattern was different among males: their sexual behavior dropped off significantly from the early and late 1990s, as shown in figure 4.1 (Santelli et al. 2000; see also Risman and Schwartz 2002).

Many possible explanations, few of which are actually competing ones, might have accounted for this trend. First of all, the data could be spurious: there may have been a normative shift in what were considered the socially desirable "answers" as disapproval for premarital sex grew. However, such a trend would not account for the substantial difference in trends by gender and ethnicity. I am inclined to believe that the real change among males was attributable to a heightened awareness of the risk of HIV/AIDS and other STDs and the child support responsibilities associated with parenthood, but it is not easy to demonstrate those potential links. It is also possible that sampling attrition in the various studies biased these findings in favor of showing that males were decreasing their sexual behavior when in fact a higher proportion of sexually active males dropped out of the survey or simply were not in the sampling frame because they were incarcerated (Guzzo and Furstenberg 2006a).

It is evident that between the late 1980s and the late 1990s males became far more likely to use condoms at first intercourse. Several studies tracking condom use during this period show a steady increase in the proportion of younger males who reported using a condom at first intercourse. Again, it is possible that males were only learning the "correct" response to provide in surveys; however, it seems more likely that sexual risk-taking actually did recede over the past decade, judging from pregnancy and childbearing rates among teenage women.

Pregnancy and childbearing rates for teens, which had been trending upward since the late 1970s as a result of growing rates of sexual activity and more restrictive abortion policies, reversed course after reaching a high point in 1991. Beginning in the early 1990s, sexual activity leveled off, if not declined, and teens became more effective contraceptive users, perhaps because of the fear of HIV/AIDS and the lack of availability of abortion services. Since then, both pregnancy and childbearing rates for teens have dropped continually and sharply, right up to the present; in 2004 (the last year for which data are available) they reached their lowest level in a half-century.

Are we finally reaping the benefits of more restrictive upstream policies? There is strong evidence that abstinence-only programs have become steadily more prevalent in schools and communities.

As the federal government first encouraged an abstinence-only curriculum in the Clinton years and then mandated it in the more recent Bush administration, more and more localities have adopted the federal standards. As one critic notes:

> The real success of the abstinence-only-until-marriage movement has been the ability of its leaders to shape the debate and define the terms . . . between the god-fearing and the godless; between those who wanted to give children values and those who wanted to give them condoms; between those who valued families and those who valued the freedom of sexual expression; between the moral and the immoral. (Kreinin 2003, 3)

Virtually every study that has tracked the spread of an abstinence-only agenda concurs that the conservatives have won the day, at least for the present, when it comes to defining normative standards about the appropriateness of sexual intercourse before marriage (for documentation of the increase in abstinence-only education in schools, see Darroch, Landry, and Singh 2000 and Landry, Kaeser, and Richards 1999).

But there is a fly in the ointment when it comes to interpreting this message as causally related to the trends described earlier. Based on the largest and most continuous study, the Youth Risk Behavior Survey, conducted biennially in the schools, the trends in sexual behavior, after dipping moderately in the 1990s, leveled off in 1997 during the most recent wave of abstinence-only policies. After dropping from 54.1 percent in 1991 to 48.4 percent in 1997, the percentage of teenagers who have ever had intercourse has stubbornly persisted at just below the 50 percent mark ever since (Centers for Disease Control and Prevention 2005a). Moreover, a more reliable (and certainly more contemporary) measure of sexual activity, the proportion of sexually active teens (those who report having had intercourse during the three months preceding the survey), has not changed significantly during the last nine years, the very period when abstinence-only prevailed as public policy. Despite the spread of a more restrictive curriculum in large sections of the population, the proportion of teens who report recent sexual activity (as opposed to reporting ever having had sex) has been unvarying.

By contrast, condom use at last intercourse has risen during each of the surveys (except for the most recent, when it remained stable), going from 46.2 percent in 1991 to 63 percent in 2005 (Centers for

Disease Control and Prevention 2005a). Condom use rose while use of birth control pills at last intercourse remained stable, suggesting that teens who are sexually active have become more adept at using contraception. Do these trends indicate that teenagers are becoming more reliant on condoms at the expense of hormonal methods? Not necessarily, because newer and more user-friendly methods of hormonal contraception have been introduced in recent years. The YRBS regrettably does not ask students about the use of newer forms of contraceptive implants, patches, and injections, but it is clear from other evidence that these methods are gradually becoming more widely used.

Although systematic data are lacking on the adoption of these newer methods within the teenage population, a growing amount of evidence suggests that the relatively convenient contraceptives Depo-Provera and, to a much lesser extent, Norplant are gradually taking hold among the more sexually experienced teenage population (Darroch and Singh 1999; Piccinino and Mosher 1998). Moreover, in the latter years of the last decade, so-called emergency contraception became available. As yet, we know little about the use patterns and effects on rates of unintended pregnancy among the teenage population. Clearly, however, this new method may have begun to affect pregnancy rates in the past several years.

Remarkably, the steep decline in the rate of pregnancy and childbearing over the past decade has coincided with a steep fall in both the abortion rate and the ratio of abortions to live births. The abortion rate among teens peaked in 1985 at 45.4 per thousand and dropped by 50 percent in the ensuing decade and a half (Alan Guttmacher Institute 2004). No doubt, restrictions on accessibility contributed to this decline, as has rising public disapproval of abortion. It also seems plausible that restrictions on abortion might have encouraged teens to become more vigilant contraceptors. At the same time, neither the declining availability of abortion nor the pervasiveness of abstinence-only programs has deterred sexual activity in any striking or significant way, although it is possible that these factors helped to stem the tide of casual sex and intercourse among young teens. Still, it appears as though downstream approaches account for most of the plunging level of pregnancies and births during the past fifteen years. Notably, the largest decrease has occurred among African Americans, whose rates of sexual behavior still remain very high.

THE ROLE OF PREGNANCY
PREVENTION PROGRAMS

My tentative conclusion that upstream educational efforts that emphasize sexual abstinence have had, at best, only a limited influence on curtailing sexual activity among teens does not preclude the possibility that some abstinence-only programs have positive effects when they are well delivered. On this question, there has been a good deal of research, some of it quite careful. While many advocates of restrictive practices have claimed success in educational interventions, to our knowledge no one has yet demonstrated that restrictive programs have any large or consistent effect on sexual behaviors. Studies employing random assignment designs are the least likely to show positive results of an upstream strategy (Jemmott, Jemmott, and Fong 1998; Kirby 1997, 2001; Kirby et al. 1994). An ongoing evaluation based on random assignment techniques is currently under way. As yet, this study has not produced results on whether the programs work by postponing sexual activity or by preventing unplanned pregnancies and births. An examination of intermediate indicators, such as attitude change and peer influences, shows mixed findings.

In an analysis of survey data from one of the largest and most reliable sources, the National Longitudinal Study of Adolescent Health (ADD Health), Peter Bearman and Hannah Brückner (2001) were able to show that students who pledged to remain virgins (self-reported) were less likely to engage in sex at an early age. However, the pledge seemed to work differently in different contexts, depending on age and the level of social support for virginity, and in any event, the commitment seemed not to persist beyond the early teens. Moreover, those who broke their pledge were more likely to engage in unprotected sex, a discomforting side effect of encouraging premarital chastity (Bearman and Brückner 2001; Brückner and Bearman 2005). This claim has been disputed in an unpublished analysis by the Heritage Foundation (Rector and Johnson 2005a, 2005b), but Bearman notes that this analysis is highly suspect and has not stood the test of peer review.

What about similar efforts to evaluate downstream methods, such as sex education, for teaching contraceptive compliance and reducing sexual risk-taking? A huge literature exists on the impact of such programs on preventing pregnancy and avoiding sexually transmitted diseases (Hayes 1987; Institute of Medicine 1995). The results are generally unimpressive, to say the least. While investigators over the years have frequently touted the success of one program or another, reanalysis of data, replication, and random assignment experiments have failed to identify successful interventions at the program level, with a single exception. It is definitely possible to produce gains in short-term knowledge about the risks involved in unprotected sex and in attitudes about the desirability of avoiding such actions, but changing behaviors through specific programmatic interventions seems to be far less successful, even in the short run and especially in the long run.

Recent evidence indicates that one highly intensive program pioneered by a youth development researcher, Michael Carrera, was successful (Philliber et al. 2002). Carrera developed a model program that involved huge investments in a small group of youths sustained over a very long period of time. Youths were placed in after-school programs that provided supervision, skill building, recreation, mentoring, advocacy, and sponsorship. Evaluations of the Carrera program using random assignment strategies appear to show positive effects on reducing early and unprotected sex and thus reducing the risk of pregnancy and childbearing. The Carrera approach has promise, but it is an expensive and labor-intensive model that is unlikely to be adopted on a massive scale in a highly cost-conscious society like the United States.

Given the countless millions of public and private dollars devoted to pregnancy prevention, the poor record of success of programmatic interventions, especially in light of declining rates of pregnancy and childbearing, begs to be understood. Something has brought about the leveling off of sexual behavior and lowered the level of pregnancy and childbearing among teens. If not the thousands of local programs, what then could explain these changes? Any adequate explanation of the downward trend has to be mediated by what demographers call the "proximate determinants" of fertility—sexual behavior, contraceptive use, and abortion. For the most part, we can rule out changes in abortion as an explanation for both the long-term and short-term trends, since the incidence of abortion has declined during the past two decades. Sexual activity in the early teens has gone down slightly, but the extent of the decline is modest and appears not to be a large component of the drop in teen pregnancy and childbearing, though experts still disagree on the magnitude of the effect. We have been hampered by issues of data quality and comparability in measuring the level of sexual activity, so there could still be some room for disagreement over whether teens are significantly more likely to engage in sex than they were in the 1980s. Nonetheless, most experts now think that diminishing rates of sexual activity could account for more than a small fraction of the recent decline (Santelli et al. 2006).

It appears far more likely that teenagers are avoiding unprotected sex and becoming more adept at using contraception. Despite the efforts of upstreamers to restrict the content of contraceptive education in the schools during the past decade, it is probable that the HIV/AIDS scare, greater information about the risk of STDs, and more user-friendly methods of contraception have contributed to teens' skills at using contraception. In contrast to the generally spotty evidence that sex education programs have limited success, there is a growing body of literature suggesting that HIV/AIDS programs can increase contraceptive use (Robin et al. 2004). Very recently, the availability of emergency contraception is reducing the need for and use of abortion. Given the evidence available, I am inclined to believe that downstreamers represented in the reproductive health community have been more successful in their efforts to affect teen contraceptive practices than have upstreamers in persuading them not to engage in intercourse.

Underlying this change has been a cultural and ultimately psychological shift in the behavior of teens that is pervasive and profound. Young people no longer think of marriage as a safety valve in the event of pregnancy. Early marriage, especially among low-income teens, has virtually disappeared as teens increasingly feel unprepared economically and psychologically to make long-term commitments in relationships. Only one-third as many women were married by age twenty in the late 1990s as were married in the late 1950s—17 percent compared to 51 percent. The drop-off in teenage marriage among men was just as large, declining from 21 percent to 8 percent (Kreider 2005). Consequently, it seems that both males and females have begun to understand the necessity of avoiding pregnancy along with avoiding the health risks of unprotected sex if and when they elect to have sexual relationships, though the learning curve has been gradual and far from universal.

Both attitudinal and behavioral data suggest that Americans have long regarded sexual intercourse with ambivalence, condemning it publicly and condoning it (at least under some circumstances) privately. However, it seems that gradually throughout the latter half of the past century, the private behaviors undercut the public ones. While demographic patterns ebb and flow, sexuality among the young has remained remarkably stable, with only minor fluctuations, since the late 1970s, when about half of all teenage females (and slightly more males) reported that they were not virgins by the age of eighteen, and today virtually all Americans engage in sex before marrying, a pattern that has led one researcher to conclude that premarital sex is "normative" (Finer 2007).

This normative shift has occurred in the face of relatively little institutional support for using contraception. Unlike our European counterparts, Americans make it more rather than less difficult for teenagers in particular and young adults more generally to use contraception. Some states continue to place legal or social barriers to teens' ability to make confidential decisions about the consequences of their sexual behavior. Schools have provided less explicit information in their educational efforts over the past decade and a half. Many of our public channels of communication ban the use of contraceptive advertising. Many parents remain uncomfortable or unprepared to provide information and access to contraceptive services. Accordingly, evidence reveals that the contraceptive practices of sexually active teenagers in the United States have generally been less consistent than those of sexually active teens in other nations.

It is no wonder why. Unlike in large parts of Europe, where contraceptive use is actively promoted in advertisements by public health authorities and in schools, we have continued to regard contraception as a controversial topic in public discourse (Alan Guttmacher Institute 2001; David et al. 1990; Jones et al. 1985; Jones 1986; Lottes 2002). Remarkably, major media outlets continue to refuse to advertise condoms and other forms of birth control, even while the airways are filled with messages telling men and their partners that they can get help for erectile dysfunction by medication, suggesting that enhanced sexual capacity will improve their relationships and overall well-being.

I have already mentioned the retreat from sexual education in the public schools over the past two decades. A growing number of school districts have instituted explicit rules against discussing methods of birth control, effective use of contraception, and information about emergency contraception—a method that is still unfamiliar to many younger women. A huge body of research shows that families are not much help, providing little in the way of preparation for assuming the responsibilities of sexual decisionmaking and managing reproductive health (Jaccard, Dittus, and Gordon 2000; Luker 1996; Pearson, Muller, and Frisco 2006). Among the well-off, family physicians sometimes provide assistance, but most teens do not have access to a private physician who is willing and able to assume this responsibility.

It therefore falls upon public and private reproductive health clinics to educate teenagers, but my own long experience working with these agencies has shown that they often encounter considerable problems in providing sexual socialization for adolescents. Relatively few are free to operate in public school settings, where young people are more or less a captive population. Moreover, the high premium placed on privacy presents obstacles to getting young people to make full use of school-based clinics, which in any case do not offer contraceptive methods. Mostly, teens still visit community health centers and family planning clinics, where they are afforded a reasonable measure of privacy and good medical care. Still, a substantial number of teens, especially the younger ones, are reluctant to use these agencies even when they know about them.

Not surprisingly, then, most teens report that they do not plan their first sexual encounter. Over and over again, sexually active teens say that sex is something that "just happens" in the course of relationships. Few teens report preparing to have sexual intercourse by discussing it with their partner, visiting a family planning clinic, or seeking help from a private physician. Sex is widely regarded in American culture as "uncontrollable" and "spontaneous" and ipso facto fraught with "risk." In short, though American teens seem to be getting better at using contraception, they are doing so in the face of steady political and institutional resistance.

TEENAGE SEXUAL BEHAVIOR
IN COMPARATIVE CONTEXT

In a fascinating qualitative study, Amy Schalet (2000, 2004, 2006) compared how American and Dutch teens and their families think about the initiation of sexual relationships. Her findings are backed up by evidence that teens in many other European nations are much better prepared by mass media, schools, public health venues, and, most especially, their parents to assume responsibility for their sexual behavior (Alan Guttmacher Institute 2001).

Schalet asked a small sample of parents with children in their midteens, matched for location and socioeconomic status from each country, whether they would permit their high school–age son or daughter to have a partner spend the night at their house. About nine out of ten Americans said no, while exactly the same proportion of Dutch parents, nine out of ten, replied that they would, assuming certain conditions. Not just any partner would be acceptable, the Dutch parents were quick to explain, but one in a serious romantic relationship with their teenager whom they had met and gotten to know before the sexual debut took place. The Dutch youth basically concurred with their parents, reporting that they expected to have (or had already had) their first sexual relationship at home, although it must be said that a minority of the Dutch teenagers did in fact initiate sex outside their parents' purview when they felt that their parents might disapprove of their partner.

To American parents, this practice of parental vetting of sexual partners might seem bizarre, but to the Dutch (and the French, Scandinavians, and Germans) it is entirely consistent with what Schalet calls "the normalization of sexual behavior." Sex is viewed by the Dutch as a normal part of adolescence that contributes to a young person's emotional and social development. Parents do not talk about sex as an expression of raging hormones, and there is much less talk of adolescent rebellion and the withdrawal of children into peer group relationships. Consequently, the family offers a protective and supportive context for youth to make good and responsible decisions. Interviews with Dutch teenagers provide ample evidence that parents are not living in a fantasy world. Youth expect their parents to know about and even help plan for their sexual initiation.

A recent study that compared German and American magazines for teenagers finds collaborative evidence of the very different way in which sexual relationships are viewed in Germany (Carpenter 2001). The German magazines instruct young people on how to get pleasure from their sexual relationships, while American media address the emotional and health risks associated with having sex.

This is what Schalet refers to as the American pattern of "dramatization of sexual risk," which is part of a broader conception of managing the behavior of adolescents and young adults in this country. Americans generally regard adolescents and even young adults (age eighteen to twenty-one) as developmentally incapable of acting responsibly and actively attempt to protect them from behaviors that might be considered risky, especially access to alcohol and sex. Europeans, by contrast, believe that young people ought to be taught to manage these potential risks by gradually introducing them to adultlike responsibilities during their teenage years. Whereas Americans view adolescence as a period of rebellion and irresponsibility, Europeans are inclined to expect adolescents to behave more like adults—and at least in regard to their sexual behavior, European adolescents appear to do so.

Interestingly, these different normative regimes produce similar levels of sexual initiation, but the experiences are quite different. American youth are more likely to acquire more sexual partners in a briefer time (Darroch et al. 2001), treating sexual relationships more casually and, in all likelihood, with less regard for their emotional consequences. In effect, the two different cultural climates create the consequences that are expected by public and private policies. In the United States, our normative expectations result in less responsible behavior, while in Europe the consequence of expecting more of young people is generally more responsible practices when it comes to alcohol and sex (Moore 2000; Weaver, Smith, and Kippax 2005).

Indeed, it could be argued that the American pattern of regarding adolescents as irresponsible actors creates sharp discontinuities in behavior when young people transition from the home in their late teens and early twenties. College campuses exhibit high rates of binge drinking, especially among entering students, who are frequently ill prepared to manage alcohol consumption. Similarly, there are widespread reports about a pattern of "hooking up" among young people, a term referring to casual sexual encounters devoid of strong emotional ties. How common hooking up is as a social pattern is still not empirically established, but the pattern certainly suggests that American youth are not being well prepared to adopt the emotional responsibilities of sexual relations, just as they are unprepared for alcohol use.

This suggests that Americans need to rethink how we prepare young people to manage behaviors that, if ill handled, can have adverse consequences. "Just say no" could actually be part of the problem rather than an effective solution. Interestingly, we can contrast how we introduce young people to driving to how we introduce them to sex or alcohol. Hardly anyone doubts that driving, especially for beginners, can be dangerous, yet most states permit teens to drive at age sixteen, with or without restrictions, and teens are permitted to drive everywhere in the United States by age eighteen. Teens are gradually introduced to driving, often by their parents. Driver education courses in how to become a responsible and skilled driver help teens manage the transition. Increasingly, states have introduced harsh measures if drivers consume more than a very small amount of alcohol.

By contrast, it should be noted that Europeans have far more restrictive driving laws for teenagers, since driving is considered far more risky than alcohol use or sex. In fact it is, by any objective measure. Yet we permit teenage driving and regard it as an important rite of passage. In this particular case, our society has normalized the risk by treating it as a desirable, albeit somewhat dangerous, transition to adultlike responsibility. It seems arbitrary not to do the same with sex or, following the same logic, alcohol use.

Treating premarital sex exclusively as a categorical moral issue—right or wrong in all circumstances—prevents us from considering its important developmental consequences for young people. If young people learn to regard sex as merely a source of fun (which it can be) rather than as a locus of intimate emotional expression (which it also can be), then we might expect young people to encounter problems learning to cultivate its emotional demands and possibilities later in life. Learning of this sort does not invariably lead to earlier or more casual sexual encounters. Indeed, it might encourage more gradual, emotionally rich, and responsible sexual interactions that promote the development of empathy and emotional expression. Even if one is sympathetic to the argument that sex should be reserved for marriage, it is unfair and certainly unrealistic to impose such strictures on those who adopt the different point of view that becoming sexual is a part of human development that requires the acquisition of the ability to express physical capacities and emotions related to building strong and gratifying relationships.

In many respects, our public policies and discourse have been stuck in a moral debate that has blinded Americans to the adverse consequences of managing sex largely through social control. Think, for example, of the public hysteria that occurred during the Super Bowl halftime show in 2003 when Janet Jackson's almost naked breast was briefly revealed to a huge audience of viewers on TV, while almost no attention was paid to the commercials for sexual dysfunction and the explicit lewd expressions of male entertainers. This incident exposed the duplicitous and irrational standards of content on the airways.

Adolescents are neither ignorant nor innocent. They pick up cues in their families and communities, from their peers and the media, about how to view sex. If we care about creating a culture in which sexuality is valued, then we must think hard about the standards we currently uphold and recognize that young people are learning how to be sexual from a variety of arenas over which adults exercise imperfect control. It behooves us to engage in more active, gradual, and developmentally appropriate ways of introducing and connecting sexuality to human relationships, especially if we believe that these connections have lasting consequences for the relationships that adolescents will form later in life.

Chapter 5

Supporting Marriage

AT THE BEGINNING of the Baltimore Study, public concern about the decline of marriage was not yet on the political agenda. Most young adults in the United States still married at ages that by present-day standards seem shockingly young. In 1965 the median age of marriage had already started its upward trend but still stood at 20.6 for women and 22.8 for men. Close to 40 percent of *all* women married in their teens, and more than half of these younger women were pregnant at the time of their wedding (Bachu 1999).

The contrast to the present could hardly be more striking. The median age of marriage has risen continuously over the past four decades and stands today at nearly 26 for women and 28 for men. Teenage marriage as a resolution to premarital pregnancy has declined precipitously among women, and all but disappeared among men. Among African American teenagers, marrying to legitimate a pregnancy in the teen years has become virtually extinct. During the early 1990s, fewer than one-third of white teens married after becoming pregnant, compared to 10 percent of black teens, and these figures have continued to decline during the most recent decade (Bachu 1999; Fields 2003; Graefe and Lichter 2002).

This chapter explores why the institution of marriage seems to be losing its hold on young couples, especially young people like those in the Baltimore Study, who grew up in less than advantageous circumstances. The evidence I offer speaks directly to the plausibility of a growing number of policy initiatives aimed at restoring marriage in American society, a political project that has generated considerable public attention, contentious debate, and a growing level of government funding. The prospects of the Bush administration's program to promote marriage among low-income families as a way of reducing poverty and enhancing children's fortunes in later life rests on a better grasp of what lies behind the marriage wariness of young adults. A burgeoning social science literature is attempting to address the question of what has led to the decline of marriage in the Western world and what, if anything, might be done to restore young people's confidence in matrimony (Edin and Kefalas 2005; McLanahan, Donahue, and Haskins 2005; Moynihan, Smeeding, and Rainwater 2004).

Even in the 1960s, when the first interviews in Baltimore took place, there was an evident sense of unease about the wisdom of marrying immediately following conception among the families in the study, especially among the parents of the pregnant teens; their misgivings about marriage reflected the beginnings of a huge normative shift that was to take place in the following decades.

Myra Jackson's seventeen-year-old daughter, Jewell, became pregnant during the summer before her senior year of high school in Baltimore. After the shock of discovering that she was expecting, Jewell contemplated whether she should take time off from school to have her child and whether she should marry Mason, the father of her child. Mason, who had finished the tenth grade before he found work in the shipyards, was willing enough. But Myra strongly advised Jewell to wait at least until she graduated from high school.

> You know that you be missing going up there to get your diploma with all of us waiting for it to happen. If he can't wait for you, he ain't going to be much good for you later on. Just 'cause you made one mistake, ain't no reason to make another.

It is no great mystery why Myra advocated that Jewell delay marriage and did not encourage her to "give the child a name," as others in the Baltimore sample did. Myra explained to the interviewer, Mrs. Blau, that she thought Mason, who was almost twenty, had taken advantage of Jewell's innocence.

> I don't think he goin' to look after her too good even if they get married. He ain't got no money saved up. He just want to move in here and have me cookin' and carin' for him like he some big shot. That boy ain't going to do her no good.

Myra's pessimistic assessment of Mason's potential as a breadwinner was not unusual among the parents interviewed in the Baltimore Study. Many faced similar situations in their own lives or watched other family members deal with a pregnancy early in life. Like Myra, they often counseled their daughters not to rush into marriage. More than a few recalled their own situations when they succumbed to family pressure to marry the father of their first child. Nearly all of these marriages worked out poorly.

> I don't want her to be making the same mistake that I did. Finish your education and be prepared to support yourself. It don't do your child no good if his father can't take care of him.

The preference of a large contingent of parents for getting an education over making a hasty marriage was grounded in the harsh realities of their own lives. Fewer than one-quarter of the mothers in the Baltimore Study managed to maintain a lifelong marriage. Looking back on their circumstances, most believed that they and their partners had been ill prepared to manage a successful marriage when they had children. Suffering from limited education and poor job skills, many had been forced to take menial jobs throughout their lives. These mothers wanted to see their daughters have a better fate than they had experienced, and many, rightly or wrongly, attributed their present circumstances to the mistakes they had made in marrying men who did not hold up their end of the conjugal bargain.

Deciding whether or not to wed was as great a source of conflict for the families in the Baltimore Study as were the pregnancies that prompted this decision. The pregnant teens did not always share their parents' skepticism about the benefits of marriage or their parents' distrust of the fathers of their children. Sometimes the parents' views prevailed, and sometimes daughters ignored their advice. Close to one-third of the women married before their child was born, and almost one-third wed the father of their children in the year after the birth of their first child. Consistent with other research, the likelihood of marriage was far greater among white women, among those living in economically and educationally more advantaged households, and among those whose partners were older and accordingly had more secure jobs (Landale and Forste 1991; McLaughlin and Lichter 1997; Testa et al. 1989; Wu and Wolfe 2001; Zavodny 1999). Generally, these unions had the blessing of parents, especially when their daughters were able to complete high school before marriage.

Even taking account of these selective conditions that might have favored the marital prospects of those who wed before or shortly after childbirth, the overwhelming majority of marriages to the child's father did not work out. By the time of the five-year follow-up, only half of those who had wed the father of their child remained married. Just one in six of these women was still wed when they were reinterviewed twelve years later. By the thirty-year follow-up, the surviving marriages had dropped to one in ten. Clearly, the parents' worst fears about early marriages to the father were confirmed. Other studies reveal that the findings from Baltimore are robust: early marriages, especially in response to a premarital pregnancy, have a low likelihood of lasting (Coombs and Zumeta 1970; Upchurch, Lillard, and Panis 2001).

Waiting to marry, however, was not an effective alternative strategy. Women who delayed marriage were not more successful, whether or not they married the child's father or someone else. The sad story is that low-income, expectant mothers, especially if they are African American, have dismal prospects of achieving marital stability. But this depressing picture is incomplete without adding an important caveat. The chances of sustaining a successful marriage for low-income and poorly educated couples, particularly African Americans, are hardly any better if they are able to delay childbearing and marry later in life (Ellwood and Jencks 2004; Goldstein 1999). In short, successful marriage—at least a successful first marriage—is elusive and increasingly rare for the great majority of low-income couples, and for almost all African Americans of modest means. What Daniel Patrick Moynihan saw as a fault line in the ability to manage marriage within the black community has grown to a huge chasm that is no longer confined to blacks but applies to an ever larger share of low-income and less-educated couples (South 1999).

By the time we conducted the thirty-year follow-up in the mid-1990s, the institution of marriage in America had been placed on the critical list. When we examined the behavior of the next generation—the firstborn children who were in their late twenties—only a minority of these young adults, whether or not they had children, had entered marriage (see also Furstenberg, Levine, and Brooks-Gunn 1990). The time-honored practice of shotgun marriage had all but vanished in the United States, in large part because pregnant women saw marriage at an early age as an ill-advised and highly risky enterprise. As we heard from one of the parents in Baltimore who counseled her daughter to postpone marriage: "There's no point in making a second mistake on top of the first."

As the offspring of the teen mothers approached adulthood, my collaborator, Jeanne Brooks-Gunn, and I interviewed a subset of the young adults to find out how they viewed their lives and what plans they had for the future. Much to our surprise, we discovered that most still strongly hoped to marry someday. But we also learned that marriage was viewed as a capstone of success—a step that should be taken only when their economic fortunes were settled and secure (Edin and Kefalas 2005; Garfinkel, McLanahan, and Hanson 1998; Gibson-Davis, Edin, and McLanahan 2005; Waller 2002). In contrast to their grandparents, who regarded marriage as an inevitable and desirable decision to make when facing a premarital pregnancy, and their parents, who viewed it with a certain degree of wariness but believed it was a necessary condition for success, this generation adopted a different perspective: marriage was a privilege to be achieved or earned by dint of educational and economic accomplishments (Cherlin 2004). Marriage has become a conditional transition to be undertaken only when justified by strong indications of success. The formidable barriers to marriage that have been erected over the years are taken by young people as a warning not to enter marriage without the requisite resources (Kefalas et al. 2006).

Of course, exceptions still occurred. I had a series of conversations in the mid-1990s with Shennell Nichols, the twenty-four-year-old daughter of Agnes Nelson, one of the teen mothers who had been part of the original sample. Agnes, a practical nurse, was caring for Shennell's son during the daytime while her daughter worked at a convenience store. Shennell was planning to marry a young soldier five years her junior, and Agnes was vehemently opposed to the wedding plans. Determined to proceed with the wedding despite her mother's objections, Shennell dismissed her mother's concerns that she was too unsettled, did not know her fiancé (who was not the father of her child) well enough, and was unprepared to undertake the serious obligations of marriage. The day after the interview, at Shennell's insistence, I spoke to Agnes's sister in order to gain some perspective on the family dispute. The aunt gave me an earful, elaborating on why Shennell was not ready to get married. Several years later, I learned that the marriage occurred as planned but that, just as Agnes feared, had not survived.

Other marriages did occur among the firstborn young adults, but most of those in their mid-twenties reported that they were far from being ready to settle down with a partner for life. The exceptions were generally those youth who were unusually far along in establishing a career and had a time-tested relationship with a partner who was equally well situated (Furstenberg 2001).

SOURCES OF RELUCTANCE TO MARRY

The young adults provided a host of explanations for their skittishness about marriage, at least during their early and middle twenties. Most drew on direct observations of members of their family and community. Virtually all watched their parents go through divorce or never even make it to marriage, and they also witnessed numerous kin and friends go through painful separations. Many referred back to their childhood to explain why they were in no rush to settle down with a partner.

> My mother always taught us that romance without finance can be a nuisance. . . . I can do bad by myself.

After completing a round of interviews with the young adults in the early-1990s, I gathered together eight participants who had had children in their teens or early twenties into a focus group to talk about marriage, the fathers of their children, and their plans for the future (Furstenberg 2001; Furstenberg, Sherwood, and Sullivan 1992). Most of the women in the focus group were in a steady relationship with the father of their child, though some had migrated to a new relationship. Their commentary about marriage was sobering, to say the least. Looming large in the background was the apprehension on the part of both men and women that marriages were risky undertakings. Speaking of men, the group observed:

> BEEBEE: That's how most of them are. I mean, they get scared away.
>
> CHELSEA (sarcastically): That's the responsibility of the father.
>
> BEEBEE: Yeah. They got to grow up.
>
> CHELSEA: Even when they're older, some of them—not even the young [fathers]—they scared.

FF: What are they scared of?

CHELSEA: I guess failing, maybe failing the child or not standing up to the mother's standards or something. It takes too much for them.

AMY: Not being able to—when the child come to you specifically and ask for something—they scared because they might not be able to get it to them at that particular time.

ANGIE (speaking of the father of her child): He wasn't scared. He just spoiled and always had everything his way.

The women in the group carried on issuing a stream of complaints about the men in their lives, based on past and present experiences. They complained that the fathers and surrogate fathers of their children were jealous, controlling, unreliable, and emotionally unavailable to their children. Their strongest criticisms had less to do with failing to provide material support—though they had plenty to say about failures on this front—and more to do with failing to show up for important occasions in their children's lives, "to be a daddy to them." The single exception was a woman who had married the father of her child and who lauded his commitment to her and their children. She drew a round of incredulous responses from the other women, who seemed to feel that men like that were so rare that they had never sighted one.

Possession of adequate resources, of course, is clearly the sine qua non for getting married among women like the offspring of the teen mothers. Few could assume that the men they were living with or dating would be employed steadily and in a job that would provide an adequate income. At the bottom of the socioeconomic ladder, women were extremely cautious about entering relationships that might burden them economically with another mouth to feed. "If he can't pay, he don't stay," was an axiom frequently voiced and widely observed (see Edin 2000).

Many of the younger generation of women in my study claimed that material contributions were of less importance than emotional support. The overriding apprehension revolved around men's interest and involvement in their children's lives. Being emotionally reliable and available to their children was a huge consideration in how the women evaluated men's performance and presence in their lives. Unfortunately, few men measured up to the women's standards, as suggested by Chelsea's remark quoted earlier. Many males had relatively little experience in raising children and proved to be, in the women's view, unreliable parents. As one woman complained, "I learned about being a parent on the job. Why can't he?"

The young men I spoke to who already had children presented another side of the picture. They often felt overextended, harshly judged, or put upon when it came to caring for their children. Women were suspicious gatekeepers, they were overly protective of their children, and they misunderstood the continuous hassles of everyday life that the men were forced to endure. Men, unaccustomed to the demands of domestic life, often felt overcommitted, tied down, and controlled by their children's mothers. Jordon, the father of Amy's child, presented his side of the story to me in an interview that I conducted just after the focus group.

> I do what I can. . . . It was kind of hard for me to keep a job. . . . It was like Amy was always wanting money. . . . I give it to her, but there were times I didn't give it to her because of the fact that she spend it on her. Sometimes if I send money downtown [to the Welfare Department], then the mother only [gets] forty dollars back or twenty dollars back. So I just give to them. . . . Or sometimes I send it downtown. Long as the government know I'm taking care of my kids, I'm happy.

The biological fathers frequently found themselves in a bind, trying to satisfy the bureaucratic requirements of a child support system that is poorly aligned with the day-to-day, informal exchanges that occur between parents who live apart. And the fathers who assumed active responsibility for the care of a quasi-stepchild often were beleaguered by an array of obligations that were inherited, usually reluctantly, when they formed a relationship with a woman who had had children by someone else (see Furstenberg 2001).

MULTI-PARTNERED CHILDBEARING
AND MARITAL RELATIONSHIPS

It is hard to overestimate the problems stemming from "multi-partnered childbearing" among low-income African American families—the phenomenon of parents having children by different partners from previous relationships. Early and nonmarital childbearing frequently produces complex families in which siblings have different fathers (or mothers) because women and men migrated from one relationship to the next. The complications created by the succession of unions and efforts to honor parental commitments across households are formidable (Carlson and Furstenberg 2006; Furstenberg and King 1999; Guzzo and Furstenberg 2005, 2006b; Mincy 2002a; Mincy and Huang 2002a, 2002b).

Fathers in many impoverished families commonly care for children in more than one household, creating time and resource conflicts that are not easily resolved. It is little wonder, then, that many young men perceive the mothers of their children as making claims on them that they are unable to satisfy. And it is little wonder that women in turn feel that their partners are letting them and their children down by giving them too little—or worse yet, by providing for other women's children rather than the children in their household, who may or may not be the father's offspring. There is simply no way for many men in multi-partnered families to satisfy the mounting claims on their time and money.

In an analysis of the fertility patterns of the offspring of the Baltimore mothers, Rosalind King and I discovered that the men and women who had children in their teens were especially likely to produce complex families. The majority of women who had their first child before age twenty went on to have a second child with someone else before reaching their late twenties. Although males in the sample were less likely to have children than females by their late twenties, those who did often were highly prolific and prone to having children by more than one woman. A relatively small fraction of males (7 percent of the firstborn males) accounted for 20 percent of all the children produced in the second generation by the time they reached their late twenties. Of all the males in the sample, these men were the least educated, the most prone to substance abuse, crime, and emotional disorders, and, of course, the most economically vulnerable. In the second generation, the process of childbearing, at least early in life, created family situations that were unlikely to be followed, much less preceded, by marriage. Other studies following women and men in more recent nonmarital birth cohorts who have children by more than one partner confirm that multi-partnered fertility is far more likely among disadvantaged couples for whom childbearing occurs without the prospect of entering a viable marriage (Carlson and Furstenberg 2006).

Recognizing that most men would be an unsuitable partner, women in the sample postponed marriage when they were expecting children, and even more so when they were not. Assuming that they could do better if they waited, these women nonetheless faced a bleak marriage market. Apart from the sheer problem of finding a man with a regular and remunerative job, they needed to integrate any new partner into a household that often included another man's children. Many males were reluctant to assume the burdens of a ready-made family, especially if their own children were not members of the household.

Delaying marriage creates a new set of pressures for women with children. It exposes them to the risk of a second child with another man. A new relationship generates pressure to have another child as a precondition for thinking about marriage. Of course, if the pregnancy does not result in marriage, or leads to a marriage that lasts only briefly, it only serves to further undermine a woman's position in the marriage market. And men with children by multiple women become less and less attractive as a marriage partner, since they are frequently juggling responsibilities for children from prior relationships that require time and resources that compete with what they can offer to a new partner. Worse yet, many of these young fathers end up incarcerated and incapable of supporting their children, not only in the present but also when they are released from prison.

Family complexity created another pervasive problem for young men and women in creating stable unions. Sexual jealousy was rampant among lower-income youth. Mistrust of the opposite sex had several sources. Fidelity, although valued in the abstract, was not always practiced because relationships were uncertain, insecure, and sometimes ephemeral (England, Edin, and Linnenberg 2003). These general apprehensions were magnified when former lovers, especially those who had parented a partner's child, were still in the picture. Repeatedly, the young adults in our study who had former relationships involving children alluded to the difficulties of dealing with the emotional ambiguities of managing relationships across households. Lena Nelson, one of the young adults in the Baltimore Study, recalled the relationship she had with her boyfriend, who initially was very supportive to her child:

> He did everything that he could for me, but he was a very, very, very insecure, jealous man—very. And I couldn't stand that because, you know, I was really innocent. I mean, I had my son, but I had no reason for him to feel like that.

Reinforced by biographical experience, young people grow up in a culture where distrust of the opposite gender is rife. Suspiciousness and jealousy in relationships is pervasive, fed and enhanced by stories and gossip and rumor that are a constant force within inner-city families and neighborhoods. The absence of stable marriage makes matrimony seem more hazardous owing to the scarcity of models of success. The young adults in the study were more likely to point to their grandparents than their parents as exemplars of the marriages they wanted to emulate.

We cannot ignore the structural explanations that undergird this shift in what William Julius Wilson (1987) has called the rise of a "ghetto-specific culture." Wilson is referring to the fact that local cultures reflect and respond to the material conditions in which families reside—failing schools, high unemployment, wage discrimination in the labor market, weak social connections to help locate good jobs, and the lack of marriageable males—all contribute in varying degrees to family instability. And the absence of stable families, the ineffective schools, and the paucity of other community resources make the underground economy relatively more attractive to young people than it might otherwise be if favorable economic and social conditions prevailed. The absence of opportunities, especially for males, helps to foster and sustain a culture in inner-city neighborhoods that undermines trust, commitment, and confidence in marriage as a context for childbearing. The younger women we spoke to repeatedly complained, "There are not many good men out there to marry." This palpable reality leads to a system of conditional relationships as women hedge their bets, waiting for signs that a man is truly worthy of marriage. Men, in turn, feel constantly scrutinized, judged, and found wanting in this social system. Many resent their marginality but sometimes respond to it by behaving in ways that fulfill women's negative expectations.

This dark picture of male-female relationships in the inner city is not new. It was referred to by virtually all of the urban ethnographers who focused on gender relations among low-income families a generation ago: Elliot Liebow's classic work, *Tally's Corner* (1967), Ulf Hannerz's *Soulside* (1969), Carol Stack's study of a Midwestern ghetto in *All Our Kin* (1974), Lee Rainwater's (1970) research on a public housing site in Saint Louis, and Joyce Ladner's (1971) piercing observations of teenage parenthood in Washington, D.C. No doubt, the seeds of this culture that undermines trust in marriage were planted in the 1960s as black males found it increasingly difficult to find well-paying unskilled or semi-skilled jobs, while women were more willing to accept low-income jobs supplemented by public and private assistance; however, similar accounts of gender distrust go back at least as far as the early twentieth century (Du Bois 1908; Furstenberg 2007). It is no exaggeration to say that stable marriages in the inner city have become nearly extinct and that among low-income African Americans they have long been in scarce supply.

What my colleagues and I discovered to be pervasive among the Baltimore youth, if not universal—not only among African American youth but, to a rising extent, among lower-income populations more generally—has recently been demonstrated by a slew of studies by both qualitative and quantitative researchers. Kathryn Edin and Maria Kefalas (2005), in a recent large-scale qualitative study in Philadelphia and Camden, New Jersey, report that gender distrust is an important reason why low-income couples shy away from making marital commitments in early adulthood. In separate work based on in-depth interviews, Christina Gibson-Davis, Kathryn Edin, and Sara McLanahan (2005) report a similar reluctance to move to marriage among a subsample of "fragile families," a term that has come to describe the fledgling households created by cohabiting partners and their children. In a third study, Maureen Waller (2001), also conducting interviews from the same population used in the Fragile Families and Child Well-being Study, provides another rich account of the problems encountered by young parents in establishing stable and enduring ties.

The Fragile Families and Child Well-being Study, initiated by Sara McLanahan and Irv Garfinkel along with many distinguished collaborators, has also yielded excellent quantitative information on the precarious ties between young parents who have children out of wedlock but often in the context of a conditional relationship. Despite McLanahan's designation of premarital pregnancy as a "magic moment" to strengthen parental bonds, particularly among couples in committed relationships, the evidence provided by the study seems to point to the conclusion that the glue keeping parents together is thin and insubstantial. Only a tiny fraction of the couples who were cohabiting or who described themselves as likely to marry at some point moved to marriage during the first year of the child's life (Carlson, McLanahan, and England 2004); by three years after the birth, fewer than half of the unwed couples remained in any type of romantic relationship. In reality, the magic moment quickly fades in the face of the ominous recognition that creating a permanent union, at best, is a future aspiration and, more often, merely a fleeting fantasy.

WHAT IT TAKES TO SUCCEED IN MARRIAGE

Lest my assessment of why young people in the inner city are reluctant to marry seems too bleak and depressing, it may be useful to think of the circumstances under which marriage has a reasonable prospect of thriving. In a series of qualitative case studies based on the Baltimore data, I identified a set of preconditions that appeared to be favorable to marriage in the inner city (Furstenberg 2001). Predictably, many of these are the flip side of the impediments to marriage I have already discussed. Other conditions, however, are worth noting because, though relatively rare, they provide insight into how some young adults from inner-city communities are managing to beat the long odds of establishing a stable union.

The first and probably most important component of becoming marriageable is gaining a strong position in the labor market through educational attainment and occupational experience. Judging from the data in the Baltimore Study, along with a number of other studies, young adults who grow up in the inner city are well aware of the broad outlines of what is required to attain success in the labor market; however, there is ample evidence that most youth are not well positioned to move beyond high school or find remunerative positions in the labor market.

Most youth who attended public schools in Baltimore found themselves woefully undereducated even if they graduated on schedule. The exceptions were youth who ended up in private or parochial schools or were selected into special programs within neighborhood schools that provided special assistance in making the transition to careers or to higher education. There is growing evidence that without the benefit of educational programs that offer specific training, counseling, and support, most inner-city youth are likely to founder in the years between eighteen and twenty-four, when they should be obtaining additional training and acquiring work-related skills (Osgood et al. 2005; Settersten, Furstenberg, and Rumbaut 2005; William T. Grant Foundation 1998). Credentials and experience signal to employers that young adults are prepared for work life. Incidentally, they also send the same sort of signal to romantic partners who are looking for indications of commitment, employability, and maturity.

As we watched the young adults in Baltimore move from adolescence to early adulthood, we began to detect changes in the standards applied to romantic partners. The young women in our study increasingly began to complain that many men were unwilling or unable to settle down or "were still running the streets." And many of the young men, some of whom had already become fathers, acknowledged in turn that they were unprepared to settle down (Anderson 1999; Furstenberg 2001).

This leads to an obvious but powerful observation about why marriage is such a difficult undertaking for those who grow up in unstable families, go to chaotic schools, and live in communities without much connecting tissue. As William Julius Wilson (1987, 1996) has so shrewdly observed in his analysis of the urban underclass, the skills needed to succeed in the workplace overlap to a considerable degree with the skills necessary to succeed in forming enduring emotional unions. The process of settling down occurs when young people are incorporated into the larger society through work and family roles. The skills needed to perform these roles increasingly call for discipline and self-regulation, an ability to understand the interests of others, communication, self-knowledge, and a host of other skills that are often gained through early family life, schooling, and employment.

These skills can be taught and observed in the family or acquired by mentoring and modeling outside the household; they can be learned in schools, religious and civic organizations, or even acquired from friends and coworkers in the labor market. But young people need considerable investment, cultivation, and supervision if they are to pick up these social and psychological skills before adulthood. If left largely on their own or placed in settings that do not foster these qualities, they may find these skills difficult to acquire in later life through remedial interventions.

Some of the young adults in the Baltimore Study, especially those who had continued in school and who held a steady job by the time they were in their mid-twenties, showed all the signs of acquiring the habits and practices associated with marriageability. The better-educated youth and those who had entered the labor force were more capable, more socially and psychologically mature, and came from more stable and supportive families. Furthermore, living in well-functioning neighborhoods and attending schools that offered quality education, discipline, sponsorship, and support contributed to building these personal and interpersonal capabilities.

Throughout childhood and adolescence, youth either acquire a bundle of attitudes and skills that promote successful adaptation in their early adult years or they become increasingly developmentally disabled and dysfunctional in assuming adultlike roles that involve economic independence and emotional interdependence (Settersten et al. 2005). Of course, this general proposition is only a starting point for studying the sources of marriageability, because relatively few young adults fall unambiguously on one side of this divide or the other.

Certainly among the Baltimore youth we could see the full range of adaptations. There were youth who had benefited from growing up in a stable family situation (sometimes but not usually consisting of two biological parents), who had one or two working parents or parent-surrogates, and who were provided with support, encouragement, and appropriate discipline. If these youth also went to schools with capable teachers, industrious peers, and orderly routines, they also had far better prospects of succeeding. Finally, if youth were raised in neighborhoods that afforded the same sorts of advantages, they were also likely to do better in the long run, if only because they were less inclined to get in trouble with the law or less likely to get enmeshed in the criminal justice system if they did. Many of the families who conferred these sorts of advantages had consciously employed strategies to isolate their children from the communities in which they resided, using neighbors, churches, or civic organizations to shield their children from the adversities associated with poor schools and low-resource neighborhoods (Furstenberg et al. 1999). At the other end of the continuum were youth who had few of the immediate advantages that might have shaped their development in a positive direction.

Individual characteristics of the youth inevitably and often quite powerfully enter into the picture regardless of the cumulative level of exposure to advantageous or disadvantageous circumstances. Personal attributes such as intelligence, judgment, talents, appearance, and the possession of social skills all moderated the impact of family, school, and neighborhood contexts on developmental trajectories. In short, selection and social process go hand in hand, helping to explain diverse outcomes even among populations that might otherwise appear to be relatively homogeneous. Not infrequently, children in the same household took different life paths because of these individual differences, which often triggered social opportunities, sponsorship, and mentoring that enabled some to fare better than others under seemingly similar circumstances.

Yet many young adults like those in the Baltimore Study, particularly males, fell far short of developing the qualities associated with marriageability. As we observed in chapter 3, the majority of the firstborn males were ill prepared by the time they reached early adulthood to succeed in higher education, a necessary condition for attaining a stable and well-paying job. Most had fared poorly in school systems that were poorly equipped and whose staff expected to work with students who were entering school underprepared and often lacking the soft skills necessary to manage the rigors of the classroom. Based on our interviews and the findings of many other researchers, the children who fall behind—and more often than not they are males—enter adolescence with learning and behavioral deficits that make them highly vulnerable to disengaging from school (Ferguson 2001; Jacobs 1996; Lopez 2004). They frequently experience school as a hostile institution where many of the teachers, largely female, are skeptical of their abilities and commitment to education (Dance 2002). By their own accounts, the second-generation males frequently succumbed to the attractions of street life and peer systems, which do not support conventional routes to success.

Reconsidering the results presented in chapter 3, it is hard to imagine how most of the males in the study were likely to form stable families without receiving a substantial and sustained measure of rehabilitation, training, and support. After all, by their late twenties, close to half had spent time in correctional facilities; only half had graduated from high school; most were either unemployed or working episodically; a substantial number had substance abuse problems; some suffered from mental illness; and many would have brought children from previous relationships into a marriage. This package of social attributes creates enormous impediments, to say the least, to establishing stable parental, much less conjugal, relationships. These barriers were repeatedly mentioned by both the men and the women in the Baltimore Study and are cited by almost all social researchers who have examined the formation of intimate relationships in inner-city communities (see, for example, Anderson 1989, 1990; Edin and Kefalas 2005) and among unwed parents in urban centers more broadly (Carlson, McLanahan, and England 2004; Gibson-Davis, Edin, and McLanahan 2005; Waller and Swisher 2005: Western, Lopoo, and McLanahan 2004).

These uncomfortable facts provide a necessary framework for assessing the prospects of current policy initiatives aimed at promoting stable marriage and discouraging the early family formation that typically undermines parental responsibility.

THE POLITICS OF MARRIAGE

Concerns about the decline of marriage in the United States have been festering since the 1960s, when the marriage age began to rise, the rate of marriage began to drop, and nonmarital childbearing became widespread. It was two decades or so before researchers began to delve into the sources of these changes and politicians and policymakers began to search for ways to reverse the marriage trends.

The political forces have lined up in predictable fashion, with the left observing structural changes that have eroded men's earning capacity and women's willingness to enter relationships built on the assumption of gender inequality and the right decrying the decline of parental values, commitment, and self-sacrifice. Many conservatives have also cited a second reason for the change in marriage practices: they claim that economic incentives to marry have been eroded by public assistance to single women, tax policies, and programs aimed at helping single women (Murray 1984; Wilson 2002).

Whatever set of explanations accounts for the weakening of marriage, they must apply broadly, since the trends observed in the United States are common to nearly all industrialized nations. Social demographers have sometimes referred to this package of change as the "Second Demographic Transition" (Lesthaeghe 1995), comparing it to the great transformation in family patterns that initially brought fertility rates down from pre-industrial levels. The more recent transformation involving the decoupling of sex, marriage, and fertility, along with the erosion of the gender-based division of labor, has altered family systems throughout the West and in many parts of Asia too, further pushing rates of marriage downward and partially accounting for steep declines in childbearing (Therborn 2004). In Europe the concern is less with the transformation in marriage practices than with falling fertility; in the United States, where fertility has remained relatively high, far more attention has been devoted to rehabilitating the institution of marriage. For the most part, nations that have experimented with public policies to counter demographic trends by providing economic incentives for family formation have witnessed little or no success.

Interest in devising pro-marriage policies was probably first expressed by Daniel Patrick Moynihan in his famous report on the black family, but the effort to promote marriage through public policy did not begin in earnest until the Reagan presidency, when legislators began to question and redesign the public assistance program for dependent children. I reserve for the next chapter a fuller discussion of welfare reform as it relates to the issue of teenage childbearing, but it is important to note here that many politicians and some policymakers have strongly argued that the decline of marriage can be traced to a growing dependency of women on public assistance (Murray 1984; Wilson 2002).

Their argument goes something like this: women are less inclined to marry when they can support themselves and their children on public assistance. And men in turn are more willing to risk pregnancy when they feel little or no responsibility to support their children. Taken together, many conservatives and a number of moderate policymakers feel that marriage could be reinvigorated by changing the balance of incentives and disincentives to entering wedlock. It should be said that little hard evidence has been produced by social scientists to support these claims. Showing an association between levels of government support and marriage practices at the state or, for that matter, international level has been difficult to demonstrate (Bitler et al. 2004; Gennetian and Knox

2003; Moffitt 1998; Moynihan, Smeeding, and Rainwater 2004). Many policy changes aimed at bolstering marriage have relied largely on anecdotal accounts of working and nonworking poor women about their attitudes toward men and marriage.

Nonetheless, taking the first step in changing the incentive structure—the Family Support Act of 1988—received broad legislative approval across the ideological spectrum. The aim of this legislation was to encourage work (through the Job Opportunities and Basic Skills Program) and to enforce existing regulations that permitted states to collect unpaid child support decrees by shoring up state and federal mechanisms for garnishing the wages of workers who did not pay child support and making more vigorous efforts to establish paternity at the time of delivery. The law focused especially on paternity establishment and collecting the payments of women on welfare from the fathers of their children as a means of reimbursing public expenditures. Conservatives liked the idea because it got tough on the men who fathered children out of wedlock and promised to cut down on growing welfare expenditures. Liberals hoped that such efforts would put more cash in the hands of poor women and their children as well as hold biological fathers accountable for their actions. Some believed that child support payments would eventually be assured through government funding, sometimes referred to as "child support assurance." That is, the federal and state governments, following some European countries, would guarantee a fixed level of child support payments that would be provided regardless of whether the money for support awards was collected from parents or not. This never happened.

At best, the Family Support Act could be declared a partial success. It has undoubtedly helped to account for a gradual increase in the amount of child support collection, and it may have helped to impress on men their obligations to the children they bear. But it is hard to demonstrate that poor women and their children benefited significantly from the legislation. By all accounts, there is simply not a lot of money to be collected from most of the men who father the children of women living in poverty or who are receiving public funds (Garfinkel, McLanahan, and Hanson 1998). Many women complain that, if anything, greater child support enforcement has complicated relations with the fathers of their children by erecting bureaucratic barriers to child support, replacing informal exchange and parental collaboration (Waller and Plotnick 2001).

The Family Support Act had barely been implemented when it was superseded by a fundamental reform of the welfare system that had been put in place during the Great Depression as a means of protecting single women, then mostly widows, and their children. The demographic shift from widows to divorcées and unmarried mothers increased the number of families on Aid to Families with Dependent Children (AFDC), raising the public costs to taxpayers. The limited amount of monies collected by stricter child support enforcement did little to offset the rising costs of public assistance. In 1996 a sharply divided Congress did away with AFDC, replacing it with a program of support designed to be temporary and time-limited. The reorganization, designated as Temporary Assistance for Needy Families (TANF), was designed to make women on welfare economically independent by providing them with job training, placement, and child care support while requiring them to work after two years.

Welfare reform was accompanied by a great deal of rhetoric about the need to restore marriage and change the incentive structure for poor women and men, which was believed to encourage nonmarital childbearing and discourage marriage (Duncan and Chase-Lansdale 2001a). New provisions in TANF explicitly permitted support for low-income two-parent families, but the measure was primarily aimed at reducing permanent economic support for single women and their offspring by enabling more women to find employment. Just before the passage of TANF, Congress also expanded the Earned Income Tax Credit (EITC), which provides tax credits to low-income working families with children. The shift away from public assistance to unemployed women to policies that support employment, self-sufficiency, and child support obligations was designed in part with the objective of making marriage a more attractive arrangement to couples and, accordingly, discouraging single parenthood. It was widely believed that this array of programs would also help reduce the level of intergenerational poverty—a topic I explore in great detail in the next chapter.

Clearly, TANF succeeded in at least one respect: it dramatically and swiftly reduced the welfare rolls in the late 1990s and the early years of the twenty-first century. This change was accompanied by a significant rise in the proportion of poor women who were employed full-time, though some of these gains were largely erased in the recession beginning in 2000. But did welfare reform or the EITC, which arguably might have worked in the opposite direction, have any effect on marriage practices or levels of nonmarital child-bearing? It is still too soon to tell, but the early indications from an examination of recent demographic trends provide at best a mixed picture. On the positive side, as mentioned already, nonmarital childbearing among teenagers has dropped off significantly, though the trend began well before welfare reform in 1996, and long before its implementation. Moreover, there is no evidence that the states that pioneered welfare reform before it became federal law had more notable declines in teenage childbearing in the 1990s. While the culture surrounding nonmarital childbearing among teenagers may have been affected by the public attention to the issue, it is difficult to demonstrate empirically that the policies adopted in the late 1980s and mid-1990s have played a significant part in the family formation decisions of young men and women, the poor and the near-poor, over the past decade and a half.

As yet, these broad policies aimed in part at reinforcing the institution of marriage seem to have had little influence on the marriage practices of the poor or of young couples who become pregnant outside of marriage. If anything, the trend has been in the opposite direction of what advocates of these reforms expected. Since the passage of welfare reform and the EITC, overall marriage rates in the United States have declined by more than 15 percent, dropping from 8.8 per 1,000 individuals in 1996 to 7.4 in 2004 (Brunner 2006). Some of that decline is surely due to the continued postponement of marriage to later ages, but age-specific rates of marriage continue to drop, and the waning of marriage appears to have continued apace among the less educated and those with limited earnings capabilities. This is not conclusive evidence that the policies aimed at increasing marriage among low-income families are not working, but it is hardly encouraging news (for an excellent discussion of marriage trends and marriage policies, see McLanahan, Donahue, and Haskins 2005).

There is some evidence that children in low-income families have become less likely to be living with single mothers and more likely to be living with two biological parents (regardless of marital status) since the 1996 welfare reform (Acs and Nelson 2003).

Nonetheless, the general trends of union formation among poor couples provide little evidence to date for the hypothesis that policy initiatives enacted in the late 1980s and the 1990s, such as child support enforcement, welfare reform, and the EITC, have reversed or even abated the long-term declines in marriage timing, rates, or survival in the first decade of the present century (Moynihan, Smeeding, and Rainwater 2004). All of these marital indicators have continued their relentless trend in the opposite direction from the more universal practice of marriage that existed a half-century ago (McLanahan, Donahue, and Haskins 2005).

As marriage rates have continued to fall, the proportion of couples with children cohabiting has continued to rise, and a growing share of children are living with unmarried parents or in single-parent households. Conceivably, the policies have slowed down the pace of the retreat from marriage, but they certainly have not reversed it. Among teens and young adults, wariness about marriage early in life has only increased during the past decade. In 1990, 10 percent of women in their teens and just one-third of women in their early twenties were married, and more than two-thirds of women were wed by their late twenties; by 2003 those percentages had shrunk to, respectively, 2 percent, under 20 percent, and just more than half. Obviously, these declines mean that many young couples, including those with children together, are deferring marriage or eschewing it altogether. While it is possible that some ground will be made up by marriages entered into later in life, general demographic trends provide strong evidence that the policy changes enacted in the past two decades and intended to strengthen young people's resolve to marry simply have not worked. Indeed, there is mounting evidence that the marriage gap between the college-educated and the non-college-educated has only widened in the past decade or so (Ellwood and Jencks 2004; Goldstein and Kenney 2001).

PROMOTING MARRIAGE

This reality has led the Bush administration to undertake a controversial program to promote marriage through a broad educational campaign to alter young people's attitudes about marriage. The idea of promoting marriage through community education programs emerged early after the election of George W. Bush and has been strongly embraced during his administration. Originally conceived as a program to persuade women on welfare that it was in their best interests to marry the father of their child, the program was roundly criticized as an unwarranted and unwise approach to helping single mothers and their children.

Under the leadership of Wade Horn, who was the Assistant Secretary for Children and Families at the Department of Health and Human Services and the point person in the Bush administration for these programs until 2007, there has been a steady increase in the federal budget for programs that support marriage promotion, not just among the welfare poor. Horn has argued that:

> Families are greatly strengthened by stable employment, but promoting work alone will not overcome the impediments to healthy development that many children experience. We must support positive changes in family structure as well and, in the next phase of welfare, we must focus more explicitly on [fostering] healthy marriages and [allocating] more resources to promoting it. (Moynihan, Smeeding, and Rainwater 2004, 184)

Many social scientists, myself included, concluded on the basis of existing evidence that the idea of convincing women on welfare to marry was unlikely to be successful, at least as it was initially proposed. As described earlier in this chapter, pregnant women, especially teens and women in their early twenties, face an enormous number of barriers to marrying the fathers of their children. Most of the prospective fathers are simply not marriageable because they are already married to someone else, chronically unemployed or underemployed, incarcerated or otherwise involved in the criminal justice system, coping with substance abuse problems or other mental health problems, or managing complex family lives because of children from previous relationships. Many, if not most, simply do not meet the job qualifications for marriage established by their partners and, in many instances, themselves.

The best and most current source of data on the marriageability of the men who father children, the Fragile Families and Child Well-being Study, has examined a representative sample of unmarried couples living in metropolitan communities who have just had a child together. Researchers discovered that while many of the couples were romantically involved at the time of conception and hoped someday to get married, in fact relatively few were willing or able to move into marriage. Like the younger generation in the Baltimore Study, most couples believed that a hasty marriage under less than desirable circumstances would not improve their own or their children's circumstances.

Ironically, the evidence from a variety of sources indicates that low-income women do not have to be convinced of the virtues of marriage (Edin and Kefalas 2005; Furstenberg 2001; Gibson-Davis, Edin, and McLanahan 2005; Waller 2001). The vast majority of low-income women, regardless of race, say that they aspire to marry someday. In interviews with the young adult offspring of the teen mothers in Baltimore, we were told repeatedly by males and females alike that they hoped to wed sometime in the future (Furstenberg, Levine, and Brooks-Gunn 1990). But even in their late twenties many felt ill prepared to take this momentous step. Marriage per se did not confer security for them and their children, as believed by previous generations. Marriage, we were told, was too serious an undertaking to be entered into lightly; most couples believed that it required maturity, experience, and the test of time.

A good deal of evidence from a growing literature on early adulthood suggests that young adults in the inner city do not in fact hold very different views about marriage from their more advantaged peers. Increasingly, marriage is regarded as a capstone transition that occurs only when self-sufficiency is assured. This is true for affluent and well-educated women who defer marriage (and childbearing) to achieve their professional goals (Oppenheimer 1988) and for low-SES women who have children out of wedlock but defer marriage for lack of a suitable partner (Edin and Kefalas 2005). In a comparative analysis of young adults' views of marriage using in-depth interviews from four different geographical locations around the country, Maria Kefalas, Pat Carr, Laura Napolitano, and I (2006) discovered that many adults now view entering marriage as a developmental process growing out of long-term experience in a relationship. Marriage is less a pledge of commitment (though it is certainly that too) than a recognition of commitment accomplished through ongoing experience. Little wonder, then, that many couples regard cohabitation as a necessary stage on the road to marriage.

Interestingly, my co-authors and I observed that only in one site, rural Iowa, did couples continue the marriage practices that might have prevailed a half-century ago. In Iowa, young people were more likely to marry young, with relatively little experience, and sometimes in response to a premarital pregnancy. Not surprisingly, these young marriages were prone to problems and quite vulnerable to dissolution. The vestigial pattern of early marriage remains in some regions of the United States, especially in states and localities with high concentrations of evangelical Christians, who subscribe to traditional beliefs about the desirability of marriage. No doubt, the persistent pattern of early marriage helps to explain the seemingly anomalous correlation with higher divorce rates in the so-called red states—the states with higher proportions of residents who adhere strongly to beliefs in the sanctity of marriage.

The federal government's marriage promotion efforts are likely to miss the mark if they trumpet the benefits of marriage without recognizing the considerable barriers to marriage for young people with limited means and limited experience and skills. This is as true for young people living in Iowa and Oklahoma, where the idea of marriage promotion is widely embraced, as it is for those in the inner city, where this policy has been greeted with some wariness if not outright skepticism.

The Bush administration has pledged to spend $230 million to promote marriage throughout the country. This money draws on TANF dollars but is no longer exclusively directed to the welfare population. Indeed, much of the funding is being spent by community groups, often based in churches and religious organizations that have a strong ideological commitment to encouraging young adults to wed. The more sophisticated programs appreciate the delicacy of the task and are committed to building relationship skills and resources; the less sophisticated programs rely largely on proselytizing and advocating the spiritual virtues of matrimony.

Even among the programs that are founded in clinical science, many employ largely didactic rather than experiential or therapeutic interventions, using brief courses of education that may or may not be accompanied by short opportunities for direct skill-building in communication and emotional exchange. The evaluation research using short-term strategies is limited and inconsistent (Dion 2005). It is not at all clear whether short-term interventions can either promote successful marriages or save failing ones. What little evaluation has been undertaken has almost completely been confined to middle-class populations, among whom the challenges are relatively modest compared to low-income populations (Cowan and Cowan 1992; Gottman 1999; Markman et al. 2003). Existing programs and curricula would need to be adapted in order to serve low-income couples effectively (Dion 2005).

In short, we simply do not know whether promoting marriage is feasible. Is it possible to attract and sustain programs for low-income couples prior to marriage in which both participate in a series of sessions or workshops? Many initiatives have had difficulty running programs for low-income parents in which both men and women participate if only because so many face unaccommodating work schedules and child care arrangements (Miller and Knox 2001). And even if it is possible to achieve adherence to the program schedule, can programs aimed at imparting relationship skills actually result in higher rates of marriage and marital success? It is certainly possible that the opposite result might occur: marriage promotion programs could produce greater levels of marital dissolution by enlisting into marriage couples who might otherwise have remained single but who are unable to sustain the union. In other words, is public policy running ahead of practical knowledge in ways that might result either in misspent money or, worse yet, in the promotion of behavior that would harm rather than help young parents and their children?

Understanding the daunting challenges of marriage promotion, the Administration for Children, Youth, and Families (ACYF), the federal agency charged with supervising the program, has begun to devote more services to intact but troubled marriages that are at high risk of breaking apart. Such marriages, if detected in an early stage, seem like a more propitious target for intervention. However, many of the services being envisioned may not be up to the task. Marriage counseling, a hazardous enterprise under the best of circumstances, often requires lengthy, therapeutic interventions to help couples build new attitudes and skills that often cannot be imparted in a weekend workshop or a short set of classes.

To its credit, ACYF has built into its program a strong evaluation component to test the viability of different interventions. As I write this chapter, several large-scale intervention programs are being organized and will be tested by experimental designs. As a part-time adviser to these efforts, I would describe myself as a sympathetic skeptic who does not hold out any great hope for success at a scale or level that is likely to alter the fundamental changes that have taken place in marriage and marriage-like arrangements. Even so, I think that young people with limited experience in observing successful unions should be given help in acquiring skills for making relationships work, especially low-income couples who might otherwise not be able to afford premarital or postmarital counseling.

NEW DIRECTIONS FOR POLICIES
AIMED AT STRENGTHENING UNIONS

Public education, targeted interventions, and even greater availability of therapeutic services can have only modest effects on the erosion of marriage in low-income populations. Low-income populations face a daunting array of challenges to forming stable parenting unions: most have limited exposure to successful role models for building strong emotional relations and are embedded in a culture where gender mistrust is widespread; strains on everyday family life are chronic and often intense; marriageable males are in short supply; families (and households) are complex and fraught with competing interests; and needed supports and services are limited or absent altogether. It should come as no surprise that stable unions are difficult to achieve among these populations.

The rhetoric of the Bush administration—or, for that matter, the Clinton administration that preceded it—far exceeds the commitment to making the necessary public investment to support marriages and families. There would be nothing wrong with spending a quarter of a billion dollars to help couples build relationship skills were it not for the fact that at the same time the government is scaling back on its already meager investments in health, employment and training, and day care services aimed at providing supports to low-income families (Center for Law and Social Policy 2006). Robbing one needed program to pay for another is not an intelligently crafted strategy for enhancing the well-being of America's families and children.

Consider an alternative approach to the present policy, which is based on the assumption that children's welfare is improved if marriages are strengthened. I am inclined to think that a better approach might be to assume the opposite: that marriages are strengthened by improving children's welfare. Let me explain my rationale for postulating that investments in children will improve marriage prospects.

First, I have already noted that the prospects of making stronger marriages are limited given the human, social, and psychological capital of low-income women and, especially, their partners. Without concluding that the damage has already been done, a huge amount of rehabilitation is required to improve the marriageability of the low-income population substantially enough to ensure the security of the children they bear and rear. No doubt, it is a worthy undertaking, but one that is neither easy nor cheap to implement. Many of the measures require the provision of an array of family support services to low-income parents in addition to programs designed to build relational skills.

A more plausible approach may be to invest directly in children residing in low-income households regardless of the family form of their households. All the existing evidence points to the conclusion that by promoting early education in day care and after-school programs as well as strengthening school systems, children's chances of going beyond high school are improved (Currie 2001; Currie and Thomas 2000; Heckman 2000; Waldfogel 2006). The impact of education and related employment prospects is more likely to improve the ability of young people to enter into marriage and sustain marriage than any special programs that could be devised. Based on available evidence, there is little doubt that investments in human capital pay rich dividends in social and psychological capital as well (Danziger and Waldfogel 2000). And the presence of these sorts of assets is more likely to improve marriage in the next generation than any current measures that we can contemplate in helping struggling couples to keep their relationships intact.

Of course, these two approaches are complementary rather than competing strategies for strengthening relationships. However, I suspect that primary prevention may have a better prospect of succeeding than remedial efforts. It is more difficult to enhance skills among individuals who have a history of school failure, crime, drug abuse, and relationship problems than it is to invest in human capital by better and more intense education at earlier ages (Duncan and Brooks-Gunn 1997). The second approach may be more costly than the first, but it is more likely to be cost-effective in the long term (Karoly, Kilburn, and Cannon 2005). It not only prevents a host of expensive problems over the life course but permits individuals to gain the necessary skills to become financially independent and emotionally interdependent.

One of the obvious criticisms of such an intergenerational approach is that it is time-consuming and will not yield immediate benefits. This is probably not correct if adopting a preventive strategy reduces school, health, and social problems during childhood. Conceivably, investments in child care, health care, schooling, and after-school programs also reduce the stresses on parents and hence bolster precarious relationships. But equally important, if not more so, children do not suffer as much damage in the event that their parents do not remain together.

Another rejoinder to the approach that I have suggested is that the provision of services to nonstandard families legitimates and may even encourage the decision of parents not to live together. This could further undermine marriage by making alternative forms of the family possible and attractive. This argument seems far-fetched and lacks empirical support. The United States provides fewer family supports, less income support, and more social disapproval of alternative family forms than virtually any other industrialized nation, and yet at the same time it has the lowest percentage of children living with both biological parents of any Western nation (Heuveline, Timberlake, and Furstenberg 2003). Perhaps it is time to acknowledge that people do not form, sustain, or dissolve relationships primarily because of incentives and disincentives created by public policy. In short, we have little to fear by helping children thrive regardless of their family form; such supports are not likely to have much effect on their parents' decisions about whether to live together or not. If anything, greater support for children early in life would help tip the balance in favor of parents remaining together rather than living apart.

As I discuss again in the final chapter, I have few illusions that the argument I put forth here is likely to persuade those who believe in shrinking government assistance for families that their views are misguided. Many of those who believe that the autonomy of the family is best maintained when the government stays out of the business of providing supportive services are not going to be dissuaded of their opinions, either by argument or by evidence to the contrary.

Ultimately, however, all but the most ideologically minded policymakers and politicians can be influenced by argument and evidence. One of the appealing features of the ongoing "marriage promotion" experiments funded by the government is that social scientists and policy analysts who hold differing opinions about the potential efficacy of marriage promotion programs will learn whether the promise of such efforts is real and can be implemented at reasonable costs. The latter is not a trivial consideration because the alternative path to increasing union stability through greater investment in children and families is not inexpensive, as I have already noted.

At the same time that we are learning from the marriage promotion experiments, we should be thinking about alternative ways of strengthening bonds between couples, especially those who become parents. As I discussed in the previous chapter, this calls for making parenthood a more deliberate and reasoned decision that is planned and designed to occur at a propitious time. But making parenthood more intentional is only half of the issue for building a family well designed to promote children's welfare.

The other part of building strong families involves enabling parents to sustain a commitment to rearing their children together, preferably in the same household. If we ever could, we certainly no longer can take for granted that fostering and sustaining strong ties between parents will happen when children are born, particularly given the high rates of multi-partnered fertility. Merely pronouncing the couple "husband and wife" offers little in the way of assurance that they will stay together or, for that matter, successfully parent together even if they do. This is why I believe that there is room for skill building, training, and support for couples (whether they are heterosexual or same-sex) in unions. But to form and nurture these unions, we better be prepared to provide a lot more economic and social support than we have in the recent past. The alternative is probably the continued unraveling of parental unions, whether they are marriages or cohabitations.

Finally, it is difficult to deny that strengthening unions through public policy initiatives of any sort is likely to have only modest effects on the survival of marriage as an institution. Across the Western nations, and especially in the United States, free choice is deeply rooted in both our history and the culture of capitalism. Political rights and economic roles promote individual choice. This culture permeates kinship systems and family processes in ways that make it difficult to enforce lifelong unions even when children are involved. This fact is obviously why attempts to make marriage binding meet with resistance even in religious subcultures that take the biblical scriptures as prescriptive. When given the opportunity, few couples elect to enter into "covenant marriages" that make divorce more difficult. Evidence suggests that men are far more willing than women to undertake lasting unions, in part because they perceive and probably receive greater benefits from matrimony (Nock 1998, 2005).

If for no other reason, it seems prudent not to assume that we can dramatically reverse many of the demographic trends that have weakened marriage. How can we get young people to stop having premarital sex when marriage typically now occurs in the late twenties? How do we convince young people that it is in their best interests not to live together when the economic, social, and psychological advantages of cohabitation become ever more compelling in a system where uncertainties about life paths continue well into early adulthood? And how do we persuade unhappily married (or cohabiting) couples to remain married when their day-to-day experiences tell them that their relationship is not working out? Surely we must recognize that public policy, even if it were more potent than anything currently in place, is likely to have only a weak influence on these types of personal decisions.

It is for this reason that I believe direct investment in children is a more realistic way of helping the next generation succeed than trying to shape the family forms in which children are reared. The best way to strengthen children's capacities when they grow up to sustain stable unions may be through providing them with a good education. Unequal levels of investment in children ultimately result in an uneven distribution of human, social, and psychological capital in adulthood. The distribution of these resources affects young people's chances, not only their chances of becoming good providers but also the likelihood that they will become good partners and parents later in life. I have claimed that shifting that distribution is more likely to affect the viability of marriage than any single policy or set of policies targeted at strengthening marriage that we could ever devise. If I am correct, it then follows that investing in public education and increasing support for higher education might do more to restore marriage than all our efforts to promote or privilege marriage through legal means, public education, and remedial services.

—— Chapter 6 ——

Teenage Childbearing and Welfare Reform

Soon after Rwanda Powers discovered she was pregnant, she applied for and received public assistance to help support her child while she finished school. Although the father of the baby was in jail, Rwanda explained to the interviewer, Mrs. Blau, that they were planning to marry as soon as he was released. That did not happen. A year after her first child was born, Rwanda was pregnant again with the child of another man, and she continued on public assistance. A high school dropout, Rwanda reported that she wanted to return to school so that she could find a good job. As she said, "I feel, if you have a family, you need to work, 'cause welfare doesn't give you much. [And working] beats sittin' around the house doing nothing."

Rwanda, however, did not return to complete high school or earn a GED in the immediate aftermath of her first birth. She was still receiving public assistance when interviewed at the seventeen-year follow-up, when she reported that she had never worked for any significant period. As we saw in chapter 2, Rwanda's experience, although hardly typical of the women in the study, was also not uncommon. Nearly two-thirds of the Baltimore sample had received public assistance during part or all of the five years following the birth of their first child. Close to one-third of the study participants either remained continuously on welfare or cycled on and off during the decade and a half after they entered parenthood (Furstenberg, Brooks-Gunn, and Morgan 1987). Regardless of their aspirations, it appears that many of these teenage mothers failed to escape from welfare dependency—or at least so it seemed, based on the results of the initial stages of the study.

137

How did the welfare experience mark the lives of the women we followed and their offspring, many of whom grew up relying in part on public assistance? Is there reason to believe that the reforms introduced during the 1990s to reduce welfare dependence have improved the circumstances of poor women and helped to reduce the level of teenage childbearing? The evidence from our study provides a useful baseline against which to compare the efficacy of the reforms that were part of the elimination of welfare as a lifelong entitlement. By looking backward in time and examining the experiences of the women in the Baltimore Study, we can offer some provisional assessment of the costs and benefits of the new system that is now in place.

This chapter explores these questions, examining how the experiences of the teen mothers fit the policies that aimed at replacing economic dependency with self-sufficiency, a strategy that many hoped would strengthen marriage and discourage nonmarital childbearing. It will probably come as no surprise that the evidence from the Baltimore Study and the larger literature on teen parenthood and welfare reliance often fails to match the direction of welfare policy reform intended to reduce the incentives for becoming a single parent.

WELFARE AND SINGLE MOTHERS

Government cash assistance to single mothers was a practice that began in the 1930s as part of the Social Security reforms designed to lift vulnerable families and the elderly out of poverty. The programs, which included what would later be known as Aid to Families with Dependent Children (AFDC), helped to "protect" single mothers, at the time largely widows, from being forced to enter the labor force. It was not uncommon during the Depression for mothers to work outside the home, but it was considered undesirable for the well-being of children, who, it was thought, required the care of a full-time parent during their tender years (Gordon 1994).

Not long after AFDC was established, the demographic composition of families receiving AFDC changed, and with these changes came a shift in the program's racial and ethnic makeup. In a matter of several decades, recipients of aid shifted from mostly widows to a larger number of divorcées, and beginning in the 1960s the program began to serve a growing number of never-married mothers. As the program's population shifted from whites to more blacks and Latinos, public sympathy for the welfare population began to evaporate. The relatively generous practices of the Johnson administration in the early 1960s were strongly embraced by a Democratic Congress that had made a commitment to the War on Poverty, but even during the 1960s rumbles of discontent in both political parties were evident with the mounting costs of the Vietnam War.

Discourse about public assistance had long had an ungenerous and even savage edge, but beginning in the 1960s critics began to describe public assistance as a program that promoted promiscuity and encouraged the poor to have children (Goodwin 1983; Kriesberg 1970; Placek and Hendershot 1974; Rainwater 1970). The early literature exploring the existence of a "culture of poverty" among the AFDC population found little support for the notion that women on welfare had distinctively different ideas about family formation from the rest of the population, but the steady stream of empirical evidence did little to temper the emerging political debate over public assistance as a policy that fostered dependency and instilled in the next generation bad habits that undermined the work ethic (see, for example, Banfield 1974).

During the 1970s, as the American economy soured and stagflation increased, public assistance was effectively reduced as support levels failed to keep up with inflation. By the 1980s, when the Reagan administration launched an all-out assault on welfare, the levels of support had declined sharply in real dollars, even though increases in rates of divorce and nonmarital childbearing and political efforts to organize the poor had led to increases in the welfare population (Piven and Cloward 1993). Nonetheless, a growing public consensus was emerging that women on welfare should work rather than be stay-at-home mothers (Gordon 1994). As the proportion of working mothers grew in the labor force, the protections accorded to full-time motherhood weakened. Why should women on welfare be subsidized not to work, critics asked, when a growing number of low-income women were taking jobs to help support their family? Apart from the left, which for the most part vigorously supported the continuation of family support through AFDC, sentiment in the United States shifted toward helping single mothers enter the labor force through education, job training, and child support (Ellwood 1989; Riccio, Friedlander, and Freedman 1994).

Heated disagreements continued among researchers and policy-makers on how best to achieve a work-oriented social support system that would help single mothers enter the labor force but would not produce inequities for single women and low-income couples who were not receiving public assistance. Moreover, social conservatives, who worried that welfare created incentives for single parenthood, advocated changes in welfare policy aimed at discouraging unmarried parenthood (Tanner 2003). A series of legislative changes instituted during the Reagan years, culminating in the Family Support Act of 1988, were designed to reduce the costs of public assistance to taxpayers and eliminate what were viewed as perverse incentives for having children outside of marriage. Despite these legislative initiatives, the drumbeat of criticism over public assistance and its presumed effects on the family formation patterns of low-income families continued unabated.

Critics of welfare rallied around the writings of Charles Murray, who first proposed eliminating welfare in a series of popular essays in the 1980s that were collected into his famous book on the subject, *Losing Ground* (1984). Few books on matters of public policy have had the influence of *Losing Ground,* which cogently sets out the case against public assistance for the poor. Murray's work, although documented by various studies and academic sources, relied largely on the brilliant rhetorical device of creating a fictional couple who, following Murray's logic, were compelled to rely on welfare because they were better off not marrying, not working, and having additional children as a means to increase welfare payments. Murray's analysis sought to reveal the logic of why and how AFDC had undermined the family, contributed to the growth of unemployment, and added to the rise of welfare dependency.

Teenage parenthood was featured in *Losing Ground* as both the symptom and inevitable product of a misguided and distorted system of economic incentives that encouraged young women to have children and discouraged young men from marrying them when they became pregnant. And Murray, like Moynihan before him, assumed that teenage childbearing was a critical link in the perpetuation of the cycle of social disadvantage. He writes:

The lives of such young women [teenage mothers] are irretrievably changed by the fact of their single motherhood—education, access to a job ladder, and simple freedom to mature without the pressures of raising a child are made extraordinarily more difficult. The lives of their children are affected as decisively. (Murray 1984, 129)

Critics of public assistance, such as Murray, and the architects of welfare reform, such as the political scientist Lawrence Mead (1986), claimed that the perverse incentives built into the welfare system were largely responsible for the decline of work commitment and marriage, aided by the liberal political culture of the 1960s. Lamenting this misdirection of public policy and its impact on the poor, Murray (1984, 219) writes almost mournfully:

It was wrong to take from the most industrious, most responsible poor— take safety, education, justice, status—so that we could cater to the least industrious, least responsible poor. It was wrong to impose rules that made it rational for adolescents to behave in ways that destroyed their futures.

In what must have seemed in 1984 an almost impossible vision, Murray proposes a corrective to the policies of the past, boldly advocating "scrapping the entire federal welfare and income-support structure for working-aged persons, including AFDC, Medicaid, Food Stamps, Unemployment Insurance, Worker's Compensation, subsidized housing, disability insurance, and the rest." He adds: "It would leave the working-aged person with no recourse whatsoever except the job market, family members, friends, and public or private locally funded services" (227–8).

In fact, Murray's solution called for providing minimal assistance to poor families, and even that was to be made contingent on their good behavior. To the single mother, Murray makes the suggestion that she go to work.

The question we must now ask is: What is so bad about that? If children were always better off being with their mother all day and if, by the act of giving birth, a mother acquired the inalienable right to be with the child, then her situation would be unjust to her and injurious to her children. Neither assertion can be defended, however. (Murray 1984, 231)

The continuing pressure in the 1990s to make radical revisions to public assistance policies led some states to request federal waivers of existing welfare laws so that they could experiment with different approaches to encourage work; these policies would ultimately replace AFDC (Rogers-Dillon 2004). Some of these programs— job placement, child care, and continued health insurance for low-income parents and children—were strongly endorsed by single women who wanted to return to the labor force as quickly as possible. Others, such as time limits on welfare receipt and sanctions for noncompliance, were controversial and often regarded as efforts to make it difficult for vulnerable women to receive support. Given that many states at the time were facing deficits, some argued that these requirements were diversionary strategies designed to discourage applications for welfare, which in the more egregious cases amounted to purging the welfare rolls.

It is hard to imagine that critics of AFDC such as Murray and Mead expected that eliminating welfare as an entitlement would indeed become the blueprint for a total overhaul of public assistance, or that the reform of "welfare as we know it" would be enacted by Congress within a decade, much less that the law would be signed into law by a Democratic president. But that is exactly what happened. In 1996 President Bill Clinton oversaw the most fundamental overhaul of the welfare system since its enactment in the 1930s. The Personal Responsibility and Work Opportunity Reconciliation Act (PRWORA) replaced AFDC with Temporary Assistance for Needy Families (TANF), which limited welfare receipt to five years over a woman's lifetime and made receipt contingent on work. Cash assistance to poor single mothers was no longer an entitlement. Several supports were provided to women making the transition to the labor market, including the ability to keep a portion of the welfare check when they were employed.

WHY NOT WORK?

Scores of studies conducted both before and after welfare reform, mostly by economists, have examined the premise that public assistance creates incentives to poor people to have children, to defer marriage, and to not work (Blank 1997; Blank and Haskins 2001; Bloom and Michalopoulos 2001; Hamilton 2002). Although it is possible to read this body of evidence in different ways, most social scientists have concluded that incentives to form single-parent households are relatively small and often inconsistent. Relevant to this discussion, even less evidence exists that patterns of teenage childbearing have been sensitive to levels of public assistance over time and place (Acs 1995; Moffitt 2001; Offner 2005; Plotnick 1990; Sawhill et al. 2002; Sonestein and Acs 1995). Murray's claim that family formation patterns among low-income populations had been driven by welfare policies was either wrong or at least certainly greatly overstated.

Many of the reviews of this research take some pains to identify any significant impacts of public assistance on family formation patterns at all. The economist Robert Moffitt, who has written a series of such reviews over the past decade and a half, concluded in 1992, not long before the passage of welfare reform, that the availability of public assistance did lower women's labor force participation, but that the effect was not sufficient to explain either the rising rates of female headship or the influence of public assistance on family formation patterns. Moffitt's assessment of the literature provides little support for those who believed that marriage and childbearing patterns were affected by the level of public assistance. He notes that

> the econometric estimates of family structure effects are not large enough to explain long-run declines in marriage rates and, in any case, [they do not] explain recent upward trends in female headship because welfare benefits have been declining. (Moffitt 1992, 56–57)

Even prior to the dramatic changes in welfare policy enacted in 1996, the idea that AFDC was an important influence on declining marriage rates was not widely substantiated by economic and demographic trends.

The quantitative evidence that welfare policy has little influence on behavior is strongly supported by various qualitative studies that have allowed for more searching conversations with low-income parents (see, for example, Edin and Kefalas 2005; Stack 1974). Most of these studies find that the majority of families who received public assistance cycled in and out of the welfare system as their personal circumstances changed. Specifically, women migrated from the welfare rolls as they completed schooling, found jobs, or married. Often they signed up for welfare in a period of crisis following the dissolution of a partnership, the loss of a job, the loss of child care, or an illness in the family. Although their spells on welfare could be relatively lengthy, in fact only a very small percentage remained on public assistance continuously throughout their child rearing years (Ellwood and Bane 1994).

Among these studies was one by Kathleen Harris (1997) that examined the welfare histories of the Baltimore women in some detail and then replicated the findings using data from the National Longitudinal Survey of Youth (NLSY), the national study that was carried out over the same time period as the Baltimore Study. Harris established with both sets of data that movement in and out of the welfare system was highly patterned by the contingencies associated with poverty and an often capricious labor market. In other words, mothers were choosing welfare not because of built-in incentives that deterred them from work, but as a safety net in tough times. These results were bolstered by a series of studies showing that most welfare mothers worked off the books even while receiving public assistances because it was impossible for a family to subsist on public assistance alone (Edin and Jencks 1992; Edin and Lein 1997). Thus, many women on public assistance were, in effect, using welfare as a way of offsetting and compensating for the contingencies of being in the low-wage labor market.

More recently, several researchers who have examined the problems faced by low-income women, especially single mothers, find that securing stable child care is a major obstacle to entering the job market and remaining stably employed (Chaudry 2004; Waldfogel 2006). Costs, transportation problems, and the questionable reliability of child care providers both inside and outside the household often create havoc among overstressed, low-income parents (just as they do with moderate- and higher-income families). Jody Heymann, Alison Earle, and I (1999), using data from the Baltimore Study along with other data sources, discovered that illness in the family was frequently associated with job instability. Most poor families do not have jobs with sick leave benefits and therefore are either fired or forced to quit when their children have chronic health disabilities. Just as was the case for other low-income workers, many women in Baltimore were forced by family emergencies, job constraints, and job loss to leave the formal labor market to work off the books in jobs that provided greater leeway in combining family obligations with employment (see also Edin and Lein 1997).

The Baltimore data and similar studies of the welfare careers of teen mothers do not provide a great deal of support for the argument that welfare has pernicious effects on family formation. Welfare patterns appear to be more a consequence than a cause of family insecurity and instability. However, we revisit this question later in the chapter when we discuss the impact of welfare reform on family formation in the decade following its passage. Whatever the problems of AFDC—and they were considerable—the program seems to have exerted relatively little influence on the patterns of family change, particular rates or timing of marriage, and early and out-of-wedlock childbearing. These shifts were largely driven by structural alterations in the economy, leading to greater involvement in education, changing sexual practices, the availability of effective means of contraception, and, most of all, new and different expectations about what makes a successful marriage.

Nonetheless, a high proportion of teenage mothers did use public assistance, and some relied on it heavily during the years when they had dependent children. All the women in the Baltimore Study came of age as teenage parents prior to welfare reform. They were part of the old system that had produced so many of the political and public discontents that resulted in the remarkable revamping of one of the most fundamental parts of the American social welfare system. It is especially interesting, then, to review the long-term circumstances of teenage mothers who came of age before and after welfare reform.

Contrary to popular perception, being on public assistance had long been stigmatized among this low-income population, both by those who received public assistance and by those who did not. In the early 1970s, at the time of the three-year follow-up with the Baltimore women, we included several questions about the acceptability of public assistance. Surprisingly, no matter how the questions were phrased, feelings about welfare were almost uniformly negative. Only a handful of those receiving welfare indicated that it was better to receive welfare than to work when young children were in the home, when wages were no higher than welfare payments, or when good jobs could not be secured (Furstenberg 1976). Virtually all respondents shared Rwanda's view that it was always better to find a job than to rely on public assistance. But like Rwanda, somehow many of those who began receiving welfare in the early years of the study had difficulty finding their way into stable employment in their twenties and early thirties.

Of the more than half of all women in the study who had been on welfare by the seventeen-year follow-up, fewer than one in three was on welfare in 1984. The good news was that the two-thirds who had received public assistance in the first five years of the study had left the rolls by the seventeen-year follow-up. The not so good news, as Kathleen Harris (1997) discovered, was that some portion of the women who were not current recipients had been cycling on and off since the birth of their first child. However, it must also be said that many of those currently receiving welfare had been episodically in and out of the labor force over the years—some in regular jobs and many more in off-the-books employment. Those who did not escape, like Rwanda, had especially poor prospects in the labor market and faced formidable difficulties managing child care. As Heymann, Earle, and I (1999) reported, many poor women tended to have children or parents with chronic health problems and often suffered mental and physical problems themselves. Those who used public assistance heavily tended to be the most disadvantaged of the disadvantaged.

THE IMPACT OF WELFARE REFORM

Since the passage of welfare reform legislation in 1996, there have been literally hundreds, if not thousands, of studies to measure the impact of reform on the economic, psychological, and social well-being of parents and children (for an excellent summary of this literature, visit the website of the Center for Law and Social Policy; see also Blank and Haskins 2001; Haskins 2006; Parrott and Sherman 2006). Most observers agree that only a decade after the passage of welfare reform, it is still too early to assess the costs and benefits of the policy changes. However, it is generally agreed that the new system neither achieved all of its original aims nor created the drastic and adverse effects on most poor mothers and their children that many on the left had feared. Indeed, there is strong evidence that the changes were accompanied, at least prior to the 2001 recession, by a remarkable drop in poverty among single mothers (Haskins 2006; O'Neill and Hill 2002; Parrott and Sherman 2006).

The impact of welfare reform is so thoroughly intertwined with prevailing economic conditions that it is very difficult to disentangle specific impacts. The passage of an expanded Earned Income Tax Credit—essentially an income supplement for low-income working families—just prior to the regime change further complicates the

FIGURE 6.1 **AFDC/TANF Caseload, 1960 to 2001**

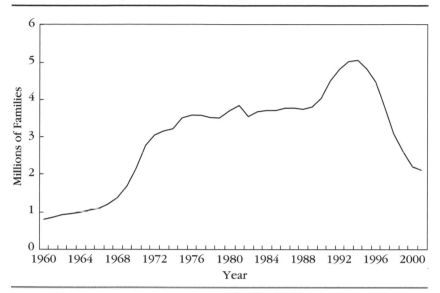

Source: U.S. Department of Health and Human Services (2002).

picture. The funding of TANF was generous when the legislation was approved because it was based on current caseload levels. As the numbers receiving TANF dropped, there was relatively ample funding to provide the job placement services and child care required to help nonworking mothers transition into the labor force. Further, during the late 1990s the booming economy created an unprecedented number of new jobs, allowing those with limited skills and education to find employment. In short, it was the perfect historical moment to introduce welfare reform.

This much we can say so far. First, the program has been judged a great success by those who wanted to shrink the number of families receiving assistance (Sawhill et al. 2002). Some combination of the bureaucratic hurdles, recipients' fear of exceeding time limits, the robust economy, and the supportive services that many states offered to low-income working parents did change the structure of opportunities for those who might otherwise have begun receiving public assistance in the past. As shown in figure 6.1, the number of women receiving cash assistance plummeted, and declines also occurred in the number of applicants for food stamps and emergency aid (Sawhill et al. 2002, 10).

Many believe that the culture surrounding the legitimacy of welfare in low-income communities also changed: women in these communities, they claim, are now less likely to expect, desire, and choose to receive public support, even on a temporary basis. I have little doubt, even though social science evidence is fragmentary on this issue, that the reform measures delegitimized welfare to some degree, although I suspect that the then-and-now comparisons are exaggerated. It is easy to forget that the stigma associated with being on welfare has long existed among the poor (Goodwin 1983; Kriesberg 1970). For the vast majority of women, it was always a last resort. Even among teenage mothers—the very group of women explicitly targeted in welfare reform—there was little support for those who remained on public assistance, and many had a strong desire to find employment, as evidenced by the cycling patterns of the teen mothers in Baltimore.

Most poor mothers like those I studied in Baltimore typically moved off the welfare rolls as their children became school-aged, but their counterparts today undoubtedly are more reluctant to go on welfare at all than they were several decades ago. Among women meeting all the eligibility requirements, fewer than half received TANF in 2002 compared to more than 85 percent in 1995, the year before the legislation was approved (Parrott and Sherman 2006). As the welfare rolls shrank, the proportion of single mothers who were employed rose from 62 percent in 1995 to a peak of 73 percent in 2001, before the recession of 2001 set in (Burtless 2004). Not only did more women enter the labor force, but their economic standing improved as earnings gains from employment, the benefits of subsidized child care, and the EITC kicked in. Between 1995 and 2001, the median income of working women rose from $22,500 to $27,500 (DeNavas-Walt and Cleveland 1996, 2002). However, it remains difficult to specify with any degree of precision the share of this change in earnings that can be attributed to the policy changes associated with welfare reform and the share that is accounted for by other economic conditions or other non-economic factors. Still, most experts believe that welfare reform deserves a good deal of the credit for encouraging single, low-income mothers to increase their labor force participation

(Blank and Haskins 2001; Colen, Geronimus, and Phipps 2006; Haskins 2006).

Since 2001, the positive picture has eroded slightly as unemployment rates have risen and remain high for low-income minority workers (Iversen and Armstrong 2006). As this book was being written, economists were still uncertain about the pace of job growth in the first decade of the twenty-first century, especially about whether the opportunities that low-income workers enjoyed in the 1990s would be fully recovered in the wake of the last recession in 2001. From 2001 to 2003—the last year for which data are available—the number of TANF recipients rose, as did the use of food stamps and supplementary TANF services. Although far below the level of AFDC families, these trends indicate that the flow on and off public support continues despite the looming threat of time limits for marginally qualified workers, an issue to which I return later in this chapter.

It is also unclear whether women previously on welfare have made out as well economically as they might have done combining work and public assistance in the era prior to TANF. Although leaving welfare signals greater economic independence, it is not always associated with economic improvement, which depends on the associated costs of working regularly, such as child care and transportation, and the level of job benefits, including health care, vacation time, and sick leave. In other words, the impact of welfare reform on former recipients has had the obvious benefit of relieving the public's tax burden as well as fostering higher self-esteem among former welfare recipients. Unquestionably, it has brought about an improvement in the lives of women who find steady and remunerative employment. In short, there is broad consensus among researchers and policymakers that welfare reform has improved the lot of single mothers who have found reasonably good jobs (O'Neill and Hill 2002).

For women with less education, fewer job skills, and more personal problems, welfare reform has probably had the opposite effect, but those whose economic situation has worsened are a distinct minority (Greenberg 2006; Haskins 2006; Moffitt 2002). How large is this portion of the welfare population? Most estimates suggest that perhaps as few as 10 percent or as many as 20 percent of former welfare recipients have fared poorly in the aftermath of welfare reform because they are not easily employable, lacking the education, skills, and mental or physical health to obtain a job with earnings that would match what they might have received on public assistance (Zedlewski and Loprest 2001). Another portion of the women who might have stayed on welfare longer in the past do not make out any better than they would had they remained on welfare, though arguably this outcome could be seen as a draw or a positive outcome of a policy that was aimed at getting poor women back in the labor force sooner rather than later.

For obvious reasons, it is more difficult to measure the impact on non-economic outcomes on mothers and children. Several studies have suggested that young children benefit when their mothers leave welfare for a job—or at least, that their development is not compromised by their mother's return to the labor force (Duncan and Chase-Lansdale 2001b; Gennetian and Miller 2002). The change from staying at home to working is, of course, more apparent than real, since we know that most women are working off the books part-time or full-time. Most of the research suggests that work, perhaps especially for less-educated women, typically involves a trade-off between mother care and alternative forms of child care. Depending on the quality of care by parents and other child care alternatives, children's circumstances may improve or worsen when their mothers spend more time in the labor force. Nonetheless, numerous studies suggest that the workplace can provide indirect benefits to the children of low-income workers by offering social capital to their parents in the form of knowledge, information, and support (Waldfogel 2006).

Interestingly, some studies hint that older children, particularly adolescents, have not fared as well under the new welfare regime (Gennetian et al. 2004). Given the paucity of after-school opportunities in many low-income neighborhoods and the family responsibilities assumed by many of the older children of former welfare recipients, older children may be inadequately supervised at home and in the neighborhood. Evidence has been accumulating that adolescents often spend time with peers after school in settings where adults are not present and opportunities for engaging in antisocial or self-destructive behavior are thus enhanced.

In 2000 Lynne Haney and Robin Rogers-Dillon interviewed women in the Baltimore Study, some of whom had received welfare consistently and some of whom had been able to leave the welfare rolls prior to the passage of TANF. In addition, they spoke with the firstborn children, many of whom had experience in both the old and new systems. Haney and Rogers-Dillon confirm many of the findings mentioned here. In particular, they note the very positive view that mothers gain of themselves after entering the workforce, but they also observe the absence of social supports for many of the women who move from welfare to work, as well as the vast burdens imposed on low-income women: managing transportation, locating quality child care, and coping with the time bind created by long working hours plus travel time (often two hours or more a day).

Some women turned to males for partial or full support, but many were wary about becoming reliant on male support. Because of the paucity of economically independent males, the unreliability of many men in providing regular support, and their distrust of men's ability to be cooperative partners, low-income women tended to keep males, especially those who did not father their children, at a distance. In contrast to the "process of unplanned parenthood" that had initiated motherhood for them many years before, they carefully tested the water, in effect, before they jumped in. One respondent beautifully captured the deep insecurity that many women felt about relying on a man:

> I think I found a good man. I mean, I hope I found a good man. Yes, I believe I have. Everything would fall apart without him. Ain't no way I could keep the job [without him]. Every day I worry: What if he doesn't show up today? What if the kids are alone now? I call every day, many times. Until now, he's always been there. I thank the Lord for this. I think he's a good man. I mean, I do believe he's a good man.

This passage may explain why by all accounts welfare reform did not alter family formation patterns. Arguably, it may have helped to discourage or reverse the prevalence of teenage childbearing, although the decline in early and out-of-wedlock childbearing preceded TANF legislation by five years and it seems likely that the combination of economic changes, tightening of child support enforcement, improvement of contraceptive methods, and fear of HIV/AIDS and STDs all contributed to the reversal in fertility among younger women. At the same time, there is little evidence that women looked more often to husbands and partners as they moved from public assistance to employment; nor, for that matter, is there evidence that they curtailed their level of childbearing outside of marriage.

Marriage rates have not risen since the passage of welfare reform. In fact, they have been falling steadily since 1990 and have declined more in the years since welfare reform than before (Centers for Disease Control and Prevention 2005b). This comes as no surprise to social demographers, who predicted that welfare reform would have little or no impact on marriage practices and indeed might aggravate economic and social disparities between low-income women and men (Lichter, Graefe, and Brown 2003; Lichter and Crowley 2004). If anything, by increasing the prospects of low-income women and doing little to change the circumstances of their potential marriage partners (low-income men), TANF, and possibly the EITC, could have even helped to further erode marriage among low-income families. Women may have become more attractive as marriage partners because of their changed economic circumstances at the same time that low-income men, whose employment rates stagnated during the 1990s, became less desirable mates. Assisting low-income women to achieve economic independence while their potential mates were foundering economically, it seems, might well have undermined the policy objective of many to strengthen the institution of marriage. In an appraisal of the impact of welfare reform on family formation, Charles Murray (2001) as much as concedes that the evidence linking the two is dubious and calls for more extreme restrictions on public assistance.

THE BALTIMORE FAMILIES IN THE WAKE
OF WELFARE REFORM

Both the qualitative and quantitative evidence from the Baltimore Study confirms what many researchers have concluded about the great social experiment of the 1990s. Changing the welfare system may have helped to alter the culture surrounding public assistance. The public and politicians are less focused on the welfare poor because fewer families use public support, and when they do, they use it for shorter periods. Reform may have altered the attitudes and expectations of those receiving public assistance, although our data, supported by many other studies, suggest that most welfare recipients never wanted or expected to remain on public assistance. As noted earlier, only a small minority of women become "dependent" on welfare: one in six of the teenage mothers remained on public assistance during most or all of our study. Although not a negligible number, the vast majority of women who were chronic recipients in Baltimore had severe problems finding employment and remaining in the labor market because of a combination of low skills, emotional difficulties, health issues, dependents who were ill, and an assortment of other obstacles (see also Heymann et al. 1999; Moffitt 2002).

We began the chapter citing the case of Rwanda Powers, a teenage mother who remained unemployed throughout the first two decades of the study. Rwanda's seemingly hopeless situation took a surprising turn just after the seventeen-year follow-up. After many years of not working, Rwanda found employment in 1986 and was still working at the same job when we conducted the thirty-year follow-up a decade later. Had her transition to the labor force occurred after welfare reform, it would have been taken as evidence that women on welfare want to work and are capable of holding a job. Had Rwanda come along thirty years later, her experience would have been chalked up as evidence of the success of TANF. Conceivably, Rwanda might have been put to work earlier had she grown up in the TANF era, when she would have been given more assistance in making a successful transition to the labor force. It is equally evident from the Baltimore Study that most women found their way into employment, leaving public assistance on their own.

Nearly half of the women in the Baltimore Study spent most of their lives gainfully employed before the passage of TANF, even when their children were dependents. When they were not working, most were caring for young children or going to school to improve their job prospects and possibly working off the books at the same time. So we might well ask: Would they have fared better under the present regime than they did in the system that was in place when the Baltimore Study was conducted? Similarly, would their children be better off now than when they were being supported by AFDC?

Based on what can be gleaned from research on the costs and benefits of the present system, the answer to these questions is certainly not clear-cut. From the point of view of taxpayers, no doubt there has been some benefit. Welfare rolls have declined, although current TANF services for transitional child care and health benefits must be taken into account in assessing the savings. No doubt, too, the current system is more geared to helping people like Rwanda find their way into the labor market more swiftly than was the case thirty years ago. That is a significant achievement, especially when it seems not to have come at significant cost to the next generation.

On the negative side, the former system offered much more leeway for women to remain in school, where they could improve their long-term economic prospects. Today, in most states, women receiving assistance are propelled more quickly into unskilled employment and left on their own to gain additional schooling or training. This may or may not compromise their long-term earning prospects, but it is unlikely that so many women on public assistance would have been able to return to school in the aftermath of their first birth. Moreover, women are now under greater stress managing child care responsibilities with a full-time job. Taking into account the costs of holding a job—child care, transportation, and related expenses—most research has shown that women on welfare do not improve their economic circumstances significantly when they move into the workforce.

Finally, and perhaps of greatest importance, are the compromised circumstances of the most vulnerable poor, those who are unemployable or responsible for caring for other dependents. In some cases, women with severe health problems have been relocated to Supplemental Security Income (SSI) for the disabled, but qualifying to receive such protection is not easy. A significant minority of those who were called "welfare dependents" have fallen through the cracks, imposing an added burden on family and community members who are already beset with economic demands. Our previously ungenerous system has become even more ungenerous. This observation raises the uncomfortable question of the prospects for public support of low-income families in the future. Can we project that the current relatively benign effects of welfare reform will continue in years to come?

LOOKING AHEAD: THE UNCERTAIN FUTURE
OF WELFARE REFORM

Many critics and some supporters of TANF fear that the success of the program in the first decade after its passage may be short-lived. The high-flying economy of the 1990s has downshifted to a moderate-growth economy in the middle of the first decade of the new century after a brief recession that is still producing lingering effects on low-income families. Job rates among the poor have not fully recovered, nor are they likely to unless the economy picks up pace, which few observers believe is likely to happen in the current era of huge budget deficits, sky-high oil costs, and a highly competitive global market that is draining jobs from this country.

A divided Congress was for several years unable to reauthorize TANF and relied on temporary budget allocations until an agreement could be hammered out. Finally, in 2006, it passed reauthorization with stricter work requirements and cutbacks in some of the support services provided to women leaving TANF. In the meantime, a growing number of unemployed mothers may be turning to other forms of income support, such as unemployment insurance or private assistance, but for some, these supports cannot be tapped or have been exhausted. While welfare rolls rose somewhat in the most recent recession, unemployed poor mothers seem to be reluctant to resort to TANF because of the threat of reaching time limits.

Predictably, since 2000 the poverty rate has risen for single women who head households and for all children under age eighteen, rising about 11 percent in the first half of the current decade; in 2005, the latest year for which data are available, the poverty rate stood at 31 percent for single women heading households and 18 percent for all children under eighteen—below the figures a decade earlier but stubbornly persistent despite the overall improvement in the economy as the United States emerged from the recession of 2001 (DeNavas-Walt, Proctor, and Lee 2006).

While health insurance remains available to most poor children through the Children's Health Insurance Program (CHIP), significant numbers of children remain unsubscribed in any program. In 2005, 11.2 percent of all children and 19 percent of children in poverty did not have health insurance. The rates of the uninsured gradually rose in the United States during the past decade, with some interruption during the booming economy of the late 1990s (DeNavas-Walt, Proctor, and Lee 2006). As work-based insurance becomes unavailable or unaffordable, many poor working women lack insurance even when their children are covered. Thus, it remains an open question whether welfare reform has contributed to the problem of uninsurance by shifting the burden of obtaining insurance to the resistant marketplace. No doubt these reversals of the favorable trends in the late 1990s are linked to the sluggish recovery from the last recession. They represent troubling indicators that the current safety net is inadequate to protect vulnerable families who rely on work to make ends meet.

Making work pay, the stated objective of the Clinton administration's approach to welfare policy and the position many advocates of welfare reform have advanced, relies on the availability of jobs that pay a living wage and the continuation of services for low-income families who may be unable to afford to work without generous subsidies for day care and health insurance. If jobs disappear and supports are reduced, low-income families could end up being no better off, and perhaps less secure, than they were under the old welfare regime.

The current administration has pinned its hopes on promoting marriage as a way of offsetting public support for poor families. No doubt some low-income families will find marriage an attractive possibility if both partners have relatively secure jobs and at least one of the jobs offers health benefits. How many parents with a high school degree or less can find such a position and wed a partner who also has a stable position? The answer is relatively few. The wages of both high school dropouts and high school graduates have been declining, even when they can find steady employment. Beyond the deteriorating levels of compensation, most less-educated and low-income workers lack health and family support benefits through their employment. For example, fully one-fifth of all workers who were earning between $25,000 and $50,000 in 2005 did not have health insurance (DeNavas-Walt, Proctor, and Lee 2006).

For reasons reviewed in the previous chapter, many low-income parents doubt the economic benefits of marriage, and their apprehensions are generally confirmed by the available social science evidence. Welfare reform has not removed the uncertainties associated with low-income employment, such as finding reliable and afford-able day care, paying transportation costs, locating jobs with decent benefits, and coordinating work demands and family life. In short, the United States has not yet made work pay for most low-income families, much less persuaded poor women that they are better off forming a union than relying on their natal family or a sometime partner. At this point, making work pay has proved to be a better slogan than a reality for a considerable fraction of the working poor. Unfortunately, the looming budget shortfalls threaten to cur-tail rather than expand the support provisions in the TANF program "as we know it."

Many of the most successful of the former welfare recipients in the Baltimore Study used the period when their children were young and their mothers were helping to provide child care to return to school. As I reported in chapter 3, nearly 50 percent of the mothers increased their education between the birth of their first child and the final wave of surveys. In effect, welfare enabled them to invest in education and training. When they entered the labor force, they were often in a position to get relatively good jobs, especially local or federal government positions that conferred relatively generous benefits. Of all the women who had received welfare, nearly 60 percent were employed in positions that provided health benefits, in addition to vacation, sick leave, and often a pension. For most of these women, public assistance was a route out of poverty rather than a rut in which they became permanently stuck.

It is especially troubling, therefore, that the advent of TANF has, in many states, foreclosed the possibility of schooling in place of work. The reauthorization of TANF passed in 2005 made it more difficult to use TANF benefits while attending school, the only real-istic way for most poor mothers to obtain a well-paying job. The absence of support for education robs poor women of a chance to escape lifelong poverty and undermines the future prospects of their children—including the hope of entering a stable marriage.

So far I have primarily focused on the misfit between TANF and the needs of single mothers. As I noted in the last chapter, the neglect of men's schooling and employment prospects has ominous impli-cations for family formation and the well-being of children. By direct-ing policies at single women and their children and largely ignoring the role of men, especially the partners of the women and the fathers of their children, TANF has probably widened the gap between poor women and men even further and reproduced the same deterrents to stable family formation that existed during the AFDC regime. The welfare regime's focus on women evolved naturally from its origins in the Social Security program, which sought to protect single mothers and their children. However, it is high time to develop an anti-poverty, pro-family policy that is simultaneously aimed at low-income mothers and fathers.

Child support enforcement, necessary and desirable as it may be, hardly represents such a program. For many low-income families, demanding that men pay their fair share is a pipe dream when men do not have jobs and have no reasonable prospects of employment. A more practical approach would be to offer the same services and level of assistance to parents of children living in poverty, regardless of the parent's gender. This approach would help families build a future on the basis of their ability to combine resources for an adequate income and the necessary supports to raise a family. The piecemeal approach adopted in the TANF legislation (past and present) provides too little in the way of help for low-income fathers, many of whom need education and job training, job placement, and supportive services just as much as low-income mothers. As things stand, we are even more punitive toward men than we are toward women in our welfare policies. If we expect fathers to pay child support—and we should—then we must also offer more adequate support and services to those who cannot pay. This means providing the same sorts of income supports and educational training for a period of time that are afforded to low-income mothers with dependent children. In the next chapter, I return to a discussion of policies that might lift working poor families out of poverty.

CONCLUSION

American policymakers and politicians have become obsessed with the possibility that we will create incentives for individuals to have children they can ill afford. Welfare reform set out to change the mix of incentives to encourage individuals and young couples to better time their childbearing to fit with their capacity to care for and invest in their children. TANF could be seen as a promising step in this direction, despite its obvious limitations. The reauthorization of TANF did little to address the limitations and may have made matters more difficult for single poor mothers. If government reneges on its promise to make work pay, then we are likely to see two trends.

First, poor people will have fewer children. Such a shift will be applauded by many politicians and taxpayers, but fertility decline in the United States brings its own set of economic and social problems. It will complicate the already difficult situation of solving the economic shortfall in the Social Security trust fund and require that all but the most affluent elderly work longer, or it will necessitate greater reliance on immigrants to supply labor and contribute to Social Security. During the past two decades, we have witnessed a doubling of the rate of childlessness among Americans, rising from 11 percent in 1985 to 19 percent in 2004 (Dye 2005). While childlessness is still more common among affluent and better-educated women, it is not inconceivable that the strongly pro-natal attitudes among poorer women that have long been an important source of the relatively high fertility levels in the United States will give way to the reality that children are becoming ever more costly.

Second, among those individuals having children, the inability to provide sufficient care and investment promises to perpetuate the already high proportion of young people who have been inadequately nurtured, supervised, and educated. Although it is not easy to reckon the precise costs of underinvesting in children, few experts doubt that these costs are considerable and have only been growing. The current antipoverty policy is largely built on the premise that discouraging out-of-wedlock childbearing, especially among teens, will reduce poverty. The fact is that while early childbearing has declined and welfare as we knew it has been eliminated, the problem of economic disadvantage has hardly changed at all. Poverty rates declined during the 1990s as the economy grew but are threatening to return to their pre-TANF levels. If TANF support levels are further reduced in the next funding cycle, the current, largely optimistic assessment of the impact of welfare reform will surely assume a darker cast. There may yet come a time when AFDC will be regarded with some nostalgia as representing an era when we were still protecting poor women and their offspring.

Chapter 7

Destinies of the Disadvantaged

T HE EARLY CHAPTERS of this book describe the experiences of the teenage mothers in Baltimore and their families, whose lives I followed for more than three decades. Their experiences reveal a surprising fact: early childbearing, which most policymakers believe to be a powerful source of disadvantage to young mothers, had only modest effects on their prospects in later life, after taking into account their circumstances prior to becoming pregnant. This finding is widely supported by a growing body of research reviewed in this book. Although for obvious reasons we can never measure the "true" causal effects of early childbearing with the precision of a random assignment experiment, we can now approximate what such an experiment might show. If poor minority women such as those in this study (and the majority of teenage mothers, both then and now, are poor and minority) were to delay childbearing, their lives would be altered slightly for the better, but only modestly so.

Most mothers in this population would still not attend—and surely not complete—college in higher numbers if they became parents later rather than in their teens. If parenthood were delayed, most would eventually wed, as did the women in the Baltimore Study, but they would probably not remain married, judging from the experiences of low-income minority women who begin childbearing in their twenties instead of their teens. Most would find employment, but except for the most talented and persistent, they would not find their way into middle-class jobs. There would be some positive effects: family size would be slightly smaller on average, and fewer would spend time receiving public assistance. This is not to suggest that the decline in early childbearing during

160

the past fifteen years has not been a positive development. It is undoubtedly positive, because most teens do not want to become parents and are not ready to take on the responsibilities of raising children. Many of the burdens of early parenthood are shared by their families, who usually can ill afford another dependent.

Nonetheless, teenage parenthood is simply not the disastrous and life-compromising event that it has been portrayed to be. And as such, our policies, which have focused inordinately on reducing teen pregnancy as a strategy for reducing poverty, increasing social mobility, and enhancing marriage, are likely to have been mistaken or, at least, unable to meet expectations. Diminishing teen pregnancy is not, as claimed by many social scientists and policymakers, the silver bullet that, if properly aimed at the right target population, could make a huge dent in the level of poverty and disadvantage in our nation. Curbing early childbearing, it is believed, would put younger women in a far stronger position to complete their education, gain work experience, and find more desirable marriage partners. It would reduce the number of female-headed households and cut the proportion of children growing up in poverty.

Now, after a decade and a half of witnessing a steep decline in early childbearing, especially among low-income black women, it is difficult to sustain those claims. Although the age of first births has risen dramatically among African Americans and, to a lesser extent, among Latinos and whites, marriage has not increased (Fields 2003). Marriage rates have continued to fall for younger black women ages twenty to twenty-nine, despite a larger proportion entering their twenties without children (U.S. Bureau of the Census 2006a). Younger African American women, for whom the rates of childbearing have dropped most steeply, were no more likely in 2005 than in 1995 to graduate from high school. Similarly, for black females between ages twenty-five and twenty-nine, the rate of college completion has remained stable, although it did increase modestly from 2003 to 2005 (U.S. Bureau of the Census 2006b). Poverty rates in family households plummeted during the 1990s as the economy boomed, the Earned Income Tax Credit was expanded, and women on welfare were helped to transition into the labor force, but these favorable trends have not continued into the current decade, even as early childbearing has fallen to historic lows. The poverty rate for children (under age eighteen) fell from 22 percent to 16 percent between 1990 and 1999, but it increased by 12 percent from 2000 to 2005, just when we might have expected an even greater dividend from the drop in early childbearing (DeNavas-Walt, Proctor, and Lee 2006).

These results suggest that the campaign to lower teen childbearing, while certainly desirable from a public policy perspective, was fueled by a misguided contention that it would reap large benefits as both an antipoverty strategy and a way of strengthening the family. It could not deliver on either of these objectives because policymakers failed to account for the fact that the timing of first births among highly disadvantaged women is largely a marker of, not an important causal factor in shaping, the life course of low-income women and their children. Added to a multitude of other conditions that are part and parcel of growing up in disadvantage—poverty, poor education, minority status, family instability, lack of stable paternal involvement, health deficiencies, and so on—early childbearing may well contribute to poor outcomes in later life, on average, but it does not play a singular or even an especially powerful role in the creation of social disadvantage, as many social scientists, myself once included, believe. The handicaps that teen mothers face in school, the workplace, and the marriage market were not mitigated merely because teens began to wait longer to have their first child during the 1990s. On the whole, the group that should have benefited the most appears to have little to show for postponing parenthood.

The impact of early childbearing was also not as large as researchers had predicted because we may have oversubscribed to the belief that one's life course is set early in life. Most researchers who identified teenage childbearing as a serious problem believed that if schooling and work experience did not occur in adolescence and early adulthood, women would be irretrievably damaged as a result. This turned out to be less true than many of us once believed because it ignored the possibility that many young mothers, with the help of their families, would be able to respond to an early birth by rearranging their life course. When their children reached school age, and often before then, most early childbearers in the Baltimore Study were able to figure out the next steps to take to return to school and gain work experience later in life. Most did not continue to have one child after another merely to remain on welfare. Our findings confirm Paul Placek and Gerry Hendershot's (1974) observation several decades ago that receiving welfare did not encourage women to become "brood sows," an image actively promulgated in discussions of public assistance in the 1980s. Most women, according to their children's accounts, became able and committed mothers, notwithstanding the considerable help they needed in the early stages of parenthood. Or put less positively, their parenting skills might not have been greatly improved had they delayed parenthood until their twenties—unless, of course, they gained education and greater resources as a result.

However, the majority remained poor or near-poor even when they found employment. Although three out of four of these mothers worked most of their lives, they could not generally find good jobs. All but one-fifth got married, many to the fathers of their children, but few of these marriages survived. By their mid-forties, most were single and the head of their household. The wear and tear of living in poverty, raising children, and caring for family members was visible. By their mid-forties, the lives of the mothers in the Baltimore Study were marked by ill health. A significant portion of them suffered from depression, others were drug- or alcohol-dependent, and at least half who remained in poverty or near-poverty continued to battle the chronic stress of living through hard times.

A significant minority did overcome the long odds of remaining poor by returning to school. By their mid-forties, one in ten had completed college, an almost unimaginable feat given their circumstances when the study began. Some of these women prospered in white-collar jobs and were able to move out of the crime-ridden inner-city neighborhoods of Baltimore. About one-quarter of the mothers managed to enter a stable union that seemed to be working well. Nonetheless, a significant proportion of even these resilient women revealed the wounds incurred along the route to success. They, too, experienced high levels of stress, obesity, and other health problems.

Researchers, policymakers, and practitioners have too often confused correlation for causality, believing that if only poor teens behaved like those in the middle class, they would reap the same benefits when they grew up. This fiction misses the simple fact that the vast majority of those who are born poor, grow up in impoverished and unstable families, reside in disadvantaged neighborhoods, and go to inadequate schools have long odds of escaping poverty. True, some do make it, by dint of talent, hard work, and good fortune, but given average talent, motivation, and happenstance, the odds of success are drastically lower than for their middle class counterparts (Furstenberg 2006). Our deeply embedded value of self-reliance leads most Americans to believe that motivation and hard work permit anyone to overcome the obstacles imposed by economic and social disadvantage (Stonecash 2007).

In some respects, the Baltimore Study can be read as a testament to the ability of many families to overcome extreme adversity and beat the odds of poverty and racial and gender discrimination. If one half can make it, then, we are inclined to ask, why not the other half (who we suspect may not have worked as hard or used their talents as effectively)? But is it right that we should expect the poor to be more motivated or talented than the middle class, much less the affluent, in order to succeed? The middle class need only to be motivated, while the poor need to be supermotivated to rise above their circumstances. Ordinary levels of talent and motivation will not suffice for the disadvantaged, as it does for the more affluent. A stratification system that requires more of those with fewer assets is manifestly unjust, but that is precisely what is required of low-income families in American society.

Taking note of this blatant contradiction in the democratic and egalitarian creed of the United States is hardly a remedy for remedial action. Pious observations such as the ones that are issued here don't get us very far in the world of politics and public policy. We need low-cost and highly effective measures, policy analysts counter. However, it is also fair to observe that peeling away supports for low-income families, as we are currently in the process of doing, is hardly a rational response to the rapidly growing chasm between the poor and the middle class or between the middle class and the affluent. Wringing out cost savings from child care, education, health, food stamps—the list goes on—appears to be a recipe for imposing more strain on already overburdened families. While legislators continue to slice away at slender supports for parents and children, we are busy inventing novel policy initiatives, new silver bullets such as abstinence-only and marriage promotion, that probably have no more than symbolic value at best, and at worst may be counterproductive. It seems highly unlikely that we will either reduce poverty and income inequality or promote family stability without a sharp change in public priorities.

The conclusion I draw from the evidence on the impact of teenage childbearing is that we need to rethink our approach to lifting low-income children out of poverty, to aiding low-income families, and to helping couples form stable and secure unions. Categorical approaches that target special populations have their uses, but they also have their limitations. On balance, I would suggest that we invest our funds in more general approaches aimed at low-income individuals and households who could benefit from a range of economic and non-economic supports. The problem is that we resort to gimmicks, magic bullets, and inexpensive palliatives that provide too little for too few families. Our programs become symbolic campaigns to lower early childbearing rather than effective policies to eradicate poverty and disadvantage.

I fully understand the argument made by conservatives that we cannot achieve these goals without at the same time increasing a sense of responsibility, a willingness to work hard, and a sense of self-sacrifice for the family. However, I would ask commentators who lament the decline of these values to take a hard look at the behavior of low income, middle income, and high income Americans. What they will find is not a conspicuous gap in values or practices. The families I have observed appear to be every bit as willing to assume responsibility, work hard, and make sacrifices for their children as those in the middle or the privileged classes. No doubt, those who possess more of these strengths have a greater likelihood of success, but many make assiduous efforts on all these fronts, at great personal cost, only to barely get by. If their children possess only ordinary abilities and talents, they are virtually doomed to remain poor or near-poor.

Given the neighborhoods they can afford, the quality of day care they must settle for, the schools their children attend, and the lack of after-school programs in their communities, it is hardly surprising that only one in five children who grow up in the bottom quintile of the income distribution make it to the middle class. The game of getting ahead is rigged. Yes, it helps to believe in working hard, but this personal conviction is much more likely to take hold when the fruits of hard work are assured from the start, when knowledge of how the system really operates is widely available to children, when second and third chances are available, and when sponsors and promoters are abundant (Furstenberg 2006). Although we regard the United States as the land of opportunity—and it surely is compared with many nations—it provides far greater opportunity for those who start life in an advantaged rather than a disadvantaged family.

Policymakers are fond of citing comparative data on teenage childbearing showing that the United States continues to lag behind other nations in its ability to control unwanted pregnancy, abortion, and STDs. We stand out from our counterparts in industrialized countries in other regards as well. The United States leads all advanced economies in economic inequality, child and family poverty, and family instability. Many argue that the source of all these problems is family instability, which produces inequality and poverty. Other experts believe that the causality goes in the other direction: poor education and low income lead to high levels of instability. The fact is that causality runs in both directions: high rates of instability produce poor families, and poor families reproduce high rates of instability.

How do we break this chicken-and-egg cycle? Merely getting couples to take the marital pledge will do little. My analysis of three broad areas of intervention uncovered serious mismatches between current policies and programs and the needs of teen mothers. Since they are discussed extensively in the second part of this book, I reiterate them only briefly here.

First, despite the plateau in sexual activity and increased use of contraceptives by teens, far too many adolescents and young adults still become pregnant without intending to do so. Sexual education, contraceptive instruction, and access to effective means of preventing unwanted pregnancies continue to be contested issues in American society. Over the past two decades, government at both the federal and state level has reversed course, no longer providing accurate information and services in the schools, insisting instead on preaching the doctrine of abstinence-only. This policy has been enforced despite growing evidence that programs lacking specific contraceptive information ill prepare teens to manage the transition to having intercourse. Advocating abstinence also appears to do little to deter sexual activity.

The cultural battle over reproductive health services that I described in chapter 4 continues unabated. There are many ways of preserving parental prerogatives, but the current policy protects a very small minority of parents who do not want their children to be informed about contraception while depriving the vast majority who do. Bypassing the schools as a site for education might be imaginable if other sources of education were available. However, resistance to speaking openly and candidly about the risks and responsibilities associated with initiating sexual intercourse is widespread. Broadcast media are free to parade the benefits of treating erectile dysfunction but effectively censor the advantages of using contraception or providing information about options for preventing pregnancy. I also contend that American parents must abandon the fiction that their children should behave differently than they themselves did when they were teenagers. In a society in which most people will not marry until their mid- or late twenties, we must assume—as has been the case for several decades—that most young people will initiate sex sometime in their teens. By eschewing the pragmatic public health approach taken by most industrialized countries when it comes to preparing youth to manage sexual relationships, we have designed a system that does not diminish sexual activity while often failing to prevent unintended pregnancies.

Policies aimed at helping young people establish and maintain stable unions are equally ineffectual. Part of the problem is surely that many young people enter marriage without being well prepared to sustain a lasting relationship. There is plenty of room for advice and counseling, though we must acknowledge that the science of making relationships more rewarding, effective, and durable is still at a very primitive stage. I suspect that we will discover that counseling and education do not work unless accompanied by support in other arenas that sustain family life, including economic resources and assistance for working parents. Almost no one doubts that families are overburdened today, especially low-income families.

Our current marriage policies aimed at strengthening marital commitment will, I predict, be ineffectual unless they also provide more resources to low-income couples who are under constant stress in providing the basics for their children. It seems unlikely that the decline of marriage will abate until low- and moderate-income couples have both the interpersonal skills to manage relationships *and* the resources to maintain them.

The evidence suggests that both of these objectives are advanced by ensuring a good education for the large percentage of the population that currently does not have access to effective schools. Far too many children are ill prepared to go on to higher education, the necessary prerequisite for acquiring not only a good job but also, it seems, the skills that foster viable emotional relationships. Investing in schooling, I contend in chapter 4, may be our best hope for restoring stable unions, whether they take the form of marriage or de facto marriage. This requires a greater commitment not only to preparing children for higher education but also to assisting those who lack the funds to go to college without assuming unacceptable levels of family or personal debt.

Fledgling families are likely to become fragile families unless they are also given more supports from the larger community. We acknowledged in the passage of welfare reform that low-income working mothers require an array of services if they are going to achieve a successful balance in work and family responsibilities. Yet these services provided to women on welfare have been time-limited, on the unrealistic assumption that women can soon find jobs that provide (or allow them to afford) health care, child care, after-school programs, and other forms of assistance that affluent families can either purchase or receive through their employment.

No one doubts that the United States has the money to provide assistance to low- and middle-income families, but if anything, the tide has been in the reverse. The flow of tax subsidies and support has been directed at more affluent households. The tax relief given to high-income households in the early years of the Bush administration, supported not only by Republicans but by many Democrats, set the stage for eventual cutbacks in social programs for low- and middle-income families. Recent statistics published by Brian Bucks and his colleagues (2006) in the *Federal Reserve Bulletin* show a continued flow of wealth from lower- to higher-income families (from 1995 to 2004). Whereas families in the top 10 percent more than doubled their net worth during the past decade, families in the bottom two-fifths of the income distribution experienced a much lower growth rate, despite the recent run-up in housing values (their principal source of wealth). At the same time, the median debt among low-income families rose, leaving most no better or worse off than a decade earlier.

We have no simple way of calculating the impact of withdrawing resources that might otherwise have been used for education, child care, or mental health services. We only know that when low-income families become poorer, they are more likely to dissolve and children are less likely to have health insurance or to receive high-quality child care, schooling, and the like. As the costs of higher education rise and public support for education decreases, it is inevitable that fewer students from lower-income families will complete college. Without greater efforts to understand the relationship of public and private investments in education, health, and human services for children, we cannot offer precise policy analyses of how this shift in public investment has affected the family lives of the less fortunate (Folbre 2007).

This much is known: the United States, still one of a handful of the richest nations in the world, has the greatest level of family instability, the highest level of child poverty, and one of the highest levels of income inequality of any industrialized country. These correlations are suggestive but hardly definitive proof of the relationship between public investment and the well-being of children and families. Few social scientists would be so naive as to believe that funding alone could change our national standing. Cultural beliefs, demographic complexity, and institutional arrangements are but a few of the differences that divide the United States from other industrial nations. There are many sources that could explain the simultaneous correspondence of inequality, family instability, and children's outcomes.

Nonetheless, as Edward Wolff (2003, 14), the noted authority on wealth distribution, observes:

> One reason we have such high levels of inequality, compared to other advanced industrial countries, is because of our tax and . . . our social expenditure system. We have much lower taxes than almost every Western European country. And we have a less progressive tax system. . . . [T]he rich in this country manage to retain a much higher amount of wealth than the rich in other countries.

In the same interview, Wolff notes that the United States provides less support for poor families than other nations with advanced economies. He notes that a very modest wealth tax of less than 1 percent on families making more than $250,000 per year would raise more than $60 billion annually that could be used to assist low-income families. How best that money could be used to improve the circumstances of low- and moderate-income families is an open question, but there are many competing proposals that would have reasonable prospects of succeeding, such as investments in upgrading education, health, child care, and, not the least, making higher education more affordable to low-income families.

Americans strongly believe that welfare benefits ought to be associated with work for able-bodied men and women. Making work pay has been a worthy objective, and it is a goal that conveys a promise to both America's welfare poor and working poor, but most research conducted in the aftermath of welfare reform tells us that the dismantling of the welfare system failed to achieve this objective, despite the simultaneous introduction of the Earned Income Tax Credit, a significant achievement of the Clinton administration. Evidence shows that many, if not most, poor women are not better off economically by trading labor force participation for public assistance, and some are distinctly worse off. Welfare reform probably made a dent in poverty levels, but it did not come close to eliminating poverty. Welfare reform also did not achieve its lofty goals of promoting marriage and increasing family stability.

Building on welfare reform and the EITC, Gordon Berlin, the president of Manpower Demonstration Research Corporation (MDRC), an organization devoted to spawning and evaluating public policies aimed at disadvantaged children, youth, and families, has proposed revising EITC so that it applies to individual earners instead of families with children. Berlin shows that, paradoxically, such an approach could do more to improve the situation of poor families than the EITC has done by targeting families directly. First of all, this change would make work pay for single men with limited education and skills, and it would help less-educated males bring more resources into their families by offsetting the decline in their real wages. By providing an incentive to low-income males to enter the labor force and increase the value of their contributions to families, Berlin's scheme might also reverse the decline of marriage, or at least slow the rate of single-parent family formation. Couples who pool earnings from low-income jobs would do far better under Berlin's scheme than they do facing a family cap under the current policy. He estimates that it would cost $30 billion to lift virtually all working individuals out of poverty.

Raising taxes to implement this plan or any alternative approach to reducing poverty is singularly unpopular in the United States, and any proposal to raise taxes would be tantamount to political suicide for most officeholders. Although taxed at lower rates than other countries, Americans continue to believe that they are over-taxed. Therefore, this nation finds itself in a political bind that is not easily resolved without a large shift in political will. As I write this book, there are few encouraging signs to suggest that the political tides are likely to reverse in the near term.

What could change the situation? My best guess is nothing more than speculation, but I believe that in the next decade or two we may begin to see a major shift in fertility in the United States. To date, the United States has been singularly able to resist the trend toward lower population growth that has occurred in most nations with a post-industrial economy. Our fertility rate continues to be relatively robust, standing close to replacement levels, as it has for several decades. Therefore, we do not face the imminent population crisis that many European and Asian nations face.

There are many reasons why fertility has been higher in this country than in others. A very high rate of immigration, high levels of early marriage and early fertility, and high levels of fertility among the poor are among the most important reasons. However, I suspect that most of these circumstances are likely to change in the next several decades.

Immigration has slowed and probably will continue to subside from its recent levels. Most immigrant groups bring higher levels of fertility, contributing to the robust level of childbearing in this country. Demographers have shown, however, that these patterns do not persist as immigrant populations begin to assimilate. By the third generation, immigrant fertility levels are virtually indistinguishable from the general level in the population. Thus, we probably cannot count on immigration to be as important a component of our current levels of fertility as it has been in the recent past.

As this volume attests, the rate of teenage childbearing has dropped dramatically in the past decade and a half, and there are no signs of it returning to the relatively high levels of the past. The rising age of marriage and fertility in the general population makes teenage childbearing more of an anomaly than it once was. Just as middle class youth now find it virtually unthinkable to have a child in their teen years, I strongly suspect that lower-income youth are beginning to feel the same way about early childbearing. Like early marriage, early childbearing is gradually becoming non-normative in the United States, as it has long been in most of Western Europe.

The high rate of single parenthood and marital instability, surprisingly, is also likely to reduce fertility. A growing number of studies show that women outside of marriage have fewer children than those who are stably married. The reasons are obvious. The cost of raising children is greater for single women, and the comfort of doing so is lower. The women in the Baltimore Study had remarkably low levels of childbearing compared with their parents; the next generation appears to be headed for even lower levels of fertility. Although the poor have more children, the differential between levels of fertility by education and income has been declining.

The ease and accessibility of contraception is an important factor in lowering the level of fertility. Although disadvantaged couples are far more likely to have unintended births, they are gradually becoming more adept at using contraception. Moreover, methods of contraception are increasingly more user-friendly and more effective. As the cost of children rises and the subsidies for raising them diminish, more Americans are likely to have fewer children or no children at all.

If fertility reaches below replacement levels, policymakers will be forced to consider ways of bolstering population growth. Presently, population policies are not notably effective in doing so, as the European experience makes evident. However, this does not mean that increases in incentives, supports, and subsidies cannot or will not work. Many demographers believe that the long record of the French in sustaining population growth by providing generous assistance to families has helped to sustain relatively high levels of fertility. My hunch is that the United States may begin to do the same if and when fertility begins to drop below replacement levels.

If population growth falters, the pending crisis in Social Security will worsen. This is the second reason why we can ill afford to squander the human capital potential of low- and moderate-income families. Our current benefits for the elderly depend on contributions by succeeding generations. The ratio of dependents to workers will rise dramatically as baby boomers retire. This situation will be worsened in decades to come if fertility declines and investment in education and training wanes.

In the meantime, we are, I fear, committed to underinvesting in a public sense in our young. Our strong and enduring commitments to privatizing family decisions by making parents almost exclusively responsible for the welfare of their children is likely to continue. It follows that a great many children will never realize their full potential unless they happen to be born into affluent families. The sad fact is that while Americans speak reverentially of the sanctity of the family and developing the full potential of each American child, our public actions belie our political pronouncements.

It should come as no surprise that American children, despite our nation's considerable wealth, do not fare especially well by international standards in educational attainment, health, or mental health. A recent report issued by UNICEF (2007) ranked the United States second from the bottom among twenty-one Western nations in the performance of children on a wide variety of domains such as material well-being, health and safety, educational performance, family relationships, social and antisocial behavior, and subjective well-being. Part of the reason for our low standing, no doubt, is our continuing high level of family instability, but a large share must go to the limited and wavering commitment to children of low- and moderate-income parents. Growing levels of income inequality and high levels of income insufficiency have helped to cement America's standing in the industrialized world as the land of unequal opportunities for children. The growth of inequality has led to an underinvestment in moderate and low income families and an over-investment in children from well-off families, who in addition to the support they receive from parents and kin, benefit in numerous ways by tax subsidies that are unavailable to moderate- and low-income families.

Can we do better? Perhaps, but not until we change the fact that this situation is treated with indifference by those who could afford to invest a greater share to ensure that children get what they need. Until this attitude changes, we will remain a society known for its vast waste of its most precious resource—the next generation.

References

Acs, Gregory. 1995. "Do Welfare Benefits Promote Out-of-Wedlock Child-bearing?" In *Welfare Reform: An Analysis of the Issues,* edited by Isabel V. Sawhill. Washington: Urban Institute Press.

Acs, Gregory, and Sandi Nelson. 2003. "The More Things Change? Children's Living Arrangements Since Welfare Reform." Snapshots of American Families 3, no. 10, October 2003. Washington: Urban Institute. Accessed at http://www.urban.org/UploadedPDF/310859_snapshots3_no10.pdf.

Alan Guttmacher Institute. 1976. *Eleven Million Teenagers.* New York: Wiley.

————. 1981. *Teenage Pregnancy: The Problem That Hasn't Gone Away.* New York: Alan Guttmacher Institute.

————. 2001. *Teenage Sexual and Reproductive Behavior in Developed Countries—Country Report for the United States: Can More Progress Be Made?* Occasional report 8. New York: Alan Guttmacher Institute.

————. 2004. *U.S. Teenage Pregnancy Statistics: Overall Trends, Trends by Race and Ethnicity, and State-by-State Information.* New York: Alan Guttmacher Institute.

————. 2006a. "Pregnancy." Accessed at http://www.guttmacher.org/sections/pregnancy.php.

————. 2006b. *U.S. Teenage Pregnancy Statistics: National and State Trends and Trends by Race and Ethnicity.* New York: Alan Guttmacher Institute.

————. 2007. *Parental Involvement in Minors' Abortions.* New York: Alan Guttmacher Institute.

Amato, Paul R., and Alan Booth. 1997. *A Generation at Risk: Growing Up in an Era of Family Upheaval.* Cambridge, Mass.: Harvard University Press.

Anderson, Elijah. 1989. "Sex Codes and Family Life Among Poor Inner-City Youth." *Annals of the American Academy of Political and Social Sciences* 501(January): 59–78.

————. 1990. *Streetwise: Race, Class, and Change in an Urban Community.* Chicago, Ill.: University of Chicago Press.

————. 1999. *Code of the Street: Decency, Violence, and the Moral Life of the Inner City.* New York: W. W. Norton.

Armstrong, Elizabeth M., and Frank F. Furstenberg. 1998. "Taking the Road Less Traveled: Divergent Life Courses of Teen Mothers and Their Daughters." Unpublished paper. University of Pennsylvania, Philadelphia, Penn.

Ashcraft, Adam B., and Kevin Lang. 2006. "The Consequences of Teenage Childbearing." NBER Working Paper No. W12 485. Accessed at Social Science Research Network (SSRN), http://ssrn.com/abstract=926063.

Bachu, Amara. 1999. "Trends in Premarital Childbearing, 1930–1994." *Current Population Reports* P23-197, October 1999. Washington: U.S. Department of Commerce, Economics and Statistics Administration, U.S. Bureau of the Census. Accessed at http://www.census.gov/prod/99pubs/p23-197.pdf.

Bailey, Beth L. 1988. *From Front Porch to Back Seat: Courtship in Twentieth-Century America.* Baltimore, Md.: Johns Hopkins University Press.

Banfield, Edward C. 1974. *The Unheavenly City Revisited.* Boston, Mass.: Little, Brown.

Bankole, Akinrinola, Jacqueline E. Darroch, and Susheela Singh. 1999. "Determinants of Trends in Condom Use in the United States, 1988–1995." *Family Planning Perspectives* 31(6): 264–71.

Bearman, Peter S., and Hannah Brückner. 2001. "Promising the Future: Virginity Pledges and First Intercourse." *American Journal of Sociology* 106(4): 859–912.

Becker, Howard. 1973. *Outsiders: Studies in the Sociology of Deviance.* New York: Free Press.

Bitler, Marianne P., Jonah B. Gelbach, Hilary W. Hoynes, and Madeline Zavodny. 2004. "The Impact of Welfare Reform on Marriage and Divorce." *Demography* 41(2): 213–36.

Blank, Rebecca M. 1997. *It Takes a Nation.* New York: Russell Sage Foundation.

Blank, Rebecca M., and Ron Haskins. 2001. *The New World of Welfare.* Washington: Brookings Institution Press.

Blankenhorn, David. 1990. "American Family Dilemmas." In *Rebuilding the Nest: A New Commitment to the American Family,* edited by David Blankenhorn, Steven Bayme, and Jean Bethke Elshtain. Milwaukee, Wisc.: Family Service America.

Bloom, Dan, and Charles Michalopoulos. 2001. *How Welfare and Work Policies Affect Employment and Income: A Synthesis of Research.* New York: Manpower Demonstration Research Corporation.

Bongaarts, John. 1978. "A Framework for Analyzing the Proximate Determinants of Fertility." *Population and Development Review* 4(1): 105–32.

Bosk, Charles. 2005. *What Would You Do? The Collision of Ethics and Ethnography*. Chicago, Ill.: University of Chicago Press.

Brim, Orville Gilbert, Carol D. Ryff, and Ronald C. Kessler, editors. 2004. *How Healthy Are We? A National Study of Well-Being at Midlife*. Chicago, Ill.: University of Chicago Press.

Brückner, Hannah, and Peter S. Bearman. 2005. "After the Promise: The STD Consequences of Adolescent Virginity Pledges." *Journal of Adolescent Health* 36(4): 271–8.

Brunner, Borgna. 2006. *TIME Almanac with Information Please*. New York: Time Almanac.

Bucks, Brian K., Arthur B. Kennickell, and Kevin B. Moore. 2006. "Recent Changes in U.S. Family Finances: Evidence from the 2001 and 2004 Survey of Consumer Finances." *Federal Reserve Bulletin* March 22, 2006. Accessed at http://federalreserve.gov/pubs/bulletin/2006/finance-survey.pdf.

Burtless, Gary. 2004. "The Labor Force Status of Mothers Who Are Most Likely to Receive Welfare: Changes Following Reform." Web editorial, March 30, 2004. Washington: Brookings Institution. Accessed at http://www.brookings.edu/views/op-ed/burtless/20040330.htm.

Campbell, Arthur. 1968. "The Role of Family Planning in the Reduction of Poverty." *Journal of Marriage and the Family* 30(2): 236–45.

Carlson, Marcia J., and Frank F. Furstenberg, Jr. 2006. "The Prevalence and Correlates of Multi-Partnered Fertility Among Urban U.S. Parents." *Journal of Marriage and Family* 68(3): 718–32.

Carlson, Marcia, Sara McLanahan, and Paula England. 2004. "Union Formation in Fragile Families." *Demography* 41(2): 237–62.

Carpenter, Laura M. 2001. "The First Time/Das Erstes Mal—Approaches to Virginity Loss in U.S. and German Teen Magazines." *Youth and Society* 33(1): 31–61.

Carter, Hugh, and Paul C. Glick. 1976. *Marriage and Divorce: A Social and Economic Study*. Cambridge, Mass.: Harvard University Press.

Center for Law and Social Policy (CLASP). 2006. "CLASP Federal Budget Resources." July 12, 2006. Accessed at http://www.clasp.org/publications/federal_budget_resources.htm.

Centers for Disease Control and Prevention. 2000. *National Vital Statistics Report* 48(16, October 18).

———. National Center for Chronic Disease Prevention and Health Promotion. 2005a. "YRBSS: Youth Risk Behavior Surveillance System: Data and Statistics." Accessed at http://www.cdc.gov/yrbs.

———. National Center for Health Statistics. Division of Labor Statistics. 2005b. "Marriage Rates by State: 1990, 1995, and 1999–2004." Washington: National Center for Health Statistics. Accessed at www.cdc.gov/nchs/data/nvss/marriage90_04.pdf (updated October 19, 2005).

———. 2006. *National Vital Statistics Report* 55(1, September).

Chaudry, Ajay. 2004. *Putting Children First: How Low-Wage Working Mothers Manage Child Care.* New York: Russell Sage Foundation.

Cheeseborough, Sarah, Roger Ingham, and Douglas Massey. 1999. *A Review of the International Evidence on Preventing and Reducing Teenage Conceptions: The United States, Canada, Australia, and New Zealand.* London: Health Education Authority.

Cherlin, Andrew J. 1981. *Marriage, Divorce, Remarriage: Social Trends in the United States.* Cambridge, Mass.: Harvard University Press.

———. 2001. "New Developments in the Study of Nonmarital Child-bearing." In *Out of Wedlock: Causes and Consequences of Nonmarital Fertility,* edited by Lawrence L. Wu and Barbara Wolfe. New York: Russell Sage Foundation.

———. 2004. "The Deinstitutionalization of American Marriage." *Journal of Marriage and Family* 66(4): 848–61.

———. 2006. "On Single Mothers 'Doing' Family." *Journal of Marriage and Family* 68(6): 800–803.

Clarke-Stewart, Alison, Judy Dunn, and Michael Rutter. 2006. *Families Count: Effects on Child and Adolescent Development.* Cambridge: Cambridge University Press.

Colen, Cynthia, Arline T. Geronimus, and Maureen G. Phipps. 2006. "Getting a Piece of the Pie?: The Economic Boom of the 1990s and Declining Teen Birth Rates." *Social Science and Medicine* 63(6): 1531–45.

Coombs, Lolagene, and Zena Zumeta. 1970. "Correlates of Marital Dissolution in a Prospective Fertility Study: A Research Note." *Social Problems* 18(1): 92–101.

Coontz, Stephanie. 1992. *The Way We Never Were: American Families and the Nostalgia Trap.* New York: Basic Books.

———. 2005. *Marriage, a History: From Obedience to Intimacy, or How Love Conquered Marriage.* New York: Viking Press.

Cowan, Carolyn Pape, and Philip A. Cowan. 1992. *When Partners Become Parents: The Big Life Change for Couples.* New York: Lawrence Erlbaum Associates.

Currie, Janet. 2001. "Early Childhood Intervention Programs: What Do We Know?" *Journal of Economic Perspectives* 15(2): 213–38.

Currie, Janet, and Duncan Thomas. 2000. "School Quality and the Longer-Term Effects of Head Start." *Journal of Human Resources* 35(4): 755–74.

Cutright, Phillips, and Frederick S. Jaffe. 1977. *Impact of Family Planning Programs on Fertility: The U.S. Experience.* New York: Praeger.

Dance, Lory. 2002. *Tough Fronts: The Impact of Street Culture on Schooling.* New York: Routledge Press.

Danziger, Sheldon, and Jane Waldfogel, editors. 2000. *Securing the Future: Investing in Children from Birth to Adulthood.* New York: Russell Sage Foundation.

Darroch, Jacqueline E., David J. Landry, and Susheela Singh. 2000. "Changing Emphases in Sexuality Education in U.S. Public Secondary Schools, 1988–1999." *Family Planning Perspectives* 32(5): 204–11, 265.

Darroch, Jacqueline, and Susheela Singh. 1999. *Why Is Teenage Pregnancy Declining? The Roles of Abstinence, Sexual Activity, and Contraceptive Use.* Occasional report 1. New York: Alan Guttmacher Institute.

Darroch, Jacqueline E., Susheela Singh, and Jennifer J. Frost. 2001. "Differences in Teenage Pregnancy Rates Among Five Developed Countries: The Roles of Sexual Activity and Contraceptive Use." *Family Planning Perspectives* 33(6): 244–50, 281 (for erratum, see *Family Planning Perspectives* 34(1): 56).

David, Henry P., Janine M. Morgall, Mogens Osler, Niels K. Rasmussen, and Birgitte Jensen. 1990. "United States and Denmark: Different Approaches to Health Care and Family Planning." *Studies in Family Planning* 21(1): 1–19.

Davis, Kingsley, and Judith Blake. 1956. "Social Structure and Fertility: An Analytical Framework." *Economic Development and Cultural Change* 4(3): 211–35.

Degler, Carl N. 1980. *At Odds: Women and the Family in America from the Revolution to the Present.* New York: Oxford University Press.

D'Emilio, John, and Estelle B. Freedman. 1997. *Intimate Matters: A History of Sexuality in America.* 2nd ed. Chicago, Ill.: University of Chicago Press.

DeNavas-Walt, Carmen, and Robert W. Cleveland. 1996. "Money Income in the United States: 1995." *Current Population Reports* P60-193, September 1996. Washington: U.S. Bureau of the Census. Accessed at http://www.census.gov/prod/2/pop/p60/p60 193.pdf.

———. 2002. "Money Income in the United States: 2001." *Current Population Reports* P60-218, September 2001. Washington: U.S. Bureau of the Census. Accessed at http://www.census.gov/prod/2002pubs/p60-218.pdf.

DeNavas-Walt, Carmen, Bernadette D. Proctor, and Cheryl Hill Lee. 2006. "Income, Poverty, and Health Insurance Coverage in the United States: 2005." *Current Population Reports* P60-231, August 2006. Washington: U.S. Bureau of the Census. Accessed at http://www.census.gov/prod/2006pubs/p60-231.pdf.

Dion, M. Robin. 2005. "Healthy Marriage Programs: Learning What Works." *The Future of Children* 15(2): 137–56.

Downs, Anthony. 1972. "Up and Down with Ecology: The Issue-Attention Cycle." *The Public Interest* 28(Summer): 38–50.

Du Bois, W. E. B. 1908. *The Negro American Family.* Atlanta, Ga.: Atlanta University Press.

Duncan, Greg, and Jeanne Brooks-Gunn, editors. 1997. *The Consequences of Growing Up Poor.* New York: Russell Sage Foundation.

Duncan, Greg J., and P. Lindsay Chase-Lansdale, eds. 2001a. *For Better and for Worse: Welfare Reform and the Well-being of Children and Families.* New York: Russell Sage Foundation.

——. 2001b. "Welfare Reform and Children's Well-being." In *The New World of Welfare,* edited by Rebecca M. Blank and Ron Haskins. Washington: Brookings Institution Press.

Durkheim, Émile. 1951. *Suicide: A Study in Sociology.* New York: Free Press of Glencoe.

Dye, Jane Lawler. 2005. "Fertility of American Women: June 2004." *Current Population Reports* P20-555, December 2005. Washington: U.S. Bureau of the Census. Accessed at http://www.census.gov/prod/2005pubs/p20-555.pdf.

Easterlin, Richard. 1985. *The Fertility Revolution: A Supply-Demand Analysis.* Chicago, Ill.: University of Chicago Press.

Edin, Kathryn. 2000. "Few Good Men: Why Poor Women Don't Remarry." *The American Prospect* 11(4): 26–31.

Edin, Kathryn, and Christopher Jencks. 1992. "Rethinking Welfare." In *Rethinking Social Policy,* edited by Christopher Jencks. Cambridge, Mass.: Harvard University Press.

Edin, Kathryn, and Maria Kefalas. 2005. *Promises I Can Keep: Why Poor Women Put Motherhood Before Marriage.* Berkeley, Calif.: University of California Press.

Edin, Kathryn, and Laura Lein. 1997. *Making Ends Meet: How Single Mothers Survive Welfare and Low-Wage Work.* New York: Russell Sage Foundation.

Ellwood, David T. 1989. *Poor Support: Poverty in the American Family.* New York: Basic Books.

Ellwood, David, and Mary Jo Bane. 1994. *Welfare Realities: From Rhetoric to Reform.* Cambridge, Mass.: Harvard University Press.

Ellwood, David T., and Christopher Jencks. 2001. "The Spread of Single-Parent Families in the United States Since 1960." In *The Future of the Family,* edited by Daniel A. Moynihan, Timothy M. Smeeding, and Lee Rainwater. New York: Russel Sage Foundation.

England, Paula, Kathryn Edin, and Kate Linnenberg. 2003. "Love and Distrust Among Unmarried Parents." Paper presented to the National Poverty Center conference "Marriage and Family Formation Among Low-Income Couples." Washington, September 4–5, 2003.

Ferguson, Ann. 2001. *Bad Boys: Public Schools and the Making of Black Masculinity.* Ann Arbor, Mich.: University of Michigan Press.

Fields, Jason. 2003. "America's Families and Living Arrangements: 2003." *Current Population Reports* P20-553, November, 2003. Washington:

U.S. Bureau of the Census. Accessed at http://www.census.gov/prod/2004pubs/p20-553.pdf.

Finer, Lawrence B. 2007. "Trends in Premarital Sex in the United States, 1954–2003." *Public Health Reports* 122(1): 73–78.

Folbre, Nancy. 2007. *Valuing Children: Rethinking the Economics of the Family.* Cambridge, Mass.: Harvard University Press.

Fuller, Richard C., and Richard R. Myers. 1941. "The Natural History of a Social Problem." *American Sociological Review* 6(3): 320–9.

Furstenberg, Frank F. 1976. *Unplanned Parenthood: The Social Consequences of Teenage Childbearing.* New York: Free Press.

———. 1980. "Burdens and Benefits: The Impact of Early Childbearing on the Family." *Journal of Social Issues* 36(1): 64–87.

———. 1991. "As the Pendulum Swings: Teenage Childbearing and Social Concern." *Family Relations* 40(2): 127–38.

———. 1998. "When Will Teenage Childbearing Become a Problem? The Implications of Western Experience for Developing Countries." *Studies in Family Planning* 29(2): 246–53.

———. 2001. "The Fading Dream: Prospects for Marriage in the Inner City." In *Problem of the Century: Racial Stratification in the United States at Century's End,* edited by Elijah Anderson and Douglas Massey. New York: Russell Sage Foundation.

———. 2002a. "How It Takes Thirty Years to Do a Study." In *Looking at Lives: American Longitudinal Studies of the Twentieth Century,* edited by Erin Phelps, Frank F. Furstenberg, and Anne Colby. New York: Russell Sage Foundation.

———. 2002b. "From Teenage Mother to Middle-Age Matriarch: A Journey Between Two Racial Stereotypes." Paper presented to the "Race/Ethnicity, Self/Culture, and Inequality Conference," Princeton University, Princeton, N.J., April 19–20, 2002.

———. 2003. "Teenage Childbearing as a Public Issue and Private Concern." *Annual Review of Sociology* 29. 23–39.

———. 2006. "Diverging Development: The Not So Invisible Hand of Social Class in the United States." Paper presented to the biennial meeting of the Society for Research on Adolescence. San Francisco, Calif., March 23–26, 2006.

———. 2007. "The Making of the Black Family: Race and Class Revisited." *Annual Review of Sociology* 33.

Furstenberg, Frank F., and Kathleen Mullan Harris. 1993. "When and Why Fathers Matter: Impacts of Father Involvement on the Children of Adolescent Mothers." In *Young Unwed Fathers,* edited by Robert Lerman and Theodora J. Ooms. Philadelphia, Penn.: Temple University Press.

Furstenberg, Frank F., Jr., and Rosalind Berkowitz King. 1999. "Multi-Partnered Fertility Sequences: Documenting an Alternative Family

Form." Paper presented, in an earlier version, to the annual meeting of the Population Association of America, Chicago, Ill., April 1999.

Furstenberg, Frank F., and Christopher Weiss. 2000. "Intergenerational Transmission of Fathering Roles in At-Risk Families." *Marriage and Family Review* 29(2–3): 181–203.

Furstenberg, Frank F., Jeanne Brooks-Gunn, and S. Philip Morgan. 1987. *Adolescent Mothers in Later Life.* New York: Cambridge University Press.

Furstenberg, Frank F., Leon Gordis, and Milton Markowitz. 1969. "Birth Control Knowledge and Attitudes Among Unmarried Pregnant Adolescents." *Journal of Marriage and the Family* 30(1): 34–42.

Furstenberg, Frank F., Mary Elizabeth Hughes, and Jeanne Brooks-Gunn. 1992. "The Next Generation: The Children of Teenage Mothers Grow Up." In *Early Parenthood and Coming of Age in the 1990s,* edited by Margaret K. Rosenheim and Mark F. Testa. New Brunswick, N.J.: Rutgers University Press.

Furstenberg, Frank F., Judith A. Levine, and Jeanne Brooks-Gunn. 1990. "The Children of Teenage Mothers: Patterns of Early Childbearing in Two Generations." *Family Planning Perspectives* 22(2): 54–61.

Furstenberg, Frank F., George Masnick, and Susan A. Ricketts. 1972. "How Can Family Planning Programs Delay Repeated Teenage Pregnancies?" *Family Planning Perspectives* 4(3): 54–60.

Furstenberg, Frank F., Kay E. Sherwood, and Mercer L. Sullivan. 1992. *Caring and Paying: What Fathers and Mothers Say About Child Support.* New York: Manpower Demonstration Research Corporation.

Furstenberg, Frank F., Thomas D. Cook, Jacquelynne Eccles, Glen H. Elder Jr., and Arnold Sameroff. 1999. *Managing to Make It: Urban Families and Adolescent Success.* Chicago, Ill.: University of Chicago Press.

Garfinkel, Irwin, Sara S. McLanahan, and Thomas L. Hanson. 1998. "A Patchwork Portrait of Nonresident Fathers." In *Fathers Under Fire,* edited by Irwin Garfinkel, Sara S. McLanahan, Daniel R. Meyer, and Judith A. Seltzer. New York: Russell Sage Foundation.

Garfinkel, Irwin, Sara McLanahan, Daniel Meyer, and Judith Seltzer. 1998. *Fathers Under Fire: The Revolution in Child Support Enforcement.* New York: Russell Sage Foundation.

Gennetian, Lisa A., and Virginia Knox. 2003. "Staying Single: The Effects of Welfare Reform Policies on Marriage and Cohabitation." The Next Generation Working Paper Series 13. New York: Manpower Demonstration Research Corporation.

Gennetian, Lisa A., and Cynthia Miller. 2002. "Children and Welfare Reform: A View from an Experimental Welfare Program in Minnesota." *Child Development* 73(2): 601–20.

Gennetian, Lisa, Greg Duncan, Virginia Knox, Wanda Vargas, Elizabeth Clark-Kauffman, and Andrew S. London. 2004. "How Welfare Policies Affect Adolescents' School Outcomes: A Synthesis of Evidence from Experimental Studies." *Journal of Research on Adolescence* 14(4): 399–423.

Geronimus, Arline T. 2003. "Damned if You Do: Culture, Identity, Privilege, and Teenage Childbearing in the United States." *Social Science and Medicine* 57(5): 881–93.

Geronimus, Arline, and Sanders Korenman. 1992. "The Socioeconomic Consequences of Teen Childbearing Reconsidered." *Quarterly Journal of Economics* 107(4): 1187–1214.

———. 1993. "The Socioeconomic Costs of Teenage Childbearing: Evidence and Interpretation." *Demography* 30(2): 281–90.

Geronimus, Arline T., Sanders Korenman, and Marianne M. Hillemeier. 1994. "Does Young Maternal Age Adversely Affect Child Development? Evidence from Cousin Comparisons in the United States." *Population and Development Review* 20(3): 585–609.

Gibson-Davis, Christina, Kathryn Edin, and Sara McLanahan. 2005. "High Hopes but Even Higher Expectations: The Retreat from Marriage Among Low-Income Couples." *Journal of Marriage and Family* 67(5): 1301–12.

Goldstein, Joshua R. 1999. "The Level of Divorce in the United States." *Demography* 36(3): 409–14.

Goldstein, Joshua R., and Catherine T. Kenney. 2001. "Marriage Delayed or Forgone? New Cohort Forecasts of First Marriage for U.S. Women." *American Sociological Review* 66(4): 506–19.

Goodwin, Leonard. 1983. *Causes and Cures of Welfare: New Evidence on the Social Psychology of the Poor.* Lexington, Mass.: Lexington Books.

Gordon, Linda. 1994. *Pitied but Not Entitled: Single Mothers and the History of Welfare.* New York: Free Press.

Gottman, John M. 1999. *The Seven Principles for Making Marriage Work: A Practical Guide from the Country's Foremost Relationship Expert.* New York: Crown.

Graefe, Deborah R., and Daniel T. Lichter. 2002. "Marriage Among Unwed Mothers: Whites, Blacks, and Hispanics Compared." *Family Planning Perspectives* 34(6): 286–93.

Green, Arnold W. 1941. "The Cult of Personality and Sexual Relations." *Psychiatry* 4(August): 343–8.

Greenberg, Mark. 2006. "Welfare Reform: Success or Failure?" Washington: Center for Law and Social Policy, March 2006. Accessed at www.aphsa .org/Publications/Doc/PP/0603ART1/pdf.

Grogger, Jeffrey. 1997. "Incarceration-Related Costs of Early Childbearing." In *Kids Having Kids,* edited by Rebecca Maynard. Washington: Urban Institute Press.

Gusfield, Joseph. 1963. *Symbolic Crusade: Status Politics and the American Temperance Movement.* Urbana, Ill.: University of Illinois Press.

Guzzo, Karen, and Frank F. Furstenberg. 2005. "Starting Off on the Wrong Foot: First Birth Characteristics and Multi-Partnered Fertility Among Young Women." Paper presented to the annual meeting of the Eastern Sociological Society. Washington, March 17–20, 2005.

———. 2006a. "The Role of Sample Differences in Comparing Absolute Levels: A Standardization Exercise on Teenage Male Sexuality Activity in the U.S." Unpublished paper. University of Pennsylvania, Philadelphia, Penn.

———. 2006b. "Multi-Partnered Fertility Among American Men." Paper presented to the annual meeting of the Population Association of America. Los Angeles, Calif., April 1, 2006.

Haggerty, Robert J., Lonnie R. Sherrod, Norman Garmezy, and Michael Rutter. 1994. *Stress, Risk, and Resilience in Children and Adolescents: Processes, Mechanisms, and Interventions.* Cambridge: Cambridge University Press.

Haines, Michael R., and Richard H. Steckel. 2000. *A Population History of North America.* Cambridge: Cambridge University Press.

Hamilton, Gayle. 2002. *Moving People from Welfare to Work: Lessons from the National Evaluation of Welfare-to-Work Strategies.* Washington: U.S. Department of Health and Human Services.

Hannerz, Ulf. 1969. *Soulside: Inquiries into Ghetto Culture and Community.* New York: Columbia University Press.

Hareven, Tamara K. 1994. "Recent Research on the History of the Family" In *Time, Family and Community: Perspectives on Family and Community History,* edited by Michael Drake. Buckingham, U.K.: Open University Press.

Harris, Kathleen Mullan. 1997. *Teen Mothers and the Revolving Welfare Door.* Philadelphia, Penn.: Temple University Press.

Haskins, Ron. 2006. *Work over Welfare: The Inside Story of the 1996 Welfare Reform Law.* Washington: Brookings Institution Press.

Haveman, Robert H., Barbara Wolfe, and Elaine Peterson. 1997. "Children of Early Childbearers as Young Adults." In *Kids Having Kids,* edited by Rebecca Maynard. Washington: Urban Institute Press.

Hayes, Cheryl D. 1987. *Risking the Future: Adolescent Sexuality, Pregnancy, and Childbearing,* Vol. 1. Washington: National Academy Press.

Heckman, James J. 2000. "Policies to Foster Human Capital." *Research in Economics* 54(1): 3–56.

Henshaw, Stanley K. 1993. "Teenage Abortion, Birth, and Pregnancy Statistics by State, 1988." *Family Planning Perspectives* 25(3): 122–26.

Heuveline, Patrick, Jeffrey M. Timberlake, and Frank F. Furstenberg. 2003. "Shifting Childrearing to Single Mothers." *Population and Development Review* 29(1): 47–71.

Heymann, Jody, Alison Earle, and Frank F. Furstenberg. 1999. "Working Parents: What Factors Are Involved in Their Ability to Take Time Off from Work When Their Children Are Sick?" *Archives of Pediatrics and Adolescent Medicine* 153(8): 870–74.

Hofferth, Sandra, and Cheryl D. Hayes, editors. 1987. *Risking the Future: Adolescent Sexuality, Pregnancy, and Childbearing,* Vol. 2. Washington: National Academy Press.

Hofferth, Sandra L., and Lori Reid. 2002. "Early Childbearing and Children's Achievement and Behavior over Time." *Perspectives on Sexual and Reproductive Health* 34(1): 41–49.

Hoffman, Saul. 1998. "Teen Childbearing Isn't So Bad After All . . . Or Is It? A Review of the New Literature on the Consequences of Teen Childbearing." *Family Planning Perspectives* 30(5): 236–43.

Hoffman, Saul D., E. Michael Foster, and Frank F. Furstenberg, Jr. 1993. "Reevaluating the Costs of Teenage Childbearing." *Demography* 30(1): 1–13.

Holzer, Harry, and Paul Offner. 2001. "Trends in Employment Outcomes of Young Black Men, 1979–2000." Joint Center for Poverty Research Papers 245. Chicago, Ill.: Northwestern University/University of Chicago.

Institute of Medicine. 1995. *The Best Intentions: Unintended Pregnancy and the Well-Being of Children and Families.* Washington: Institute of Medicine.

Irvine, Janice M. 2002. *Talk About Sex: The Battles over Sex Education in the United States.* Berkeley, Calif.: University of California Press.

Iversen, Roberta Rehner, and Annie Laurie Armstrong. 2006. *Jobs Aren't Enough: Toward a New Economic Mobility for Low-Income Families.* Philadelphia, Penn.: Temple University Press.

Jaccard, James, Patricia J. Dittus, and Vivian V. Gordon. 2000. "Parent-Teen Communication About Premarital Sex: Factors Associated with the Extent of Communication." *Journal of Adolescent Research* 15(2): 187–208.

Jacobs, Jerry A. 1996. "Gender Inequality in Higher Education." *Annual Review of Sociology* 22: 153–85.

Jacobs, Jerry, and Scott Stoner-Eby. 1998. "Adult Enrollment and Educational Attainment." *Annals of the American Academy of Political and Social Science* 559(1): 91–108.

Jemmott, John B., Loretta S. Jemmott, and Geoffrey T. Fong. 1998. "Abstinence and Safer Sex HIV Risk-Reduction Interventions for African American Adolescents: A Randomized Controlled Trial." *Journal of the American Medical Association* 279(19): 1529–36.

Jones, Elise F. 1986. *Teenage Pregnancy in Industrialized Countries.* New Haven, Conn.: Yale University Press.

Jones, Elise F., Jacqueline Darroch Forrest, Stanley K. Henshaw, Jane Silverman, and Aida Torres. 1988. "Unintended Pregnancy, Contraceptive Practice, and Family Planning Services in Developed Countries." *Family Planning Perspectives* 20(2): 53–67.

Jones, Elise F., Jacqueline Darroch Forrest, Noreen Goldman, Stanley K. Henshaw, Richard Lincoln, Jeannie I. Rosoff, Charles F. Westoff, and Deirdre Wulf. 1985. "Teenage Pregnancy in Developed Countries: Determinants and Policy Implications." *Family Planning Perspectives* 17(2): 53–63.

Karoly, Lynn A., M. Rebecca Kilburn, and Jill S. Cannon. 2005. *Early Childhood Interventions: Proven Results, Future Promise.* Santa Monica, Calif.: Rand Corporation.

Kefalas, Maria, Frank F. Furstenberg, Patrick Carr, and Laura Napolitano. 2006. "Marriage Is More Than Being Together: The Meaning of Marriage Among Young Americans." Unpublished paper. St. Joseph's University, Philadelphia, Penn.

King, Valerie. 1994. "Nonresident Father Involvement and Child Well-being: Can Dads Make a Difference?" *Journal of Family Issues* 15(1): 78–96.

Kinsey, Alfred C. 1953. *Sexual Behavior in the Human Female.* Philadelphia, Penn.: W. B. Saunders.

Kinsey, Alfred C., Wardell B. Pomeroy, and Clyde E. Martin. 1948. *Sexual Behavior in the Human Male.* Philadelphia, Penn.: W. B. Saunders.

Kirby, Douglas. 1997. *No Easy Answers: Research Findings on Programs to Reduce Teen Pregnancy.* Washington: National Campaign to Prevent Teen Pregnancy.

———. 2001. *Emerging Answers: Research Findings on Programs to Reduce Teen Pregnancy* (summary). Washington: National Campaign to Prevent Teen Pregnancy.

Kirby, Douglas, Lynn Short, Janet Collins, Deborah Rugg, Lloyd Kolbe, Marion Howard, Brent Miller, Freya Sonestein, and Laurie S. Zabin. 1994. "School-Based Programs to Reduce Sexual Risk Behaviors: A Review of Effectiveness" (review). *Public Health Reports* 109(3): 339–60.

Kreider, Rose M. 2005. "Number, Timing, and Duration of Marriages and Divorces: 2001." *Current Population Reports* P70-97, February 2005. Washington: U.S. Bureau of the Census.

Kreinin, Tamara. 2003. "The Framing of a Debate: Ten Years of the Abstinence-Only-Until-Marriage Message." SIECUS report, September 22, 2003. Accessed June 21, 2007 at http://www.siecus.com/pubs/srpt/srpt0046.html.

Kriesberg, Louis. 1970. *Mothers in Poverty: A Study of Fatherless Families.* Chicago, Ill.: Aldine Press.

Ladner, Joyce A. 1971. *Tomorrow's Tomorrow: The Black Woman*. Garden City, N.Y.: Doubleday.

Landale, Nancy S., and Renate Forste. 1991. "Patterns of Entry into Cohabitation and Marriage Among Mainland Puerto Rican Women." *Demography* 28(4): 587–607.

Landry, David J., Lisa Kaeser, and Cory L. Richards. 1999. "Abstinence Promotion and the Provision of Information About Contraception in Public School District Sexuality Education Policies." *Family Planning Perspectives* 31(6): 280–86.

Laumann, Edward O., Robert T. Michael, Stuart Michaels, and John H. Gagnon. 1994. *The Social Organization of Sexuality: Sexual Practices in the United States*. Chicago, Ill.: University of Chicago Press.

Leadbetter, Bonnie J., and Niobe Way. 2001. *Growing Up Fast: Transitions to Adulthood Among Adolescent Mothers*. New York: Guilford Press.

Lesthaeghe, Ronald. 1995. "The Second Demographic Transition in Western Countries: An Interpretation." In *Gender and Family Change in Industrialized Countries,* edited by Karen O. Mason and An-Magritt Jensen. Oxford: Clarendon Press.

Levine, David I., and Gary Painter. 2003. "The Schooling Costs of Teenage Out-of-Wedlock Childbearing: Analysis with a Within-School Propensity-Score-Matching Estimator." *The Review of Economics and Statistics* 85(4): 884–900.

Levine, Judith. 2002. *Harmful to Minors: The Perils of Protecting Children from Sex*. Minneapolis, Minn.: University of Minnesota Press.

Levine, Judith A., Clifton R. Emery, and Harold Pollack. 2007. "The Well-Being of Children Born to Teen Mothers." *Journal of Marriage and Family* 69(1): 105–22.

Levine, Judith A., Harold Pollack, and Maureen E. Comfort. 2001. "Academic and Behavioral Outcomes Among the Children of Young Mothers." *Journal of Marriage and the Family* 63(2): 355–69.

Lichter, Daniel T., and Martha L. Crowley. 2004. "Welfare Reform and Child Poverty: Effects of Maternal Employment, Marriage, and Cohabitation." *Social Science Research* 33(3): 385–408.

Lichter, Daniel T., Deborah R. Graefe, and J. Brian Brown. 2003. "Is Marriage a Panacea? Union Formation Among Economically Disadvantaged Unwed Mothers." *Social Problems* 50(1): 60–86.

Lieberson, Stanley. 1985. *Making It Count: The Improvement of Social Research and Theory*. Berkeley, Calif.: University of California Press.

Liebow, Elliot. 1967. *Tally's Corner*. Boston, Mass.: Little, Brown.

Lopez, Nancy. 2004. *Hopeful Girls, Troubled Boys: Race and Gender Disparity in Urban Education*. New York: Routledge Press.

Lottes, Ilsa L. 2002. "Sexual Health Policies in Other Industrialized Countries: Are There Lessons for the United States?" *Journal of Sex Research* 39(1): 79–83.

Luker, Kristin. 1996. *Dubious Conceptions: The Politics of Teenage Pregnancy*. Cambridge, Mass.: Harvard University Press.

————. 1999. "A Reminder That Human Behavior Frequently Refuses to Conform to Models Created by Researchers." *Family Planning Perspectives* 31(5): 248–49.

Markman, Howard J., Scott M. Stanley, Natalie H. Jenkins, Susan L. Blumberg, and Carol Whitely. 2003. *Two Hours to a Great Marriage: A Step-by-Step Guide for Making Love Last*. San Francisco, Calif.: Jossey-Bass.

Mauldin, Jane. 1998. "Families Started by Teenagers." In *All Our Families: New Policies for a New Century*, edited by Mary Ann Mason, Arlene Skolnick, and Stephen D. Sugarman. New York: Oxford University Press.

May, Elaine Tyler. 1988. *Homeward Bound*. New York: Basic Books.

Maynard, Rebecca A., editor. 1997. *Kids Having Kids: Economic Costs and Social Consequences of Teen Pregnancy*. Washington: Urban Institute Press.

McDonald, Katrina Bell, and Elizabeth M. Armstrong. 2001. "De-Romanticizing Black Intergenerational Support: The Questionable Expectations of Welfare Reform." *Journal of Marriage and Family* 63(1): 213–23.

McLanahan, Sara. 2004. "Diverging Destinies: How Children Fare Under the Second Demographic Transition." *Demography* 41(4): 607–27.

McLanahan, Sara, and Gary Sandefur. 1994. *Growing Up with a Single Parent*. Cambridge, Mass.: Harvard University Press.

McLanahan, Sara, Elisabeth Donahue, and Ron Haskins, editors. 2005. *The Future of Children: Marriage and Child Well-being* 15(2, Fall). Washington: Brookings Institution Press.

McLaughlin, Diane K., and Daniel T. Lichter. 1997. "Poverty and the Marital Behavior of Young Women." *Journal of Marriage and the Family* 59(3): 582–94.

Mead, Lawrence. 1986. *Beyond Entitlement: The Social Obligations of Citizenship*. New York: Free Press.

Miller, Cynthia, and Virginia Knox. 2001. "The Challenge of Helping Low-Income Fathers Support Their Children: Final Lessons from Parents' Fair Share." New York: Manpower Demonstration Research Corporation.

Mincy, Ronald B. 2002a. "Who Should Marry Whom: Multi-Partnered Fertility Among New Parents." Working paper 02-03-FF. Center for Research on Child Well-Being, Princeton University.

————. 2002b. "What About Black Fathers?" *The American Prospect* 13(7).

Mincy, Ronald B., and Chien-Chung Huang. 2002a. "Just Get Me to the Church: Assessing Policies to Promote Marriage Among Fragile Families." Working paper 02-02-FF. Center for Research on Child Well-Being, Princeton University.

————. 2002b. "The 'M' Word: The Rise and Fall of Interracial Coalitions on Fathers and Welfare Reform." Working paper 02-07-FF. Center for Research on Child Well-Being, Princeton University.

Moffitt, Robert A. 1992. "Incentive Effects of the U.S. Welfare System: A Review." *Journal of Economic Literature* 30(1): 1–61.

————. 1998. "The Effect of Welfare on Marriage and Fertility." In *Welfare, the Family, and Reproductive Behavior,* edited by Robert Moffitt. Washington: National Academy Press.

————. 2001. "Welfare Benefits and Female Headship in U.S. Time Series." In *Out of Wedlock: Causes and Consequences of Nonmarital Fertility,* edited by Lawrence Wu and Barbara Wolfe. New York: Russell Sage Foundation.

————. 2002. "From Welfare to Work: What the Evidence Shows." Welfare Reform and Beyond Brief 13. Washington: Brookings Institution.

Moore, Kristen A., Donna R. Morrison, and A. D. Greene. 1997. "Effects on the Children Born to Adolescent Mothers." In *Kids Having Kids,* edited by Rebecca Maynard. Washington: Urban Institute Press.

Moore, Kristen A., and Nancy O. Snyder. 1991. "Cognitive Attainment Among Firstborn Children of Adolescent Mothers." *American Sociological Review* 56(5): 612–24.

Moore, Mary Lou. 2000. "Adolescent Pregnancy Rates in Three European Countries: Lessons to Be Learned?" *Journal of Obstetric, Gynecologic, and Neonatal Nursing* 29(4): 355–62.

Moran, Jeffrey P. 2000. *Teaching Sex: The Shaping of Adolescence in the Twentieth Century.* Cambridge, Mass.: Harvard University Press.

Mott, Frank L. 1990. "When Is a Father Really Gone? Paternal-Child Contact in Father-Absent Homes." *Demography* 27(4): 499–517.

Moynihan, Daniel Patrick. 1965. *The Negro Family: The Case for National Action.* Washington: U.S. Department of Labor, Office of Political Planning Research.

Moynihan, Daniel P., Timothy M. Smeeding, and Lee Rainwater, editors. 2004. *The Future of the Family.* New York: Russell Sage Foundation.

Murray, Charles. 1984. *Losing Ground: American Social Policy.* New York: Basic Books.

————. 2001. "Family Formation." In *The New World of Welfare,* edited by Rebecca M. Blank and Ron Haskins. Washington: Brookings Institution Press.

Nagin, Daniel S., Greg Pogarsky, and David P. Farrington. 1997. "Adolescent Mothers and the Criminal Behavior of Their Children." *Law and Society Review* 31(1): 137–62.

Nathanson, Constance A. 1991. *Dangerous Passage: The Social Control of Sexuality in Women's Adolescence.* Philadelphia, Penn.: Temple University Press.

National Campaign to Prevent Teen Pregnancy. 1997. "What the Polling Data Tell Us: A Summary of Past Surveys on Teen Pregnancy." April 1997. Accessed at http://www.teenpregnancy.org/resources/data/polling97.asp.

————. 2007. "Fact Sheet: The Next Best Thing: Encouraging Contraceptive Use Among Sexually Active Teens." Accessed at http://www.teenpregnancy.org/resources/reading/fact_sheets/bestthfs.asp.

Nock, Steven L. 1998. *Marriage in Men's Lives.* New York: Oxford University Press.

————. 2005. "Marriage as a Public Issue." *The Future of Children* 15(2): 13–32.

O'Connell Martin, and Maurice J. Moore. 1980. "The Legitimacy Status of First Births to U.S. Women Aged 15–24, 1939–1978." *Family Planning Perspectives* 12(1): 16–23, 25.

Offner, Paul. 2005. "Welfare Reform and Teenage Girls." *Social Science Quarterly* 86(2): 306–32.

O'Neill, June E., and M. Anne Hill. 2002. "Gaining Ground: Women, Welfare Reform, and Work." Policy report 251. Dallas, Tex.: National Center for Policy Analysis.

Oppenheimer, Valerie K. 1988. "A Theory of Marriage Timing." *American Journal of Sociology* 94(3): 563–91.

Osgood, Wayne, E. Michael Foster, Constance Flanagan, and Gretchen R. Ruth, eds. 2005. *On Your Own Without a Net: The Transition to Adulthood for Vulnerable Populations.* Chicago: University of Chicago Press.

Pager, Devah, and Bruce Western. 2005a. "Discrimination in Low Trust Labor Markets." Paper presented to the annual meeting of the American Sociological Association. Philadelphia, Penn., August 13–16, 2005.

————. 2005b. "Discrimination in Low Wage Labor Markets: Evidence from New York City." Paper presented to the Population Association of America. Philadelphia, Penn., March 31, 2005.

Parrott, Sharon, and Arloc Sherman. 2006. "TANF at Ten: Program Results Are More Mixed Than Often Understood." Washington: Center on Budget and Policy Priorities.

Pearson, Jennifer, Chandra Muller, and Michelle L. Frisco. 2006. "Parental Involvement, Family Structure, and Adolescent Sexual Decision Making." *Sociological Perspectives* 49(1): 67–90.

Philliber, Susan, Jacqueline Williams Kaye, Scott Herrling, and Emily West. 2002. "Preventing Pregnancy and Improving Health Care Access Among Teenagers: An Evaluation of the Children's Aid Society–Carrera Program." *Perspectives on Sexual and Reproductive Health* 34(5): 244–51.

Piccinino, Linda J., and William D. Mosher. 1998. "Trends in Contraceptive Use in the United States: 1982–1995." *Family Planning Perspectives* 30(1): 4–10, 46.

Piven, Frances Fox, and Richard Cloward. 1993. *Regulating the Poor: The Functions of Public Welfare*. New York: Vintage.

Placek, Paul J., and Gerry E. Hendershot. 1974. "Public Welfare and Family Planning: An Empirical Study of the 'Brood Sow' Myth." *Social Problems* 21(5): 658–73.

Plotnick, Robert. 1990. "Welfare and Teenage Out-of-Wedlock Childbearing: Evidence from the 1980s." *Journal of Marriage and the Family* 52(3): 735–46.

Popenoe, David. 1996. *Life Without Father*. New York: Free Press.

Rains, Prudence Mors. 1971. *Becoming an Unwed Mother*. Chicago, Ill.: Aldine-Atherton.

Rainwater, Lee. 1970. *Behind Ghetto Walls*. Chicago, Ill.: Aldine Press.

Rainwater, Lee, and William L. Yancey. 1967. *The Moynihan Report and the Politics of Controversy*. Cambridge, Mass.: MIT Press.

Rector, Robert, and Kirk A. Johnson. 2005a. *Adolescent Virginity Pledges, Condom Use, and Sexually Transmitted Diseases Among Young Adults*. Washington: Heritage Foundation.

———. 2005b. *Adolescent Virginity Pledges and Risky Sexual Behaviors*. Washington: Heritage Foundation.

Reiss, Ira L. 1964. "Premarital Sexual Permissiveness Among Negroes and Whites." *American Sociological Review* 29(5): 688–98.

Riccio, James, Daniel Friedlander, and Stephen Freedman. 1994. *Benefits, Costs, and Three-Year Impacts of a Welfare-to-Work Program*. New York: Manpower Demonstration Research Corporation.

Risman, Barbara, and Pepper Schwartz. 2002. "After the Sexual Revolution: Gender and Politics in Teen Dating." *Contexts* 1(1): 16–24.

Robin, Leah, Patricia Dittus, Daniel Whitaker, Richard Crosby, Kathleen Ethier, Jane Mezoff, Kim Miller, and Katina Pappas-Deluca. 2004. "Behavioral Interventions to Reduce Incidence of HIV, STD, and Pregnancy Among Adolescents: A Decade in Review, 2004." *Journal of Adolescent Health* 34(1): 3–26.

Rogers-Dillon, Robin. 2004. *The Welfare Experiments: Politics and Policy Evaluation*. Stanford, Calif.: Stanford University Press.

Rogers-Dillon, Robin, and Lynne Haney. 2005. "Minimizing Vulnerability: Selective Interdependencies After Welfare Reform." *Qualitative Sociology* 28(3): 235–54.

Rosoff, Jeannie I. 1975. "Is Support of Abortion Political Suicide?" *Family Planning Perspectives* 7(1): 13–22.

Rothman, Ellen R. 1984. *Hands and Hearts: A History of Courtship in America*. New York: Basic Books.

Santelli, John S., Brian Morrow, John E. Anderson, and Laura Duberstein Lindberg. 2006. "Contraceptive Use and Pregnancy Risk Among U.S. High

School Students, 1991–2003." *Perspectives on Sexual and Reproductive Health* 38(2): 106–11.

Santelli, John S., Laura Duberstein Lindberg, Joyce Abma, Clea Sucoff McNeely, and Michael Resnick. 2000. "Adolescent Sexual Behavior: Estimates and Trends from Four Nationally Representative Surveys." *Family Planning Perspectives* 32(4): 156–66.

Sawhill, Isabel V., R. Kent Weaver, Ron Haskins, and Andrea Kane, eds. 2002. *Welfare Reform and Beyond: The Future of the Safety Net*. Washington: Brookings Institution.

Schalet, Amy T. 2000. "Raging Hormones, Regulated Love: Adolescent Sexuality and the Constitution of the Modern Individual in the United States and the Netherlands." *Body and Society* 6(1): 75–105.

———. 2004. "Must We Fear Adolescent Sexuality?" *Medscape General Medicine* 6(4): 1–22.

———. 2006. *Raging Hormones, Regulated Love*. Chicago, Ill.: University of Chicago Press.

Seltzer, Judith. 1998. "Father by Law: Effects of Joint Legal Custody on Father's Involvement with Children." *Demography* 35(2): 135–46.

Settersten, Richard A., Jr., Frank F. Furstenberg, and Rubén G. Rumbaut. 2005. *On the Frontier of Adulthood: Theory, Research, and Public Policy*. Chicago, Ill.: University of Chicago Press.

Singh, Susheela, and Jacqueline E. Darroch. 1999. "Trends in Sexual Activity Among Adolescent American Women: 1982–1995." *Family Planning Perspectives* 31(5): 212–9.

———. 2000. "Adolescent Pregnancy and Childbearing: Levels and Trends in Developed Countries." *Family Planning Perspectives* 32(1): 14–23.

Singh, Susheela, Jacqueline E. Darroch, and Jennifer J. Frost. 2001. "Socioeconomic Disadvantage and Adolescent Women's Sexual and Reproductive Behavior: The Case of Five Developed Countries." *Family Planning Perspectives* 33(6): 251–58, 289.

Sklar, June, and Beth Berkov. 1974. "Abortion, Illegitimacy, and the American Birth Rate." *Science* 185(4155): 909.

Smith, Daniel Scott, and Michael S. Hindus. 1975. "Premarital Pregnancy in America, 1640–1971." *Journal of Interdisciplinary History* 5(4): 537–70.

Smith, Herbert L., S. Philip Morgan, and Tanya Koropeckyj-Cox. 1996. "A Decomposition of Trends in the Nonmarital Fertility Ratios of Blacks and Whites in the United States, 1960–1992." *Demography* 33(2): 141–51.

Smith, Tom. 1998. "American Sexual Behavior: Trends, Socio-demographic Differences, and Risk Behavior." GSS Topical Report 25. Chicago, Ill.: National Opinion Research Center/University of Chicago.

———. 2000. "Changes in the Generation Gap, 1972–1998." GSS Social Change Reports 43. Chicago, Ill.: National Opinion Research Center/ University of Chicago.

Smith Battle, Lee. 1996. "Intergenerational Ethics of Caring for Adolescent Mothers and Their Children." *Family Relations* 45(1): 56–64.

Sonestein, Freya L., and Gregory Acs. 1995. "Teenage Childbearing: The Trends and Their Implications." In *Welfare Reform: An Analysis of the Issues,* edited by Isabel V. Sawhill. Washington: Urban Institute.

South, Scott J. 1999. "Historical Changes and Life Course Variation in the Determinants of Premarital Childbearing." *Journal of Marriage and the Family* 61(3): 752–63.

Stack, Carol. 1974. *All Our Kin.* Chicago, Ill.: Aldine Press.

Stack, Carol, and Linda M. Burton. 1993. "Kinscripts." *Journal of Comparative Family Studies* 24(2): 157–70.

Stonecash, Jeffrey. 2007. "Inequality and the American Public: Results of the Third Annual Maxwell School Survey." Syracuse, N.Y.: Campbell Public Affairs Institute, Syracuse University.

Tanner, Michael. 2003. *The Poverty of Welfare: Helping Others in Civil Society.* Washington: Cato Institute.

Testa, Mark, Nan Marie Astone, Marilyn Krogh, and Kathryn Neckerman. 1989. "Employment and Marriage Among Inner-City Fathers." *Annals of the American Academy of Political and Social Science* 501(1): 87, 90–91.

Therborn, Goran. 2004. *Between Sex and Power: Family in the World, 1900–2000.* Oxford: Routledge Press.

UNICEF. 2007. "Child Poverty in Perspective: An Overview of Child Well-being in Rich Countries." Innocenti Report Card 7. Accessed at http://www.unicef.org/media/files/ChildPovertyReport.pdf

Upchurch, Dawn M., Lee A. Lillard, and Constantijn W. A. Panis. 2001. "The Impact of Nonmarital Childbearing on Subsequent Marital Formation and Dissolution." In *Out of Wedlock: Causes and Consequences of Nonmarital Fertility,* edited by Lawrence Wu and Barbara Wolfe. New York: Russell Sage Foundation.

U.S. Bureau of the Census. 1975. *Historical Statistics of the United States, Colonial Times to 1970.* Washington: U.S. Bureau of the Census.

———. 2006a. "America's Families and Living Arrangements: 2005." Washington: U.S. Bureau of the Census. Accessed at http://www.census.gov/population/www/socdemo/hh-fam/cps2005.html.

———. 2006b. "Educational Attainment in the United States: 2005." Washington: U.S. Bureau of the Census. Accessed at http://www.census.gov/population/www/socdemo/education/cps2005.html.

———. 2007. *Statistical Abstract of the United States: 2007.* 126th edition. Washington: U.S. Department of Labor. Accessed at http://www.census.gov/compendia/statab/.

U.S. Department of Health and Human Services. Administration for Children and Families. 2002. "ACF News: Statistics." Accessed at http://www.acf.hhs.gov/news/stats/3697.htm. Last updated May 23, 2002.

U.S. Public Health Service. 1986. *Surgeon General's Report on Acquired Immune Deficiency Syndrome.* Rockville, Md.: U.S. Public Health Service.

Ventura, Stephanie J., and Christine A. Bachrach. 2000. "Nonmarital Childbearing in the United States, 1940–1999." *National Vital Statistics Report* 48(16): 1–39. Washington: National Center for Health Statistics.

Ventura, Stephanie J., T. J. Mathews, and Brady E. Hamilton. 2001. "Births to Teenagers in the United States, 1940–2000." *National Vital Statistics Report* 49(10): 1–23. Washington: National Center for Health Statistics.

Vincent, Clark E. 1961. *Unmarried Mothers.* New York: Free Press of Glencoe.

Vinovskis, Maris. 1988. *An "Epidemic" of Adolescent Pregnancy?* New York: Oxford University Press.

Waldfogel, Jane. 2006. *What Children Need.* Cambridge, Mass.: Harvard University Press.

Waller, Maureen. 2001. "High Hopes: Unwed Parents' Expectations About Marriage." *Children and Youth Services Review* 23(6–7): 457–84.

———. 2002. *My Baby's Father.* Ithaca, N.Y.: Cornell University Press.

Waller, Maureen R., and Robert Plotnick. 2001. "Effective Child Support Policy for Low-Income Families: Evidence from Street-Level Research" *Journal of Policy Analysis and Management* 20(1): 89–110.

Waller, Maureen, and Raymond R. Swisher. 2005. "Fathers' Risk Behaviors in Fragile Families: Implications for 'Healthy Marriages.' " Working paper 2002-18-FF. Center for Research on Child Well-Being, Princeton University.

Waller, Willard W. 1936. "Social Problems and the Mores." *American Sociological Review* 1(6): 922–33.

Weaver, Heather, Gary Smith, and Susan Kippax. 2005. "School-Based Sex Education Policies and Indicators of Sexual Health Among Young People: A Comparison of the Netherlands, France, Australia, and the United States." *Sex Education: Sexuality, Society, and Learning* 5(2): 171–88.

Weeks, John R. 1976. *Teenage Marriages: A Demographic Analysis.* Westport, Conn.: Greenwood Press.

Weiss, Christopher O., and Frank F. Furstenberg. 1997. "Schooling Together: Mutual Influences on Educational Success of Teenage Mothers and Their Children." Presented to the annual meetings of the Society for Research on Child Development. Washington, April 1997.

Western, Bruce, Leonard Lopoo, and Sara McLanahan. 2004. "Incarceration and the Bonds Between Parents in Fragile Families." In *Imprisoning America: The Social Effects of Mass Incarceration,* edited by Mary Patillo, David Weiman, and Bruce Western. New York: Russell Sage Foundation.

Westoff, Charles F. 1988. "Unintended Pregnancy in America and Abroad." *Family Planning Perspectives* 20(6): 254, 257–61.

Westoff, Charles F., Gerard Calot, and Andrew D. Foster. 1983. "Teenage Fertility in Developed Nations: 1971–1980." *Family Planning Perspectives* 15(3): 105–11.

Whitman, Thomas L., John G. Borkowski, Deborah A. Keogh, and Keri Weed. 2001. *Interwoven Lives: Adolescent Mothers and Their Children.* Mahwah, N.J.: Lawrence Erlbaum Associates.

Whyte, William F. 1943. "A Slum Sex Code." *American Journal of Sociology* 49(1): 24–31.

William T. Grant Foundation. 1998. *The Forgotten Half: Pathways to Success for America's Youth and Young Families.* Washington: William T. Grant Commission on Work, Family, and Citizenship.

Wilson, James Q. 2002. *The Marriage Problem: How Our Culture Has Weakened Families.* New York: HarperCollins.

Wilson, William Julius. 1987. *The Truly Disadvantaged: The Inner City, the Underclass, and Public Policy.* Chicago, Ill.: University of Chicago Press.

———. 1996. *When Work Disappears: The World of the New Urban Poor.* New York: Alfred A. Knopf.

Wolff, Edward. 2003. "The Wealth Divide. The Growing Gap in the United States Between the Rich and the Rest." *Multinational Monitor* 24(5): 7–9.

Wu, Lawrence L., and Barbara Wolfe, editors. 2001. *Out of Wedlock: Causes and Consequences of Nonmarital Fertility.* New York: Russell Sage Foundation.

Zaslow, Martha J., and Cheryl D. Hayes. 1986. "Sex Differences in Children's Response to Psychosocial Stress: Towards a Cross-Context Analysis." In *Advances in Developmental Psychology,* Vol. 4, edited by Michael E. Lamb, Ann L. Brown, and Barbara Rogoff. Hillsdale, N.J.: Lawrence Erlbaum Associates.

Zavodny, Madeline. 1999. "Do Men's Characteristics Affect Whether a Nonmarital Pregnancy Results in Marriage?" *Journal of Marriage and the Family* 61: 764–73.

Zedlewski, Sheila R., and Pamela Loprest. 2001. "Will TANF Work for the Most Disadvantaged Families?" In *The New World of Welfare,* edited by Rebecca M. Blank and Ron Haskins. Washington: Brookings Institution.

Zelnik, Melvin, John F. Kantner, and Kathleen Ford. 1981. *Sex and Pregnancy in Adolescence.* Sage Library of Social Research, Vol. 133. Beverly Hills, Calif.: Sage Publications.

—— Index ——

Boldface numbers refer to figures and tables.

public policy aimed at supporting
marriage (*continued*)
new directions for, 132–6; plausibility of, 106–7; politics of, 122–7
public policy aimed at teenage childbearing, 73–74; "epidemic" of
teenage pregnancy, belief in, 81–84;
the politics of, 84–96; poverty and
inequality, misguided beliefs regarding linkage to, 160–5; pregnancy
prevention (*see* pregnancy prevention efforts); problems of, 4–5; welfare reform (*see* welfare reform)
Public Policy Institute of California, 2
Puritans, the, 78–79

race: likelihood of marriage by pregnant teens distinguished by, 108;
public attitudes toward welfare
recipients and, 138–9; public concern about declining rates of
marriage/teenage pregnancy and,
85; stereotypes based on, 13–14
(*see also* stereotypes). *See also*
African Americans
Rainwater, Lee, 116
Reagan, Ronald, 87–88, 92
reproductive health services: advocates for, 15–16, 81–83; conservative
attack of the 1980s directed at,
87–88; contraception and family
planning (*see* contraception; family
planning); controversy/debate over,
76, 166–7; political alliance during
the 1970s supporting, 84–86;
teenage population, legal actions
opening up access for, 17, 81–82
Risking the Future (National Academy
of Sciences), 47
Roe v. Wade, 18, 83, 85
Rogers-Dillon, Robin, 150–1

Schalet, Amy, 101–3
"Second Demographic Transition," 123
selectivity, 47–49, 69

sex education, 86–88, 90–92, 166
single parenthood: increase in, 11–13,
127; increasing among teens, 12–13,
16; perceived as viable option, 11;
poverty rate for women heading
households, 155; teenage childbearing and, policymakers' linkage of,
73–74 (*see also* public policy aimed
at teenage childbearing); welfare
and, 138–9 (*see also* welfare; welfare reform). *See also* marriage
social science: the Baltimore Study (*see*
Baltimore Study); Campbell on the
consequences facing teenage mothers, 15, 19–20, 24–25, 51; children of
teenage mothers, conclusions regarding negative effects experienced by,
67–71; long-term effects of teenage
childbearing, overestimation of
effects of, 46–52; marriage promotion
policies, skepticism regarding, 128–9;
the selectivity problem, 47–49, 69;
teenage childbearing as a research
agenda, 19–20; welfare's impact on
the behavior of recipients, 142–5
Social Security, 172
Stack, Carol, 116
stereotypes: of teenage mothers, 4, 16,
20, 42; of unmarried African American teen mothers, 13–14
sterilization, 33–34
Supreme Court, United States, Griswold decision and contraception,
81–82
*Surgeon General's Report on Acquired
Immune Deficiency Syndrome* (U.S.
Public Health Service), 91

TANF. *See* Temporary Assistance to
Needy Families
tax policy, 168, 170–1. *See also* Earned
Income Tax Credit
teenage childbearing: beliefs regarding, intensity and inaccuracy of, 1–4
(*see also* stereotypes); causal linkage to poverty and disadvantage,